PUT ON THE
FULL
COMBAT
GEAR
of GOD*

EPHESIANS 6 FROM A MODERN SOLDIER'S PERSPECTIVE

JIM WAGNER

* Put on the whole armor of God, that you may be able to stand against the wiles of the devil.

Ephesians 6:11

PUT ON THE FULL COMBAT GEAR OF GOD
© 2021 by Jim Wagner and Kariné Wagner. All rights reserved.

June 2021
Printed in the United States of America

 **GodsArmySurvivalTraining.com**

All Scripture quotations, unless otherwise indicated, are taken from the New King James Version®. Copyright © 1982 by Thomas Nelson. All rights reserved.

ISBN: 978-0-9863269-5-0

ACKNOWLEDGMENTS

My wife and I had been friends with Laci (pronounced *Lot-see*) and his wife Elizabeth for almost two decades, and as long as we had known them they had always been solid church-going Christians. Then in 2020 life changed for all us, along with everyone else in the United States for that matter: the Coronavirus pandemic, lockdowns, the early release of thousands of prisoners into the streets, skyrocketing crime, race and social riots all across the country, and political turmoil that tested God's people physically, emotionally, and spiritually.

Laci and Elizabeth, who never dreamed of having a gun in their house before the troubles began, had a change of heart when events kept getting worse and worse. They had always known about my tactical background, but they finally came to a decision to tap into my skills by soliciting my help in guiding them through the process of purchasing some firearms and giving them private shooting lessons to be proficient enough to protect their home and successful manufacturing buisiness.

During this very turbulent time, the four of us also got together every Friday evening, along with a few other veteran believers, to "break bread together," like the 1st Century church had also done under persecution, and we prayed harder than we had ever prayed before: for each other, for our families and friends, for the nation, and for the church to "wake up," as stated in Romans 13:11 *And do this, understanding the present time: The hour has already come for you to* **wake up** *from your slumber, because our salvation is nearer now than when we first believed.*

In California, where we all lived, our Governor singled out churches and home Bible studies prohibiting them from meeting together, at any capacity during COVID-19. When the U.S. Supreme Court eventually ruled that churches had the Constitutional right ro be treated in the exact same manner as any secular business or organization during the pandemic, the Governor "permitted" us to meet, but we were not allowed to sing songs of praise to the Lord when we did. "Peaceful demonstrators" screaming profanities, looting businesses, and torching buildings was okay during the same time, but not singing. Of course, none of his mandates ever stopped my church or our Friday Night Prayer group from meeting together to *shout joyfully to the Lord, all the earth, break forth in song, rejoice, and sing praises. Psalm 98:4* We chose to obey God rather than man, and we never agreed to suspend the U.S. Constitution in "the land of the Free and the Home of the Brave." We just continued to live as free Americans, while so many others lived in fear, because it was our right.

During those difficult days, yet exciting as far as the fulfillment of Bible prophecy was concerned, I made many comparisons to the combat skills that I was teaching Laci and Elizabeth on the gun range to the spiritual warfare we were all facing as Christians on a daily basis. They shared with me that God had used me to helped them better understand what it meant to be a "Christian Soldier," and the Scriptures they had read about spiritual warfare "made more sense now." When I received the same positive feedback from several other believers that I was teaching at the time, I just knew that I had to share my teachings with other believers beyond my inner circle, so they too could be "toughened up" for the even more difficult days that still lie ahead - the very "birth pangs" that Jesus warned us would come.

I want to thank the following people who inspired me or helped me with the making of this book, and the ministry opportunities it has brought me:

My wife Kariné
Laci and Elizabeth
Don and Gloria
Pastor Barry, Vahe, Ariel, Garth, Richard, Big Mike, Mikael, Dee,
my brother-in-law Greg, and Big Mamma

TABLE OF CONTENTS

INTRODUCTION

FOR A MUSEUM OR THE BATTLEFIELD?

The Apostle Paul instructs us in Ephesians 6:11 to *Put on the whole armor of God, that you may be able to stand against the wiles of the devil.* Then he gives us a detailed inventory of the various pieces of armor and war equipment used by a foot soldier in the 1st Century Roman Empire. Many Christians, and perhaps yourself included, can't really relate strongly to this metaphor. After all, "armor" is something that belongs in a museum, behind glass cases or mounted on the walls with descriptions next to it. It may be interesting to gaze upon as you stroll through the quiet rooms displaying it, and it is educational, but suits of armor are relics of the past, and hardly relevant today. Or, are they?

We are keenly aware that *All Scripture is given by inspiration of God, and is profitable for doctrine, for reproof, for correction, for instruction in righteousness,* as stated in 2 Timothy 3:16. Therefore, this curious metaphor used by Paul, the "whole armor" thing, must also apply to us 21st Century believers as much as it did for the 1st Century church. This being the case, we cannot get hung up on the word "armor," and make the mistake of linking it only to a distant past. This metaphor is for today.

Since God obviously wants us to have an understanding of armor, as it pertains to our faith and service to Him, the logical question that needs to be asked is, "Does anyone today wear armor?" Knowing the answer to this question may bring us to a closer understanding of this portion of scripture.

The answer to the question is, "Yes. There are certain people today who wear armor." Both law enforcement officers on the streets, and combat Soldiers wear armor; only today we call it "body armor." Body armor is just that, it is worn on the body to protect against bullets and fragmentation. All of the pieces described by Paul are pieces still in use today. The materials, shapes, and sizes may have changed over the past two millennia, but the purpose of each one remains exactly the same. Today's warriors refer to these pieces as "full combat gear."

Before we go any further, let's take a cursory look at Ephesians 6:10 through 20, our topic of study, which is often referred to as "The Whole Armor of God." Then throughout this book we'll examine each verse in greater detail.

*Finally, my brethren, be strong in the Lord and in the power of His might. **Put on the whole armor of God,** that you may be able to stand against the wiles of the devil. For we do not wrestle against flesh and blood, but against principalities, against powers, against the rulers of the darkness of this age, against spiritual hosts of wickedness in the heavenly places. Therefore **take up the whole armor of God,** that you may be able to withstand in the evil day, and having done all, to stand. Stand therefore, having girded your waist with truth, having put on the breastplate of righteousness, and having shod your feet with the preparation of the gospel of peace; above all, taking the shield of faith with which you will be able to quench all the fiery darts of the wicked one. And take the helmet of salvation, and the sword of the Spirit, which is the word of God; praying always with all prayer and supplication in the Spirit, being watchful to this end with all perseverance and supplication for all the saints - and for me, that utterance may be given to me, that I may open my mouth boldly to make known the mystery of the gospel, for which I am an ambassador in chains; that in it I may speak boldly, as I ought to speak.*

How then are we to completely understand the meaning of this portion of scripture when less than one-half of 1% of the population has served, or is currently serving, in the United States Armed Forces? And, of that one-half of 1% only 10% of those in the military have had, or currently have, combat occupations; meaning, those who *fight for a living.*

When it comes to law enforcement, which is a paramilitary organization due to its similar structure to that of the military and the use of much of the same equipment, the number of those serving as federal agents, police officers and deputies is even lower than that of the military. Compared to the population of the United States, only one quarter of 1% protect the citizens. This is why they are referred to as "The Thin Blue Line;" *blue* represents the generic term "police," and the *thin line* is the metaphoric line between law & order and anarchy. You may have seen the symbol that is used to represent the "The Thin Blue Line" on the back of someone's pick-up truck or flying on a flagpole. It's a black and white American flag with a blue line where the 8th stripe is located.

If you've made the mistake of thinking of Paul's metaphor of armor as an antiquated example, or you just could never quite relate to it, having never put on body armor or picked up a weapon to protect your country or community before, then I'm convinced that my background as a former soldier in a combat unit, a police officer, a S.W.A.T. officer, the team leader of a sheriff's department Dignitary Protection Unit, a U.S. federal counterterrorist agent, then an additional 10 years as a Reserve Soldier in a Military Police unit and then a Security Forces unit, which included being the team leader of a Special Reaction Team (the military equivalent of a civilian S.W.A.T. team), will give you the perspective you need to better understand Ephesians 6. Notice that I stated, "better understand it," and not "fully understand it." That was intentional, because only the Holy Spirit can lead you to fully understand a passage of Scripture. I can only give you the technical aspects of the metaphor, along with some real-world examples, and throw in a few of my own colorful experiences that will prepare you to put on your own body armor; spiritual body armor, and perhaps even physical body armor the way the country seems to be going lately.

So, let's have you take your first step in becoming a Christian Soldier. Instead of reading the scripture *Put on the whole armor of God, that you may be able to stand against the wiles of the devil* as most believers do, giving it homage as a quaint metaphor, it's time to read it as if your life depends upon it, for it does! In case you haven't been paying much attention to the news lately, or you've turned it off altogether because it's depressing, keep in mind that the "birth pangs" that Jesus warned us about, concerning the End Times, are increasing in amount and intensity. Therefore Christian Soldier, here are your direct orders, reading Ephesians 6:13 using today's language and definitions:

Put on your full combat gear issued to you, by the authority of the Commander in Chief, to destroy the enemy.

Chapter 1

JOINING THE ARMY

IT'S ALL IN THE FIELD MANUALS

Modern military techniques and tactics are found in Field Manuals. The acronym for "Field Manual," because the military loves to use acronyms for just about everything under the sun, is "FM." An FM is a publication, in soft cover book form published by the United States Army Publishing Directorate, that contains detailed how-to procedures for Soldiers in the field. There are currently some 542 Field Manuals used by the United States Army.

Each FM has a designated number. For example, FM 3-39 is all about Military Police Operations. FM 3-99 covers Airborne and Air Assault Operations, while FM 4-40 is a guide to Quartermaster Operations, which simply means getting supplies to Soldiers. Each of these operations manuals are broad in their scope.

Then there are other FMs that go into great detail on certain tasks and equipment. For example, FM 3-21.5 *Drill & Ceremony* is a step-by-step "rule book" on marching. As a Noncommissioned Officer, an NCO if you want another acronym to remember, I had to know this book inside and out, because you just can't have a platoon of Soldiers lollygag on a military base going from point A to point B. FM 3-22.9 *Rifle Marksmanship M4* is just that, how to properly use and care for the M4 rifle. You get the idea. That's why there are so many FMs.

Each Field Manual is divided into numbered chapters, and each technique or tactic is chronologically numbered. Does this sound familiar? The Holy

Bible is arranged nearly the same way.

When the Scriptures were first written they were individual books, psalms, and letters, such as Genesis, Exodus, The Gospel of John, Letter to the Hebrews, and so forth. When the early church fathers compiled all these elements into one complete book, the "canon" as it was called, there were not individually numbered chapters and verses. It was not until the Byzantine Empire (395-1453 AD) that "chapters," (κεφάλαια in Greek, pronounced kef-ah-lay-ah) were inserted. Then, it wasn't until the year 1551 that French Bible scholar and printer Robert Estienne assigned standard numbered verses within the chapters, which we still use today. Since the Bible came first, long before military Field Manuals, it's safe to say that FMs imitated the Bible's format.

There are 66 books, written by 40 authors, all of whom were inspired by God, in the Holy Bible. Therefore, Christian Soldier, there are 66 Field Manuals you must learn inside and out. Yes, it is a daunting task, but they were all written to keep you "alive," on the battlefield, which is this earth, and prepare you for eternity. Therefore, we will be studying FM 2-10. No, not the U.S. Army's FM 2-10, which is *Cavalry Field Manual Mechanized Elements,* but the FM that points us to Calvary, the 2nd book of the Bible, which is the New Testament, and the 10th book of the New Testament is Ephesians.

INSIDE THE RECRUITING CENTER

What I'm going to do now is have you experience joining the United States Army. That's right, I'm going to take you through all the experiences that every recruit soldier would have, from recruiting to being discharged after years of service, for illustrative purposes. By doing it this way I'll be able to better explain the spiritual parallels between the U.S. Army and God's Army. Granted, the U.S. Army is an imperfect model to use, and so was the Roman Army that Paul used, but it's the best model we have here on earth to teach us the spiritual truths of Ephesians 6.

Are you ready? Let's do it. FOLLOW ME!

One day, while you're at a county fair or some other community event, you notice some military recruiters who have a table set up. It's very professional with a table skirt, brochures in neat piles, and some giveaways: pencils, pens, and stickers with the U.S. Army emblem on them. Sharp looking Soldiers are passing out double-fold brochures to anyone coming up to the table. On the covers of these slick brochures are eye-catching action photos of Soldiers doing incredible things: jumping out of airplanes, SCUBA diving under a turquoise ocean, fierce looking men wading waist deep in a muddy green swamp each covered in green face paint and toting intimidating looking rifles. You're interested, they seem to be friendly by the smiles on their faces, and so you go up to the table to hear what they have to say.

You talk to one of the recruiters, which is easier than you thought, and before taking off you grab a few of their brochures, along with a few freebies they have. You especially like the fridge magnet.

Later that evening you look over the three brochures you took, and you entertain the idea of being a Soldier in the United States Army. However, you're going to have to give it some more serious thought, but not until you sleep on it. After all, it would be a life changing event.

After a few days of surfing on the U.S. Army's official website you decide that you want to enlist, and so you look up the nearest U.S. Armed Forces Recruiting Center, which is not very far from your home.

When you get to the location the next day you walk right past the U.S. Marine Corps office, the U.S. Navy office, the U.S. Air Force office, and even the U.S. Space Force office that are in the same building, and head straight to the U.S. Army recruiting office at the end of the hallway. You have nothing against the other services, but being a Soldier appeals to you the most.

As soon as you step into the U.S. Army Recruiting office, you see a sharp, well-groomed Soldier in his uniform, who greets you with a warm, "Welcome."

You expected him to remain seated behind his desk, and for you to walk up to him, but instead he stands up immediately and walks to you as a friendly gesture. This makes you feel rather important.

The sergeant walks over to where you are standing, and introduces himself to you by firmly shaking your hand, looks you right in the eye, and says, "My name is Sergeant First Class Owens, and you are?"

After telling him your name he politely points to the nearest of the two chairs that are in front of his desk. He insists, "Please, take a seat," and then the two of you begin to talk.

You immediately notice that there's quite a contrast between you and the recruiter. You're very casual, but he has a command presence about him. It's his uniform, his demeanor, and the backing of the United States government.

God is also in the business of recruiting for His all-volunteer Army. The "brochures" that He has been using for centuries to draw people in, and to fight for Christendom, are all the books of the Bible. As I mentioned before, there are 66 books in the Bible, written by 40 authors, over a span of 1,546 years. There is no other "book" like this in history. Yes, they also double as our Field Manuals.

These 66 books explain everything an interested person needs to know for making an informed decision on whether to "join" or not. These books contain vast amounts of information on the nature of God, the history of the world from beginning to end, the "rules and regulations" we ought to live by, a list of the heroes, a list of the enemies past and present, many scientific facts that were not verified until modern history, and even the strategy that will lead to final victory. Of course, not every detail we'd like to know is contained in this single volume we call the Bible. John, one of Jesus' disciples, said it best so that we would understand, *and there are also many things that Jesus did, which if they were written one by one, I suppose that even the world itself could not contain the books that would be written. Amen. John 21:25*

When it comes to recruiting, God has a big quota to fill, and He uses both His Word and His people in the recruiting process. In fact, the order for every believer is to, *Go into all the world and preach the gospel to every creature. Mark 16:15*

"All the world" includes your family, friends, coworkers, neighbors, and even becoming a missionary in some remote corner of the world, if that is what God calls you to do. Whatever corner of the world you are in at the moment, is your recruiting field. Recruiting a grade school child is just as important as recruiting a Hollywood star. "All the world" means just that - ALL THE WORLD, because God is *not willing that any should perish, but that all should come to repentance. 2 Peter 3:9*

When believers share the Gospel, they are, in a sense, "recruiters." Just as the U.S. Army uses former civilians, who became soldiers, to recruit new civilians to join their ranks, God uses former sinners, who became saints, to get current sinners into His kingdom. We call the Christian Soldiers' recruiting method "witnessing."

Then comes that day that the interested person takes the "recruiting information" seriously, and wishes to talk to someone about joining, or he or she has already made up their mind that they're ready to "sign on the dotted line," and all they need to know is the next step to become saved.

TESTING & MEDICAL EXAM

Before the United States Army will allow you to join them, you must take a written test that measures your intelligence and aptitude. This test is called the Armed Services Vocational Aptitude Battery, and like any phrase in the military it has an acronym, ASVAB. It's pronounced as-vab. The ASVAB determines what 190 jobs in the U.S. Army a candidate is qualified to do. They're not going to allow a soldier to be a mechanic, fixing multi-million-dollar helicopters, if he or she doesn't have the natural ability to do so. To do that job, or Military Occupational Specialty (MOS) as they call it, one needs to be good at math, and good at fixing things. Likewise, if someone comes to the recruiter with a bachelor's degree in hand, the recruiter is going to suggest to them that they go to Officer Candidate School (OCS) in order to become a commissioned officer, because having a college degree is a condition to become a second lieutenant.

How's your health? If you have any health issues that would disqualify you from service, then no amount of smarts is going to get you in. This is why every prospective recruit is required to have a physical examination by military medical personnel. They examine every inch of you, both inside and out, and it even requires you removing all your clothing at one point. It's a little unnerving seeing the physician putting on a pair of blue Nitrile gloves in front of you as you are stark naked, but it's got to be done.

Unlike the U.S. Army, that must test every recruit at every physical and mental level, known as Military Entrance Processing Stations, God already knows everything about you, "both inside and out." He knows every cell of your body, all your habits, and every thought in your brain. Even before you had the thought pop into your mind about joining God's Army, He knew it before you did. Addressing this very issue, King David (1035 – 970 BC), a Warrior King, wrote this:

O Lord, you have searched me and known me. You know my sitting down and rising up; You understand my thought afar off. You comprehend my path and my laying down, and are acquainted with all my ways. For there is not a word on my tongue, but behold, O Lord, You know it altogether. Psalm 139:1-4

Concerning your physical body, God said, *but the very hairs of your head are all numbered. Luke 12:7* That's pretty amazing since there are approximately 100,000 to 150,000 hairs on the average human head. Yet, it's not like He just counted them all yesterday. God formed all those hair follicles when you were yet still in your mother's womb, *for you created my inmost being; You knit me together in my mother's womb. Psalm 139:13*

And, speaking of your prenatal days, Isaiah 44:24 proclaims, *Thus says the Lord, your Redeemer, and **He who formed you from the womb:** "I am the Lord, who makes all things, **Who stretches out the heavens** all alone, **Who spreads abroad the earth** by Myself."*

So, not only did He personally make you in your mother's womb, but He puts this event on an equal par with creating the universe. Yes, you! The creation of your body is just as marvelous as the forming of the heavens and the earth in His eyes.

Unlike the United States Army that rejects people with disqualifying physical defects, or those with less than average intelligence or aptitude, God accepts all recruits into His glorious Army. In fact, He even overlooks disqualifiers that the U.S. Army wouldn't dare to, like committing a felony. That's right, two Biblical warriors, Moses and King David, the second of whom wrote Psalm 139 that you just read two paragraphs ago, were both murderers. Of course, the key to their continued "service," and why God did not give them a "dishonorable discharge" along with the death penalty that they deserved, was because they repented of these murders, and wholeheartedly turned back to Him.

In case you're wondering, the only sin that will disqualify you from being in God's Army, and banished from His kingdom forever, is what Christians have labeled "The Unpardonable Sin."

*Therefore I say to you, every sin and blasphemy will be forgiven men, but blasphemy against the Spirit will not be forgiven men. Anyone who speaks a word against the Son of Man, it will be forgiven him, **but whoever speaks against the Holy Spirit, it will not be forgiven him,** either in this age or the* *age to come. Matthew 12:31-32*

So, what exactly does this verse mean? It seems clear, but at the same time a bit confusing. Well, let's peel this theological onion to find out.

It is the Holy Spirit, the third part of the Godhead (the Father, Son, and Holy Spirit), who draws people to Jesus Christ as Savior. The definition of the word "savior" is *a person who saves someone from danger.* Only Jesus can save a person from sin (crimes against God) and the second death (punishment in hell), but it is the Holy Spirit that convicts a person to repent. *And when He has come, **He will convict the world of sin,** and of righteousness, and of judgment: of sin, because they do not believe in Me. John 16:8*

Those who keep rejecting the Holy Spirit, who is your GET OUT OF JAIL FREE card, will not be forgiven – ever! It's that simple. When a person dies in that state of rebellion their fate is sealed, and eternal judgment awaits them. Therefore, all other sins (murder, lying, stealing, sexual immorality, gossip, and the rest of the charges) "will be forgiven." Accepting God's only plan of salvation, believing that Jesus the Christ paid the price for your rotten sins by shedding His own blood on the cross, means that He took upon Himself your punishment and you go scot-free. Not only that, but *as far as the east is from the west, so far has He removed our transgressions from us. Psalm 103:12*

Aren't you glad He didn't say, "as far as the north is from the south?"

What does that mean?

Well, when I went back into the military as a Reserve Soldier, while the Iraq and Afghanistan Wars were in full swing, one of the tasks I had to do from time to time as a military instructor was to teach Military Map Reading & Land Navigation. You guessed it! There is a Field Manual for this subject, and it is FM 3-25.26

So, here's your first military Land Nav lesson. If you start at the Prime Meridian, that's in Greenwich, England, and take an airplane west, and keep flying and flying, at what point would the plane start going east, assuming you never ran out of jet fuel? I'll give you a second to think about it.

The answer is, "You'll never stop going west." Likewise, if you start at Greenwich and fly east, with unlimited fuel, you would be forever going east around the globe. Around and around, you'd go. On the other hand, if you were in an airplane starting from the North Pole, Burrrr! and you flew down to the South Pole, which is in a southerly direction, your direction would eventually change to the opposite direction. The moment your plane passes over the South Pole, and keeps flying in the same straight line, the direction changes to a northerly direction. You would now be flying north to the North Pole. Then, when you pass over the North Pole again, you'd be heading south. You'd keep changing directions over the poles. It has everything to do with the earth's axis.

With this Land Nav lesson in mind, you can see why we should be relieved that the Bible informs us, "as far as the east is from the west, so far has He removed our transgressions from us." Your transgressions, your sins, will never catch up with you. There will be no change of direction - ever.

I find this verse fascinating, because when Psalm 103 was written, approximately 3,000 years ago, the writer was fully aware that the earth was a sphere and spun on an axis, along with the differences between latitude and longitude. Of course, I'm not surprised by the tremendous insight of this verse, because this verse is God's Word. He created the world, He knows how it works, and He revealed to the psalmist some Land Nav facts.

MILITARY OCCUPATIONAL SPECIALTY (MOS)

Your ASVAB and medical testing have been successfully completed. Congratulations! Therefore, your U.S. Army recruiter works with you to determine the best job for you, and the availability of that job. Of course, the military does not call it a job, but a "Military Occupational Specialty." If you ever want to know what someone does in the military, then you will ask them this way, "What is your MOS?" pronounced em-oh-es. The same goes for asking a veteran, "When you served, what was your MOS?" and they'll give you a number and title. For example, a response may be, "My MOS was 111.10 Infantry."

If you go to the official U.S. Army website it will give a "job description" of what an Infantryman does: *As a first step toward becoming an Infantryman, you'll train in the use of small arms, anti-tank, and other weapons systems. You will be responsible for capturing, destroying, and repelling enemy ground forces during missions. This is also the starting point for many advanced schools, such as Special Forces, Airborne School, Ranger School, Sniper School, and Pathfinder School.*

Obviously, an Infantryman is a combat MOS, and there are many combat roles. However, only a small percentage of people in the military do the actual fighting. Most MOSs are combat support roles: cooks, dentists, chaplains, clerks, mechanics, and so forth. However, all these Soldiers learn how to use a rifle, throw a hand grenade, and fire a machine gun, but once they leave Basic Combat Training after ten weeks, they eventually become detached from the combat mentality.

The U.S. Marine Corps also has an MOS for Infantryman, only they have a different MOS number and title for it. They call it "0311 Rifleman." The mindset of Marines is a little different than the other services, especially among their combat support personnel. Let me explain why.

When I was on my police department's S.W.A.T. team, I had the opportunity to train Marines at Camp Pendleton, California as a tactics instructor (it's a long story on how I ended up in that position), and in turn, I was permitted to go through many Marine courses: Military Operations Urban Terrain (MOUT), Helicopter Rope Suspension Training (HRST), Ship Assault, Tactical Swimmer, Scout Sniper School, Range Safety Officer (RSO), and I spent countless hours on various pistol and rifle ranges throwing lead downrange. I really honed my shooting skills with the Special Operations Training Group (SOTG) in their Shoot House; a 360-degree realistic indoor shooting environment. It was a symbiotic relationship that lasted nine years.

One of many things that I admire about Marines is their combat orientated attitude. You can ask any Marine in the Corps, from an F-18 jet pilot to a cook, the question, "What is your primary job as a Marine?" and they will all answer exactly the same way, "I am a Rifleman." Then they'll let you know their MOS after that.

The philosophy of the United State Marine Corps is that everyone in uniform is a "Rifleman" first, and their specialty comes second. Every Marine is expected to pick up a weapon and defend themselves or their fellow Marines when the need arises. OORAH!

"OORAH! is a loud guttural response that Marines give after they've been given orders, break formation, or are in agreement with something. Being with the Marines for nine years, while I was a law enforcement officer, I belted it out countless times with them. However, I had to recondition myself when I became a Reserve Soldier. I had to say it the U.S. Army way again, which is HOOAH!

As a Yankee I'm proud that the U.S. Army had HOOAH! long before the U.S. Marines had OORAH! Ours, and I say "ours," because during the reading of this book you are now in the U.S. Army, figuratively, and you need to know that HOOAH! started during the Second Seminole War from 1835 to 1842 by the 2nd Cavalry Regiment.

The U.S. Army's meaning of HOOAH! is defined as *anything and everything except "no."* I know, it sounds like a weak definition. In my own words, *HOOAH! is total agreement with what was just said, or what we are about to do.* Here's an example of how it would be used practically. I give you, and those in your squad, the order, "Move up that hill along the south side, and take out that machine gun nest."

You, and those in your squad, respond, "HOOAH!" which translated means, "Oh yes, we're going to destroy the enemy and take that hill the way you just ordered us to!" Then you go do it with Violence of Action.

That's a good term you should learn right now, "Violence of Action." It means, *employing lethal force with overwhelming impact to such an extent as to cause enemy combatants fear and confusion that allows the assaulting unit to seize the tactical advantage, even though they may be outnumbered.*

It's no coincidence that the Bible has its own HOOAH! It's the Hebrew word AMEN.

Amen means *so be it.* It's a declaration of affirmation, and we Christian Soldiers say this word at the end of a prayer, at the end of singing a hymn, or shout it out joyfully when we're in agreement with something the pastor or a believer has just proclaimed that really rouses our spirit. This is also why we Christians use a period punctuation (.) instead of an exclamation punctuation (!) after the word Amen, because God's ways are final - period.

Where do you think the U.S. Army got the idea of using acronyms from? They got it from God's people course, just as we found out that's how they got the idea of dividing Field Manuals into chapters and verses.

According to the Babylonian Talmud, the primary source of Jewish religious law that was completed in the year 500 BC, the word אמן, *Amen,* is actually a Hebrew acronym. It comes from three words אל מלך נאמן (read from right to left, El Melek Neh-eman, which means *God, trustworthy King*). But, again, we Christian Soldiers use it to mean *so be it.* Jesus, God Himself, used the word "Amen" in The Lord's Prayer, which ends with a request for a hostage rescue operation, a proclamation of ultimate victory as a superpower, and a confirmation with the word Amen:

> *But deliver us from the evil one.*
> *For Yours is the kingdom and the power and the glory forever.*
> **Amen.** *Matthew 6:13*

Going back to your own MOS, Hebrews 12:2 informs us that Jesus is the "author and finisher of our faith." That means He has a plan for you. He has a Military Occupational Specialty just for you, so to speak.

The interesting thing about God choosing your specialty for you, is that it may not be exactly what you had in mind for yourself. For example, He took an uneducated fisherman, Saint Peter, and had him preach to the educated elite: the Pharisees, Sadducees, and the scribes. Then he took an educated Jewish Pharisee, the Apostle Paul, who even listed his elite pedigree in the New Testament, and he ended up preaching to uneducated gentiles, sailors, and Roman soldiers chained to him when he was a prisoner. Moses was a Prince of Egypt who ended up tending sheep for 40 years. David tended sheep as a child and teenager and ended up being the King of Israel. It seems that the career paths of these four men had been flipped, but God uses these examples to give us the clear message that, *"My thoughts are not your thoughts, nor are your ways My Ways," says the Lord. "For as the heavens are higher than the earth, so are My ways higher than your ways, and My thoughts than your thoughts." Isaiah 55:8-9*

Are you in a situation right now that you are not happy with? Do you feel like you're stuck in a rut? God has you there for a reason. Likewise, are you happy with your current status? Do you like the way things are going right now? God has you there for a reason, but don't get too comfortable, for He may end up rocking your world later on. If it happens, will you accept the change when it comes? Will you allow Him to change your MOS? If you do, then you'll be in agreement that *we know that all things work together for good to those who love God, to those who are the called according to His purpose. Romans 8:28*

Regardless of what occupational specialty God has you in right now, are you a "rifleman" first? Are you willing to pick up a weapon, the Word of God, and defend your faith and your fellow Christian Soldiers? The war is happening now, and it has been raging ever since Eve took that first bite of the fruit from the *tree of the knowledge of good and evil.*

OATH OF ENLISTMENT

After your MOS is decided upon the papers are drawn up, DD FORM 4 to be exact, which is titled, in bold caps to emphasis the seriousness of the commitment, ENLISTMENT/REENLISTMENT DOCUMENT – ARMED FORCES OF THE UNITED STATES.

Here's a word of caution. Read the entire document meticulously, because you need to know exactly what you're getting into. Once you sign your name to the "contract" Uncle Sam owns you. I'm serious. When you're in the U.S. Army you can't just quit or walk away when you feel like it, like you would a civilian job. If you do, it's called AWOL, **A**bsent **W**ith**o**ut **L**eave, and if you don't turn yourself in within 30 days, and they eventually find you because there will be a warrant out for your arrest, you will be arrested and thrown into a military prison. Go AWOL during a time of war, and it becomes desertion, which is punishable with life in prison or execution.

Every Soldier knows that he or she is obligated to serve a fixed number of years in order to receive their MOS, because they talked about it with their recruiter, but when it comes to signing DD FORM 4 they may end up glossing over some of the fine print that could impact their lives long after their initial service. For example, after you fulfill your Active Duty Obligation, a term for "full time Soldier," you may be required to serve in the Reserve Component of the U.S. Army. In other words, you may be required to be a "weekend warrior" once a month and serve active duty for two weeks out of each year. Not just for one year, or two years, but all the way up to eight years if the government wants you to. That's quite a commitment! Then, if there is a war, Uncle Sam can legally order you to serve on active duty without your consent, keep you for the entire duration of the war, and even up to six months after the war ends. It's all in the contract.

Of course, you've thought over all the conditions of the contract, and you're fully committed to serving as a Soldier in the United States Army.

You're handed a pen, and you initial here, sign there, initial here also, but it's still not official. You're not a Soldier yet. A minute later you receive your set of copies for your own personal records. You place it in the Manila envelope you've been carrying all morning long with the other papers you've been given.

At AFEES, Armed Forces Examining and Entrance Station, which is the same place you just signed your enlistment papers, you are ushered into a larger room by a sergeant with a dozen other recruits. You are told to take a seat.

Five minutes later an Army captain enters the room, and then goes to the front. He stands straight and tall behind a wooden lectern that has the emblem of the United States Army on the face of it, and behind him standing upright is the flag of the United States of America. It's not a cheap flag like some people mount on the side of their houses at an angle on the 4th of July or on Memorial Day, but this one is an indoor type with a gold fringe around the edges, two gold cords and tassels hanging just under the gold spear tip, bright white embroidered stars, all majestically draped on a polished oak pole.

The officer orders you to your feet after a few moments of shuffling some papers around.

He welcomes everyone, and then orders everyone in the room, "Raise your right hand, and repeat after me."

You know it's legitimate to raise your right hand, because you saw it done in a couple of courtroom movies before, so it must be official. You repeat the words that the captain reads, and you swear this oath, an affirmation, out loud with the others standing next to you in the room:

I, _____ , do solemnly swear that I will support and defend the Constitution of the United States against all enemies, foreign and domestic; that I will bear true faith and allegiance to the same; and that I will obey the orders of the President of the United States and the orders of the officers appointed over me, according to regulations and the Uniform Code of Military Justice. So help me God.

That oath makes it official. You are legally a Soldier in the United States Army.

Stop there!

I want you to notice something before we move on. The word "Soldier" is capitalized. That's intentional, because that's exactly how the U.S. Army wants the word to appear in all literature and documentation. When the word appears like this, *soldier*, which is grammatically correct in the English language, it is to be taken as a generic word. However, in October of 2003 Army Chief of Staff General Peter J. Schoomaker decreed that the word "soldier" would be capitalized "from now on." The reason given by the Office of the Chief of Public Affairs is, "The change gives Soldiers the respect and importance they've always deserved, especially now in their fight against global terrorism." Therefore, for the rest of the book you will see the word written as Soldier when it comes to a United States Soldier.

The oath you just took, figuratively, makes you an Army Soldier, but not a "fully qualified Army Soldier." That will come many weeks later.

We'll also be capitalizing the first letter of the word "soldier" for the term *Christian Soldier.* If I were to make a decree, like General Schoomaker did, it would read something like this, "The change gives Christian Soldiers the respect and importance that even *angels desire to look into, 1 Peter 1:12,* in their fight against *the gates of hell, Matthew 16:18.*"

Going back to the oath of enlistment that you took in this story, the government is now convinced of your commitment, which allows them to move forward with their plans to spend a lot of time and money on you. They're going to mold and shape you into what they want you to be. You just have to be cooperative with the process, and let it happen.

Just as you're not a Soldier in the United States Army until you raise your right hand, which is a tradition that dates back to Isaiah 62:8, *The Lord has sworn by His right hand,* and at the same time take the oath of enlistment, you're not going to be in God's Army, nor will you step one foot into heaven, until *you confess with your mouth the Lord Jesus and believe in your heart that God has raised Him from the dead, you will be saved. Romans 10:9*

The words you repeated after the U.S. Army captain were not just words that you parroted. You are not only to believe in their meaning, but the United States government expects you to obey them.

When you said, "The Sinner's Prayer," with whatever words you used, so long as they expressed to God that you believed in your heart that He raised Jesus from the dead in order to save you from your sins, this ended your rebellion against Him as an enemy combatant, and you were instantly given citizenship into God's kingdom. As a citizen you are allowed to join God's Army.

Unlike the U.S. Army, even if you can't physically speak for some reason, due to being born that way or unable to due to a sickness or an accident, you can "speak" anytime to God from the heart. That's right, He knows your thoughts, and The Sinner's Prayer can be "spoken" internally.

It's no coincidence then that the men and women in charge of our military also require the raising of the right hand and an oath, an affirmation, for recruits to enlist or be commissioned into the United States Army. After all, we are all made in God's image. So, naturally we are going to have institutions, and do certain rituals that God also does or requires. However, unlike mortals, who cannot know a man's or a woman's thoughts, God knows every thought you ever had, are having now, and will have for eternity. He knows if your "Sinner's Prayer" was genuine or not.

To illustrate this point, there once was a United States soldier, and I am purposely not capitalizing the word "soldier" for a good reason, named Nidal Hasan who gave the same oath that all enlisted Soldiers give. The U.S.

Army believed him at his word, and invested time and money into him.

Nidal Hasan worked hard and received a college education after enlisting, and then shortly after obtaining his bachelor's degree in biochemistry he was commissioned as an officer. As such, he received even more schooling, thanks to the generosity of Uncle Sam, and after completing his internship and residency in psychiatry at Walter Reed Army Medical Center he worked his way up to the rank of major.

Then came a turning point in Major Hasan's personal life. Although born an American citizen in Arlington County, Virginia, he became a "more devout Muslim," according to his brother, after the death of their parents. He absorbed the radical Islamic online teachings of U.S. citizen, turned terrorist, Nawar al-Awlaki who was spreading his jihadist propaganda from Yemen.

On November 5, 2009 Major Hasan, armed with seven semi-automatic pistols and a revolver, went on a shooting spree at Fort Hood, Texas. He murdered 14 people, which included one unborn child, and wounded 32 others. All of the victims, except for a civilian physician assistant and the unborn baby, were fellow Soldiers.

Responding security forces shot Major Hasan four times. He survived his wounds, but he was rendered a paraplegic and sent to a military prison after his trial. As such, he was stripped of his military rank, forfeiture of his pay, and dismissed (the equivalent of a dishonorable discharge for enlisted personnel) from the United States Army.

Nidal Hasan's evil mentor Nawar Al-Awlaki was killed by a U.S. drone strike by orders of President Barack Obama two years later. Al-Awlaki was the first U.S. citizen in history to be executed in this manner.

Obviously, Nidal Hasan's oath to the United States Army was merely empty words, for he did not keep the oath. It doesn't matter that for 21 years he served his country. He was the enemy, who just happened to be dormant for 21 years. The end result is part of the whole story.

Even now there are many enemies of God who proclaim to be Christians, and they are even living the "Christian life," but they are actually dormant until the moment of truth. These infiltrating "christian soldiers" are so convincing that they have even fooled themselves. Jesus warns us, *Not everyone who says to Me, "Lord, Lord," shall enter the kingdom of heaven, but he who does the will of My Father in heaven. Many will say to Me in that day, "Lord, Lord, have we not prophesied in Your name, cast out demons in Your name, and done many wonders in Your name?" And then I will declare to them, "I never knew you; depart from Me, you who practice lawlessness!" Matthew 7:21-23*

Did you notice that this warning was not a "Major Hasan situation" that Jesus was talking about? Jesus didn't say, "If you are supposed to be following Me, and calling Me 'Lord,' but you just went out and committed a mass murder, or you lied, cheated someone, or committed some other grievous sin, then I have no choice now but to tell you to depart from Me. You're out!"

No. Jesus described people who were doing many of the things that Christians are supposed to do, like casting out demons in His name or doing many wonders in His name, but then He ends up telling them, "I never knew you; depart from Me."

Any Christian who reads these words of Jesus should be terrified. I know I am every time I read it. I can't help but think, *Am I one of those people He is talking about? Have I been deceiving myself into thinking that I am a Christian, only for Him to tell me after it's too late, 'I never knew you?'*

The truth is that Jesus wants us to be terrified when we read this. Not terrified to the point of taking hope away from us, but to stir up righteous fear in us in order to bring us to a point of self-examination, and repentance if need be.

Calling yourself a Christian does not make you a Christian. Doing "Christian things" does not get you into heaven. Even using the name of "Jesus" to do good works is not the currency to buy salvation. In the second half of verse 21 Jesus stated exactly what gets someone into heaven, "but he who does the will of my Father in heaven." So, what is the will of the Father? It's what we've already covered – *confess, believe in your heart, and you will be saved.* The principle is easy, but the process is both difficult and rewarding.

A true U.S. Army Soldier is one who gives an oath, keeps that oath, and then eventually receives an Honorable Discharge. The entire process must be fulfilled to make one a genuine Soldier. The principle is easy, but the process is both difficult and rewarding.

Oh, and in case you're wondering if I am taking this *put on the full armor of God* metaphor a bit too far, let me remind you again that being a Soldier today parallels being a Soldier when Ephesians 6 was written for us. Thus, taking an oath for the military is the backstory that many Christians just don't think about. Just as a man or woman takes the oath of enlistment to become a U.S. Army Soldier today, so too did ancient Roman men take an oath, the *sacramentum militare,* to serve in the Roman army. Roman historian, Vegetius, a Christian, wrote about the oath, which was administered annually on New Year's Day or on the anniversary of the emperor's accession:

Iurant autem milites omnia se strenue facturos quae praeceperit imperator, numquam deserturos militiam nec mortem recusaturos pro Romana republica.

I don't speak Latin either, but it translates:

But the soldiers swear that they shall faithfully execute all that the Emperor commands, that they shall never desert the service, and that they shall not seek to avoid death for the Roman republic.

In 380 AD, when Emperor Theodosius made Christianity the official religion of the Roman Empire, the Christian recruits swore the same oath, but ended it with *by God, Christ, and the Holy Ghost.*

Not before signing the enlistment contract, nor at any time during the oath, are you given any guarantees that the United States Army is going to win a war. There is also no guarantee that you'll even make it out alive until the end of your enlistment.

Now for a true story about myself related to this very subject of "no guarantees."

When I, Private Wagner, made the commitment of servitude to my country on 9 September 1980 it was during the Cold War. The enemy at the time was the Union of Soviet Socialist Republic, along with the Eastern Bloc countries, and they were determined to defeat us. Their goal was to strip the Western nations of God, democracy, and capitalism, which are the three pillars that held up the USA as the freest and most prosperous country in human history, and replace it with their atheistic communism. The god to be worshiped, if we were to have lost the Cold War, was the government. That's because there is no room at all for God in communism, and her twin sister socialism. And, if that were not enough, at the time I joined the United States Army the country of Iran had been holding 52 American hostages for 10 agonizing months, and just five months earlier the United States Armed Forces had been thoroughly humiliated during a failed rescue attempt known as Operation Eagle Claw. Yet, despite the negatives on the ledger, I wanted to serve my country as a Soldier.

The great thing about joining God's Army is that it's 100% guaranteed that His kingdom is going to win the war by destroying all of our enemies: the devil, those who serve him (fallen angels and the world), and including death itself, by casting all of them into the "lake of fire," also known as "hell."

Even if you are wounded or killed in a battle in the service of God, it's kind of like a First-Person Shooter (FPS) video game where you're given a new life if you get shot or blown up. You are reanimated, so to speak. Only, the next life given to you by God is permanent and indestructible.

For we know that if our earthly house, this tent, is destroyed, we have a building from God, a house not made with hands, eternal in the heavens.
2 Corinthians 5:1

To give you a little bit more insight into my background, as it relates to taking an oath, after my military service I took the same oath four more times, although some of the wording was slightly different here and there, during my tactical career. At the end of the graduation ceremony in the police academy I, along with 20 other remaining recruits, was sworn in as a law enforcement officer. So, what exactly is a "sworn" law enforcement officer? Although law enforcement officers are civilians in relation to the military, each takes an oath to defend the Constitution of the United States "against all enemies, foreign and domestic" just like the military. In addition to this oath, I had to memorize the Law Enforcement Code of Ethics. It's quite long, four paragraphs in total, but I'll share with you a few of the lines so you'll get an idea of what it emphasizes:

As a Law Enforcement Officer, my fundamental duty is to serve mankind, to safeguard lives and property, to protect the innocent against deception, the weak against oppression or intimidation, and the peaceful against violence or disorder, and to respect the Constitutional rights of all men to liberty, equality and justice.

It ends with these words, or at least it did in my day:

...dedicating myself before God to my chosen profession – law enforcement.

When I left the police force, I then joined the nation's fifth largest sheriff's department in the country, and I was sworn in as a deputy sheriff. It was the same oath, and the same code of ethics, that included defending the United States Constitution before God.

Following the radical Islamic terrorist attacks on United States soil, on September 11, 2001, which is infamously known as "9-11," the federal government was actively recruiting anyone with Special Operations (SpecOps) training and experience in order to fight in The Global War on Terrorism. I let the federal government know that I wanted to fight terrorism. I submitted my application, went through a rather lengthy testing process out of state, and several weeks later I was selected.

My class at F.L.E.T.C., (pronounced flet-see, which is an acronym for Federal Law Enforcement Training Center) was sworn in at the beginning of our counterterrorism training as U.S. federal agents five weeks before we were scheduled to graduate. This was definitely not the norm. The reason for this *cart before the horse* approach concerning the oath was, as it was explained to us from the Special Agent In Charge (SAIC), pronounced sack, of the training center was, "In case we come under attack again, we may have to cut your training short, and send you immediately out into the field. You all came to us from law enforcement agencies or from the military, so if this scenario happens, you'll just have to do what you have to do to protect the country. You'll have to make it up as you go."

Three years later, in 2006, I decided to go back into the military, only this time as a Reserve Soldier. Once again, I raised my right hand, and I took the exact same oath that I did when I was eighteen years old. I served 10 more years, and in that time period I rose to the rank of Master Sergeant, which is three stripes up, and three rockers down. It's a high rank when it comes to enlisted personnel.

The two elements found in both the military oath and the law enforcement oath is the defense of the U.S. Constitution, with the help of God. Most countries do not swear to their national constitution, because they have an unstable document that cannot withstand the test of time. Most Western countries also do not call upon God for His help, because they are humanists. Although the God of the Bible may have been a part of their history at one time, they don't see a need for God in modern times. It's too bad, because *Jesus Christ is the same yesterday, today, and forever. Hebrews 13:8*

Someday spiritually blind men and women may succeed in doing away with the U.S. Constitution, and pushing God completely out of the public square (as if they could actually send the God who created the universe into exile), but in God's kingdom *Heaven and earth will pass away, but My words will be no means pass away. Luke 21:33*

The Bible is not only the Christian Soldier's recruiting brochures and Field Manuals, but it is also our "Constitution" if you will, and it's going to be around for eternity. God's not going anywhere either. *And He will reign over the house of Jacob forever, and of His kingdom there will be no end. Luke 1:33* Therefore, it is impossible to go wrong giving your oath, your allegiance, to God, and be a lifelong student of His Word – the Bible.

ORDERS & TRANSPORTATION

Your group is told in a loud voice, "Stand by, to stand by," from a sergeant who just walked into the room right after the oath ceremony.

In the Army you learn a lot of idioms and *stand by to stand by* is one that you'll hear frequently by those in charge of you. Simply put, it means that you have to wait without a time limit. You're actually waiting to wait. It could be a few minutes, or a few hours. You never know.

After standing by for about thirty-five minutes the sergeant comes back into the room, orders your group to follow him into an adjacent room that is filled with a bunch of office cubicles, and then he points to a desk where everyone is supposed to line up in front of. A clerk, with the rank of Specialist, an emblem with an eagle inside of a weird upside-down triangle, is sitting behind the desk pulling sheets of paper from the printer as they keep landing in the black plastic paper tray.

When the printer goes silent the clerk takes the rest of them and stacks all the papers into a single pile. He reads off the names one at a time.

"Rodriguez."

The Soldier just named steps forward directly in front of the desk, and the clerk slaps down the piece of paper and circles only the information that the Soldier needs to know for now. He then hands the paper to the new Soldier when he is finished, who is then told, "You're dismissed. Follow the red line on the floor."

Your name is finally called, and you stand a foot in front of the desk.

You look down at the paper on the desk, and it looks like a foreign language.

The Specialist looks up at you for only a second, and then back down at the paper, "These are your orders. I'm going to explain them to you."

With a standard government issued black pen the young Specialist circles your name, your Social Security number, your MOS, where your first assignment will be, and where you'll be going for Basic Combat Training and Advanced Individual Training afterwards.

You're glad he explained it to you, although rather too quickly for your liking, or you wouldn't have understood half of the acronyms and abbreviations printed on the sheet.

This single sheet of paper, your orders, determines your life for the next 20 weeks.

The name "Sanders" is called out, which is your cue to move on.

Once the last Soldier in line has her orders in hand, your group is given a ten-minute bathroom break, and told where to meet next, which is outside of the building in front of the sign DEPARTURE POINT.

When you get outside there is an idling charter bus waiting alongside the curb. After showing your new military I.D. card to the corporal, a "two striper," who is standing with a clipboard at the foot of the steps of the bus, you board the bus and find an empty seat after your name is checked off.

A few minutes later the bus pulls away from AFEES and takes the group to the airport. The corporal, sitting in the front row seat, goes along to make sure that nobody has second thoughts and gets off the bus prematurely. That was obviously his intent by the head count he did when everyone was seated just before the bus started moving.

With the sound of an occasional honking horn echoing off of concrete walls, and the steady rhythm of car doors closing and trunks slamming at the unloading zone in front of Terminal B of the airport, your group makes a semi-circle around the corporal so everyone can hear him better. The heavy smell of car exhaust fumes, in the occasional pockets of swirling heated air, blows in your face and is inhaled through your nostrils every time a large vehicle passes by.

The corporal hands out the airline tickets one at a time. When he places your hard copy ticket into your hand he repeats, "Good luck," just as he did to the first ten people that got theirs before you. Even though it is robotically repetitious, it's genuine.

Once inside the airport terminal everyone splits off and goes their separate ways. Not everyone is going to the same destination.

You have no luggage to check in, just a small carry-on bag with you, so you head straight to the TSA checkpoint.

Your flight requires changing a plane, and then a two-hour wait once you get there. Sometime around 9:30 p.m. you arrive at the final airport on your itinerary.

When that Specialist behind the desk at AFEES gave you your orders there were certain things that had to be explained to you, because you don't know much about the Army culture.

Likewise, when you invited Jesus Christ into your heart, allowing Him to be your Lord and Savior, the "oath of your enlistment" so to speak, the

Holy Spirit literally entered into you, and at that very moment you became a Christian Soldier; an untrained and inexperienced one, but a Christian Soldier, nonetheless.

With the Holy Spirit dwelling inside every believer, you have Someone to give you instructions when you need it. *When He, the Spirit of truth, has come, He will guide you into all truth; for He will not speak on His own authority, but whatever He hears He will speak; and He will tell you things to come. John 16:13*

Should there ever come a time in your service as a Christian Soldier that you end up in enemy hands, the Holy Spirit will give you the instructions you will need to get through the ordeal then and there. *But when they deliver you up, do not worry about how or what you should speak. For it will be given to you in that hour what you should speak. Matthew 10:19*

Just like you were handed your orders, and the bus transported you to the airport, so too you receive your divine orders from God, and He will transport you to the next location that you need to get to. Some of the trips will be quick trips, while others may take a little longer. If you're a drunk, He will take you to the destination "sober." If you are engaged in sexual immorality, He will take you to the destination "purity." If you are an angry person, He will take you to the destination "peace." If you are an unhappy person, He will take you to the destination "joy." He's going to get you to where you need to go, but just how long it takes is up to the Holy Spirit and your willingness to let Him mold and shape you into what he wants you to be. We just need to be cooperative with the process, and let it happen.

"There's your carry-on bag. Get it and go! Get it and go!"

You're getting on another bus, and this one is going to take you the rest of the way to Basic Combat Training (BCT), also known as "boot camp." You need to go there to be trained in the skills of Christian soldiering. HOOAH!

Chapter 2

BASIC COMBAT TRAINING

LEARNING TO BE A SOLDIER

If you never had the opportunity to attend Basic Combat Training (BCT), also known as "Boot Camp," in the United States Army, then I'll describe it to you in one sentence, so you'll have an idea of what it is like. If you've experienced it before, perhaps through another branch of the Armed Forces, then this will definitely bring back some old memories.

It's information overload, intimidating, exciting, a culture shock, mild forms of torture, a test of one's character, all rolled up into ten weeks that seems to drag on for an eternity, and yet it's all one big blur that passes quickly.

After passing the main gate of the military base, with a big sign that reads VICTORY STARTS HERE, the bus that brought you from the airport comes to a complete stop. The air brakes hiss a couple of times before the engine is turned off. For a moment it's eerily quiet, but only for a moment.

Waiting on the curb, under the floodlights, is a line of drill sergeants spaced out evenly to the length of the bus. There's about six or seven of them. They're all wearing camouflage pattern uniforms and the iconic "Smokey the Bear" hats, the ones with a round brim, which you later find out that the proper name for it is "Campaign Hat." A couple of the drill sergeants are female, and their hats look a little different. They have on what looks like an Australian bush hat; a flat brim like the male drill sergeants' hats, but with one side upturned. These sergeants are screaming in unison at everyone inside the bus to get off, and to get into formation.

What is a formation? you ask yourself. *I just got here. How am I supposed to know?*

You don't get more than a few feet away from the outside of the bus door when one of the sergeants singles you out. He has a face of flint, with piercing hazel eyes, and shouts at you with his nose almost touching your face, "What is your major malfunction private? Don't you know your own last name? Get into alphabetical order like you were told to do! Now, move it! Move it!"

You learn quickly what an Extended Rectangular Formation is, and you soon know your place in it. In just minutes you have the Position of Attention also down pat after seeing a few people corrected, and not so politely or patiently either.

Like cattle, you are then herded into a large warehouse called the Reception Station. For the next few days, you find yourself in and out of this huge building to complete what they call "processing."

The Reception Station is one room after another that you must maneuver through like a mouse maze, each room with a different purpose.

One of the first rooms you're ushered into is the barbershop. With a dozen buzzing electric clippers all cutting hair at the same time, it makes the room sound like you're inside a giant beehive. The barbers shave the heads of the males to the very scalp. Big clumps of hair continually fall to the floor around each barber chair with each pass over of the heads, while the females have theirs cut to shoulder length. There's no fashion model styles in this place. After the cape is pulled off from your shoulders, it's back in line, and then back into the maze.

In this room your body measurements are taken with a tailor's tape measure from, I guess you'd call him a "tailor," who then immediately turns around and starts yanking folded uniforms from a few of the wooden cubby holes.

"Stick out your arms," he tells you, and then piles the different types of uniforms onto your outstretched arms, which makes you look like a human forklift.

The new clothes are almost up to your nose, and you get the hint that it's time to move on when the tailor yells out, "Next!" looking right past you as if you no longer exist.

When you get to the very last table you are instructed by a civilian clerk to stuff all the contents into the duffle bag you were just handed. At least this duffle bag makes it easier to carry everything. The new combat boots go into the bag last.

You're instructed to put on the duffle bag like a backpack, and then keep following the line like a bunch of ants.

You shuffle into yet another room, following closely behind the soldier in front of you at arm's length as you were told, and a clerk at another table hands you an olive drab laundry bag that you are instructed to hold out like a Halloween trick or treat bag once you move on.

As you sidestep your way along the long table, there is a line of clerks behind it that drop small items into the opening of the bag as you pass them: a belt, toiletries, underwear, and socks.

"Please go to the next room!" the heavyset middle-aged lady at the end of the table nicely tells you. It's the first person to show you any kindness since you arrived, and for that brief moment it felt comforting. It felt like the world you had left behind.

Your momentary peace is quickly interrupted when three men in camouflage uniforms, wearing camouflage baseball caps, *That's something new,* shout at you to keep moving. You don't even know who said it. It's just all white noise now.

As you move to keep up, you stop for just a few seconds, hoping not to get caught, so you can adjust the straps of the heavy duffle bag that's on your back in order to keep it from slipping off your shoulders, while at the same time attempting to get the laundry bag to hang from the little space available on your left shoulder, but it doesn't work because the duffle bag takes up too much space back there. It's frustrating, therefore, you decide to carry the laundry bag in front of you, bear hugging it against your chest with both arms like a packed spare parachute. You feel like a homeless person carrying all your worldly possession around with you without the benefit of a shopping cart.

Having become more efficient at shuffling from one room to another, you keep moving as you are told to do, and even though you're still jet lagged from the flights, the constant verbal abuse hurled at you keeps you awake and alert. As long as there is no down time you feel that you'll be alright.

It's been a long day and night, and finally your group is marched into the barracks, your new home, in single file. You try desperately not to drop any of your items on the floor, because when it happened two hours ago it was met with a swift tongue-lashing from a drill sergeant. It's just too ener-gy-draining to go through that again.

Each of the cots, the Army's name for beds, is assigned. In the bay there are forty cots. Forty, being how many soldiers there are in a platoon. There are twenty cots on one side of the huge room, large armoire lockers running down the middle of the room that are used to store the uniforms and toilet-ry kits, which also to serve as a room divider, and then twenty more cots on the other side that are arranged the same way. All forty of the personal spaces look identical. In fact, as you sneak a couple of peeks while stand-ing at the Position of Attention, you realize that everyone looks identical to one another: the same haircut, the same clothes, and even the same way of standing. There are different facial features, and different skin colors, but that's about it.

After the 30 minutes given to put everything away in the armoire, a quick shower, and latrine (communal toilets) time, the final order is given, "Lights out!"

You lucked out that you don't have to pull any guard duty tonight.

You're out like a light when your head hits the pillow. You're completely exhausted.

During the wee hours, which started the moment the dream cycle began, you forgot all about the Army. You feel as though you are back home, because you had just been there the day before in your own warm comfy bed.

Then reality hits you. Literally.

Kaaaabang! Tink! Tink! Tink! Clunk! is the sound of a metal trash can, as it bounces a few times between the two rows of cots atop the slick waxed tiled floor, coming to a stop against the metal frame at the foot of your cot. The fluorescent lights are flipped on instantaneously. A drill sergeant had thrown the empty metal trash can in the air, that followed a trajectory between the two rows of cots on your side of the bay, just like a giant bowling ball.

"Get out of your cots now! Stand at attention! On the line! On the line!" shrills the drill sergeant.

With your sleepy squinting eyes adjusting to the bright light, you see the drill sergeant at one end of the room standing with his legs shoulder width apart, and his fists resting on his hips in the classic Superman pose. He couldn't have looked more authoritative.

You move your hand up to your forehead to brush aside your bangs out of your face, as is your morning habit when getting out of bed, but there are no bangs there to push away. You feel what's going on up there by rubbing your greatly reduced head of hair with the palm of your hand, and that is when you suddenly realize where you're at, *Oh yeah, they cut all my hair off.* Then you ask yourself, *What did I get myself into? I think I made a terrible mistake.*

You can't believe that you volunteered for this, and nothing but the unknown is ahead of you.

It is still pitch-black outside. As such, the windows may just have very well been painted over with a coat of flat black paint, because there is absolutely no difference between that, and the darkness outside. You couldn't have had any more than four hours of sleep this morning. What you wouldn't give for just two more hours of sleep.

There you are, in your green T-shirt and underwear, standing at attention with your toes on the line next to the foot of your cot as you were instructed to do. Then the next order is barked out from the same guy who just rudely threw the trash can, "Get dressed! Be in front of the building, in formation, in five minutes, for PTR!"

Nobody was moving, so he yelled out, "Now, people!"

Then the platoon bay was filled with busy activity.

What the heck is PRT? you ask yourself. You remember seeing the term on the Army's website before, but you had already forgotten what it means. Just a few hours earlier you had a ton of acronyms thrown at you, so how could you remember that one?

You find out real soon what the acronym PRT means after being marched out onto a damp grassy field some distance away from the barracks. It is Physical Readiness Training, and lots of it.

The drill sergeant, standing on the small wooden platform looking down at your platoon, in a loud commanding voice states, "Today we'll be conducting an Endurance and Mobility session, which will consist of the Preparation Drill, the Hip Stability Drill, Military Movement Drill, Ability Group Run, and Recovery Drill."

You don't know what any of it means, but it sounds like a lot of stuff to do.

The stretching and exercises are not that difficult, and they're even welcomed to stop the shivering.

When the run begins the sun has still not come up yet, although the sky is starting to show shades of yellow to the east, and it's getting brighter by the minute.

While doing Double Time, running at the speed of a jog in a tight group formation, you learn your first cadence song. It's exactly what you expected, having seen it before in many war movies. The tough-as-nails sergeant leading the cadence, who served two tours in Afghanistan and one in Iraq, has the platoon sing an Airborne song, because he had been with the 82nd Airborne when he was overseas. He belts it out:

"C-130 rolling down the strip,
forty troopers gonna take a little trip."

You repeat the lyrics to the sound of everyone's boots slapping the street asphalt.

Before the sergeant begins the next verse, he bellows out to the platoon, "Sing like you have a pair!" and continues:

"Mission top secret, destination unknown,
and they don't give a damn if they ever come home."

The cussing bothers you as a Christian, so you only lip that word when you get to it, and then continue to sing the rest of the lyrics out loud.

"Stand up, hook up, shuffle to the door,
Jump right out and count to four.
If that main don't open wide,
I've got a reserve by my side."

Oh, wow! This is cool! you can't help but think.

After the "little run," as the drill sergeant sadistically describes it, you're marched in a formation back to the company area. You start to shiver again in the crisp cool morning air, because you're now stationary wearing your sweaty PT gear: a black short sleeve T-shirt with the word ARMY in big bold street sign yellow letters across the chest, tucked into black shorts with a reflective yellow belt around the waist, finishing the ensemble with white socks and black tennis shoes. The sergeant doesn't care about your discomfort, because he's talking to the company commander, a captain.

At least the sun is up.

A few minutes later the sergeant renders a salute to the officer, and then turns his attention back to the platoon.

"Platoon, Fall Out!"

"Yes Drill Sergeant! HOOAH!"

Everyone breaks formation and yells, "Ahhhhhhhhhhhhhhhhhhhhhhh!" all the way to the barracks entrance as if rooting for the same team at a highly charged college football game.

This long yell did not come spontaneously for anyone, for you and your platoon were taught exactly what to do just minutes earlier in order to "show your esprit du corps," and that you had "better always" have esprit du corps for the entire duration of BCT.

You quickly get out of your sports clothes, change into your combat uniform, and try hard not to be the last one out. There's no doubt in your mind that the sergeant will carry out his threat to punish the last Soldier out of the barracks.

While standing at attention you sneak another quick peek down at your gig line, even though doing so while at the Position of Attention can get you into heaps of trouble if caught. God forbid if the gig line is off, for two of your fellow soldiers had been hollered at, and made to do 20 push-ups, before they even made it out of the building when their gig lines were found to be a bit off. The "gig line," as you were taught the night before when issued the uniforms, which now seems like days ago, is a military term that refers to the alignment of the seam of the uniform shirt, belt buckle, and pants fly-seam. They all have to be lined up.

Now that you are fully dressed, and the morning sun is shining its golden warm rays on the platoon, you feel comfortable. However, no good feeling lasts for long in this place. The sergeant gets the formation moving again, and it's a four-minute march to the front of a nondescript building. This one is not like the others, for it has the distinct smell of cooking bacon wafting from it.

The sergeant leaves you standing there in the Position of Parade Rest: feet spread shoulder width apart with hands flat and overlapping each other behind the small of the back. He's gone for several minutes after disappearing inside the building marked MESS HALL.

When the sergeant emerges from the mess hall, which was making you salivate from the familiar odors coming from it, and even the few vegans and vegetarians in the group whispered that the smell of meat was making them hungry, you mentally prepare yourself to move again.

The next set of instructions to the platoon is, "You will not speak inside the mess hall. You will get your chow," which is Army-speak for food, "sit down, and eat for fifteen minutes. There will be no second helpings. Then take your empty food trays to the designated area, drop them off, exit the building there," as he points to a door, "and get back out here in formation. Do you understand me?"

"Yes, Drill Sergeant!" forty voices sounding like a thunderclap.

"IIIIIIII caaaaaaaan't heeeeeaaar yooooou!" he yells even louder, and mockingly.

The voices are even louder, "YES, DRILL SERGEANT!"

Finally, you're able to eat your first meal on the military base. It's not a pleasant meal, being rushed and no socializing, but the calories are much needed. You're starving.

This is the beginning of ten weeks of Basic Combat Training (BCT), and you're only several hours into it.

God help me! you send up a quick prayer to heaven.

Now, let's look at the spiritual side of your Basic Combat Training (BCT) experience, which we'll rename **Believer's Combat Training**, which also happens to be the same acronym BCT.

What! Some Christians are offended by the word "combat." To those who are, I have to say, just as a good drill sergeant would say, and that is, "What is your major malfunction? Are you kidding me? Tell me that you are kidding me!"

Let's address this issue here and now.

Too many Christians have been wimps over the centuries, and especially in our current time. They have misinterpreted Jesus' words, *But I tell you not to resist an evil person. But whoever slaps you on your right cheek, turn the other to him also. Matthew 5:39*

The "slap" (which in Greek is ῥαπίζει, pronounced rap-iz-eye) that our Commander in Chief, Jesus, is referring to is an "insult." It's not an injurious punch to the side of your face or the thrust of an enemy combat knife into the cheek. It is a noninjury strike. Therefore, Matthew 5:39 is not to be used as a convenient excuse or rationalization for being passive in the face of injustice (law enforcement), attack on one's nation (military), or domestic physical attack (self-defense of your home, family, or those in immediate peril next to you that you choose to protect). The meaning of the verse, when viewed in its context, is about a legal issue. That's right, a legal issue. We know this because the next two examples Jesus gives right after that are legal issues, thus making this one also a legal issue.

If someone takes legal action against you, you are not to "strike back" with an equal legal action, which is from the old law *an eye for an eye and a tooth for a tooth*. Rather, you are to demonstrate to the evil person, the non-believer, God's love. In fact, the third example Jesus points out to us is dealing with an actual military situation at the time he said it. Let's read it:

And whoever compels you to go one mile, go with him two. Matthew 5:41

In Jesus' day if a man was walking on a street, on the road network that connected the vast Roman Empire, a Roman soldier could legally stop him and force him to carry the soldier's backpack or some other piece of military equipment for 1,000 paces, which is roughly 1 mile today. To refuse this order was an act of rebellion, and harsh punishment was the result of defiance. So, when Jesus said to the people of his day, "go with him two," it blew their minds, and it would have a Roman's soldier's mind as well.

Here's the backstory. Jews had no choice but to go the mile, begrudgingly at that, if they were selected by a Roman soldier. Being selected for this task was considered a great insult to the Jewish mind. Remember that Israel was under Roman occupation, and Roman soldiers were not exactly liked. In fact, they were hated. However, for Roman soldiers this law was necessary, because it helped to lighten their burden and provide occasional relief. A Roman backpack could weigh up to 60 pounds, just like an American Soldier's fully loaded pack today. Therefore, for a Jew of that day, who believed in the Lord Jesus, to respond to this obligatory service by saying, "Let me carry the load one more mile for you," once he finished the 1,000 paces, and then doing it, would not only be a welcomed relief to the Roman soldier, but it would also make him realize that Christians were different. That difference is love.

Going back to the word "combat," God is love. *Beloved, let us love one another, for love is of God. 1 John 4:7* Yet, the God of love is also the same God who warns the world, *Now consider this, you who forget God, least I tear you in pieces, and there is none to deliver: Psalm 50:22*

Oh, is that too harsh for some of you?

Some of you may even be rationalizing your own concept of God by thinking, *That was the God of the Old Testament.* As if He were a different God than in the New Testament.

Well, how about a New Testament verse then? How about this one that clearly shows the same nature of God? This one is when Jesus returns to the earth to finally put a stop to man's rebellion against Him:

*Now I saw heaven opened, and behold, a white horse. And He who sat on him was called Faithful and True, and in righteousness **He judges and***

makes war. *Revelation 19:11*

Just over 2,000 years ago, Jesus entered the city of Jerusalem riding on a donkey. Had he ridden in on a white horse, a symbol of a military conqueror in the ancient world, it would have sent the wrong message to everyone witnessing the event. Not that Jesus would have been concerned that the Roman government would have taken it as a direct threat to their authority if He had been riding on a white horse instead. The timing wasn't right. His First Coming was to "save the lost" as a humble servant, a bond slave, doing His Father's will, and so the donkey. However, at His Second Coming "He judges and makes war." Not only does He make war, which can only mean destroying and killing, *He Himself* ***treads the winepress of the fierceness and wrath*** *of Almighty God. Revelation 19:15*

Treading the winepress sounds like a lovely day in Napa Valley, but it means squishing the enemies until their blood runs out everywhere. Then a few verses later He talks about the military mop up operation, *And* ***the rest were killed with the sword, which proceeded from the mouth of Him who sat on the horse.*** *And all the birds were filled with their flesh. Revelation 19:21*

So, the God of the Old Testament, the God of the New Testament, the God of love, and the God of war, are all One and the same. Likewise, you are His Christian Soldier who also loves, but who is also willing to engage in combat spiritually, and physically if the need arises. So, the word "combat" should no longer be a taboo word for us Christians. The unbelieving world wants it to be for us, but they don't dictate our belief system. God does.

Have you noticed that God does not call new Christians "recruits" like the United States Army calls their new people, but rather He refers to them as "babes." Babes, recruits, they're the same thing. Jesus told Nicodemus, a Pharisee and ruler of the Jews, exactly how young a person is at the moment he or she believes in Him, *Most assuredly, I say to you, unless one is* ***born again,*** *he cannot see the kingdom of God. John 3:3*

Nicodemus was a bit taken back by Jesus' comment, because it was meant to be taken literally - a newborn.

Nicodemus said to Him, *"How can a man **be born** when he is old? Can he enter a second time into his mother's womb and be born?" John 3:4*

What the Pharisee failed to understand was that every human being has two possibilities to be born, and two possibilities to die. However, they are two different dimensions.

*Jesus answered, "Most assuredly, I say to you, unless one is **born of water and Spirit,** he cannot enter the kingdom of God. **That which is born of flesh is flesh, and that which is born of Spirit is spirit." John 3:5***

You had no choice being born into this world. Part of the birthing process was emerging from the embryonic fluid of your mother's womb; "born of water." However, you did have a choice of being "born again," and that process began when the Holy Spirit entered you the moment you first believed.

You will have no choice to stop your death from happening. Part of the death process will be decomposition and your elements mixing in with the dirt. However, unlike the men and women who refuse to repent of their sins, and who reject the free gift of salvation, you will not have to experience the second death, which is describe like this:

But the cowardly, unbelieving, abominable, murderers, sexually immoral, sorcerers, idolaters, and all liars shall have their part in the lake which burns with fire and brimstone, which is the second death. Revelation 21:8

So, let's look at the math:

1+1+1=3 (first birth + second birth + one death = 3)

1+1+1=3 (one birth + first death + second death = 3)

Both of these equations equal 3, and three represents the past, present, and future, and the future is obviously eternity.

An equation is written as two expressions, connected by an equals sign. The expressions on the two sides of the equals sign are called the "left-hand side" and "right-hand side" of the equation. This is important to know, because God respects people's free will by giving them two sides, which are actually two choices: the *tree of life* or the *tree of the knowledge of good and evil*, the flesh or the Spirit, and the second birth or the second death. Then when judgment finally comes, He will separate the wheat from the chaff, the sheep from the goats, and the righteous from the wicked. It's easy math.

*All the nations will be gathered before Him, and He will separate them one from another, as a shepherd divides his sheep from the goats. And **He will set the sheep on His right hand, but the goats on the left.** Matthew 25:32-33*

After birth newborn babies must be taught everything about life, from square one, even how to get nourishment into their little bodies to survive and grow. Just as the U.S. Army can't start a raw recruit with Special Forces training on day one, infants can't start with solid food to eat either.

*Therefore, **laying aside all** malice, all deceit, hypocrisy, envy, and all evil speaking, **as newborn babes**, desire the pure milk of the word, that you may grow thereby, **if indeed you have tasted** that the Lord is gracious. 1 Peter 2:1-3*

When a U.S. Army Soldier starts Basic Combat Training he or she has to lay aside their former life, meaning their normal habits of civilian life. No longer can they get out of bed whenever they feel like it, or leisurely eat their breakfast. If they love their fancy designer coffee or texting their friends first thing in the morning – forget it! It's not going to happen. There are a lot of new changes that the U.S. Army forces upon recruits in order to rid them of their old civilian habits, and they are replaced with the ones the

Army wants them to have. Likewise, when you join God's Army, He not only expects you to "lay aside all" of the sinful habits of the old life, but He replaces them with new godly habits one at a time.

When the Holy Spirit enters into a person, some sin is dealt with immediately. God's presence takes away the desire immediately. Yet, other sins may take some more time to purge. This is why Peter uses the metaphor "the pure milk of the word." Babies start their growing process by drinking milk, because their bodies can't handle solid foods.

If an infant grows, as he or she ought to, then mushy baby food is added to the diet. Then around 6 to 8 months of age, when his or her teeth are developed, they start eating solid foods. By one year old most babies born in the United States are off of their mothers' breasts or off milk bottles completely. It is believed that in Biblical times children were weaned by the age of 3 to 5, and this is still a common practice in many Third World countries today.

Just as some children do not develop normally due to health problems, some Christians are slow to grow spiritually as well, but with them it's by choice. That's because these slow developing Christians have a hard time letting go of their former life – their sins. They can't seem to get through the Believer's Combat Training in a timely manner, because they are not focused and disciplined. The apostle Paul put it this way:

*And I, brethren, could not speak to you as to spiritual people, **but as to carnal,** as to babes in Christ. I fed you with milk, and not with solid food; for until now you were not able to receive it, and even now you are still not able; 1 Corinthians 3:1-2*

In other words, Paul basically told these Greek believers in today's vernacular, "Stop being spiritual babies. Grow up! You should be a lot further along in your spiritual life by now, but you're still at square one because you are carnal."

The word "carnal" means *worldly appetites and pleasures.* That was their problem. They weren't *all in.*

It's okay to be a baby when you're a baby, but when you're much older you should no longer be strictly on a milk diet. Likewise, a new recruit in the United States Army is expected to act and behave like a new recruit, but if he or she does not keep progressing in their Basic Combat Training, working towards the goal of being a *lean mean fighting machine,* then problems arise.

Yes, you can have those flashes of doubt in the beginning, like I actually had my first morning of Boot Camp at Fort Jackson, South Carolina after being rudely awakened from my sleep, but I sucked it up and stuck it out. You're the one who asked Jesus into your heart with your *eyes wide open.* You're the one who wanted to be saved from your sins, so that you could live in the Kingdom of God forever. As such, you have to decide what kind of believer you really want to be: a Christian Soldier in the fight, or a non-combatant Christian civilian who is virtually indistinguishable from the world? You can't do both, and here's why:

No one can serve two masters; for either he will hate the one and love the other, or else he will be loyal to the one and despise the other. Matthew 6:24

Either Jesus is your "master," or the enemy (your flesh) is, in this case.

And, speaking of service, here's a well-known quote from General Joshua on making the decision of which of the two masters one should serve. He's the guy who took command of the Israelite army after Moses died, and took on several enemy armies. *But as for me and my house, we will serve the Lord. Joshua 24:15*

Wow! Not only was he a great general, but as the man of his household he decided that his whole family was going to go in the right direction, towards God, and he'd take charge. He was the type of man who wasn't afraid to say to his kids, "As long as you are under my roof…"

Of course, when a person makes this kind of commitment to God, and the family follows along, it also makes for a great support group for everyone in the household. There is unity. Jesus confirmed this principle by stating, *Every kingdom divided against itself is brought to desolation, and every city or house divided against itself will not stand. Matthew 12:25* Just look at what's happening to the United States of America as a whole, the lawlessness in many American cities, and the millions of dysfunctional homes.

The slow progression or even arrested Believer's Combat Training is because many Christian Soldiers have divided loyalties. I'm no longer referring to the division within the nation, among the people in their city, or even between those in their own household, but their own duplicitous thoughts causing the division between them and God. He makes it very clear that being double-minded doesn't work, not in the U.S. Army nor God's Army.

No one engaged in warfare entangles himself with the affairs of this life, that he may please him who enlisted him as a soldier. 2 Timothy 2:4

Just as the military does not beat around the bush when conveying a message, neither does God. The last two Scriptures I quoted are clear messages to suck it up, press on, or get out. Not out of heaven, for salvation once received will never be taken back, but it means out of God's Army – out of the fight. The choice is yours.

Oh! I'm sorry. Do you want to hear it directly from the Lord Jesus, our Commander in Chief, when it comes to half-hearted service in His Army? Very well then, here it is. *So then, because you are lukewarm, and neither cold nor hot, I will vomit you out of My mouth. Revelation 3:16*

Even if this character is not you, Private Lukewarm, it's still beneficial to hear these words as our Leader warns others standing next to us in formation. If I'm doing what I'm supposed to be doing, then these words confirm my commitment to the cause. However, if I've been slacking off, being "lukewarm," then these words will make me realize that I'm starting to lose my edge. As such, I had better get myself squared away again. If I don't, then I will not be adequately trained or be effective in the war. I may even lose my fighting spirit altogether.

This brings us to the next topic – culture shock.

Basic Combat Training in the U.S. Army is a culture shock. I say this, because it is. When going from civilian life to military life you must learn many things over again, and the new things are heaped upon you rather suddenly. It's almost the same feeling you'd get when visiting a foreign country that is totally alien to your own. I don't mean in the sense of being on vacation enjoying the tourist sites, because that's fun stress, but the uneasy feeling you'd have when you're totally immersed in a culture where you are forced to learn the language and how everything works in order to survive there. Of course, your education in this strange land is not given by a friendly local tourist guide, but with not-so-friendly task masters driving you every step of the way. The "task masters" that I'm referring to are the drill sergeants, also known as Noncommissioned Officers (NCOs). Yes, the ones with the Smokey the Bear hats. Their only job is to forge you into a real Soldier. As such, their importance to you and the Army cannot be overstated.

In late 1962 the Secretary of the Army requested a survey of the quality of training that recruits were receiving. Those new soldiers who were surveyed regarded the officers and noncommissioned officers of the U.S. Army training centers as "poor instructors." To address this concern a study was conducted on the other branches of the military to see how their instructor cadre trained their recruits. Researchers compiled the best teaching methods they had found, wrote a new curriculum, and then tested it as a pilot program in 1963. The success of the program led to the creation of the Drill Sergeant School, and the first professional drill sergeants were produced from the school in 1964.

Who are the spiritual "drill sergeants" for Christian Soldiers today? They are the godly mentors, home Bible study leaders, missionaries, and pastors of churches. Any believer who is grounded in the Word of God, and who teaches and strengthens other believers, fulfills the role of "spiritual drill sergeant."

You could consider seminary, *a college that prepares students to be church leaders,* as a type of "Drill Sergeant School," so long as they adhere to the belief that the Word of God is infallible, and they are uncompromising when it comes to Christian doctrine. Unfortunately, such seminaries are harder and harder to find nowadays, because many institutions of "higher education" have gone apostate. Case in point, Harvard University.

Harvard University is the oldest institution of higher education in the United States founded in 1636. Harvard was established to train clergy for the new commonwealth of New England. The goal of the founders was to saturate New England with godly men who were well educated in the Bible so that colonists would have good shepherds and solid Biblical teaching. Harvard University's "Rules and Precepts" of 1646 for clergy in training stated, "Everyone shall consider the main end of his life and studies to know God and Jesus Christ, which is eternal life."

Yale University, the nation's third oldest institution of higher education, was established in 1701 by clergy to also educate ministers. Sadly, both Harvard and Yale have abandoned their original purpose, and both today are actively attacking the very truths of the Bible they once taught, which is ironic since Harvard's motto is VERITAS, Latin for "truth," and Yale's motto is LUX ET VERITAS, "light and truth." Many of the graduates that these two institutions have produced are some of America's most prominent lawyers, politicians, high tech giants, and actors that have also been the most active in trying to silence the church and promote a humanist globalist agenda in its stead. Go to any online search engine and type in "famous graduates of Harvard University" or "Yale University," and you'll see many familiar infamous faces.

Despite the name of the U.S. Army's program Basic Combat Training, it's not actually learning about combat every minute of the day for 10 straight weeks. Nope, Warrior Skills are not even taught during the first week. You already know that from your first couple of days.

In BCT your weapons and body armor are not going to be issued to you until you first learn the Army culture. Before you do the "fun stuff" you've got to learn the different military ranks, and how to address each one of them. This all falls under *Military Customs and Courtesy.* You don't ever want to call a sergeant a "sir" or "ma'am," or they'll respond angrily, "What did you just call me? I work for a living!"

In BCT you learn how to stand, walk, and run. This block of instructions is called *Drill and Ceremony.* You learn proper hygiene and how to dress yourself the Army way. You've already learned about your gig line, which you can now also apply to the wearing of business casual or a business suit. You learn how to make your bed, the military way. God forbid if you don't pass the Quarter Bounce Test. That's when the drill sergeant flips a quarter, bearing the image of the nation's first Commander in Chief George Washington, in the air over your cot, and lets it land on the olive drab wool blanket. If the quarter does not bounce at least once, then that means the blanket and sheet are not taut enough, and the sergeant will overturn the cot, frame and all, right there on the spot.

In BCT you learn how to talk, for there are lots of new vocabulary words in this subculture, and we've already discovered that there are unlimited acronyms. Everything has an acronym.

In BCT you learn the history of the U.S. Army, which explains all the lithographs and portraits on the walls in all the halls and rooms all around the base.

In BCT you learn what to do when the American flag is hoisted up, when it's passing by, and when it is taken down at the end of the day to the bugle rendition of Taps that is played over the loudspeakers throughout the base. Oh, and you had better stop whatever you are doing, face the flag, and render a salute until the song is over. If you're in your car, you must pull over, get out, and do the same. After all, thousands upon thousands of Americans sacrificed their lives for that flag.

In BCT you learn, well you learn a whole lot of things.

The same is true when you first become a Christian Soldier. There are a whole lot of things the Holy Spirit has to teach you before you're issued your *full combat gear of God.* Thankfully, God does not run His Army like the Iranian army did during the Iran-Iraq War (1980-1988) where "recruiters" snatched young men from their homes in the middle of the night, while their fathers and mothers begged and cried, and the following day or two they had them walking through a minefield to "clear it." No, God places you in a spiritual BCT first, trains you one step at a time, and adequately prepares you for warfare against Satan and his army.

In BCT the U.S. Army has the Physical Readiness Training program, the components of which are *strength, mobility, and endurance.* That's because good physical fitness is essential for combat Soldiers to perform their tasks on the battlefield. The Bible also highlights physical fitness to make a spiritual point?

*For **bodily exercise** profits a little, but godliness is profitable for all things, having promise of the life that now is and that which is to come. 1 Timothy 4:8*

Some Christians use this verse as an excuse not to exercise their bodies. Why? Because, exercising to stay fit and trim is hard work. It takes a lot of discipline, time, and effort.

The thing about physical fitness is that you can't just exercise once, and you're fit. If it is neglected for more than a week it can be felt. Seven days without exercise makes one weak. Lack of exercise beyond a week certainly begins to show on the exterior.

The apostle Paul does not dismiss physical exercise. He states that it "profits a little," which means that it's still a benefit, even if "a little," and we are not to abandon it. However, compared to your spiritual life on earth, and your resurrected body that you'll enjoy for eternity, the physical body is a lesser priority in comparison. That's what he meant.

If Paul was against physical fitness, then he would not have also used running as an example to make another spiritual comparison:

*Therefore we also, since we are surrounded by so great a cloud of witnesses, let us lay aside every weight, and the sin which so easily ensnares us, and **let us run with endurance the race that is set before us,** looking unto Jesus, the author and finisher of our faith, who for the joy that was set before Him endured the cross, despising the shame, and has sat down at the right hand of the throne of God. Hebrews 12:1-2*

If you are a jogger, and you go out jogging to keep healthy, you don't carry unnecessary items along with you on your jog. Not only would carrying a suitcase, set of books, or any other item slow you down considerably, but they'd also put an additional strain on other parts of your body during the jog. Taking it a step further, pun intended, if you had to compete in a foot race, as Paul just described, and you were in it to win it, you would not only have your hands empty, but you'd even have on the lightest running shoes and the lightest sports clothes possible. Likewise, as a Christian Soldier you need to get rid of every sin or activity that is a waste of time. Walking in your sins or spending too much time on things that are going to burn in the end, not only keeps you from running effectively in God's Army but keeps you out of the war altogether. For the coward, that may be exactly what he or she wants, but for a warrior who has trained to fight, he or she actually looks forward to being deployed to the front line and fighting in the war.

THE BUILDING BACK UP PROCESS

As I stated at the beginning of the chapter, Basic Combat Training is "mild forms of torture, a test of one's character all rolled up into ten weeks that seems to drag on for an eternity, and yet it's all one big blur that passes quickly." What exactly did I mean by "mild forms of torture?" Well, now's the time I'll explain it to you.

The whole process of BCT is designed to tear you down, your individual identity, and then build you back up again – in the image of the U.S. Army. One of the methods your drill sergeants are going to accomplish this is by making things physically harder for you, and the best way to do this is through the "Fit To Win" obstacle course. The official name for it is the Teamwork Development Course.

Each obstacle on the course is named, explained, and demonstrated for familiarization and safety reasons. All of the obstacles are designed with "functional fitness" in mind, which means *performing physical tasks that simulate what Soldiers will face in a combat environment.*

You're up next, and you're slightly nervous. Not because of the physical challenge, but the possibility of screwing up.

"Move up! Get ready," the sergeant prompts you.

Once you're at the starting line he yells out, "Go!"

You sprint the 25 yards to the tall ship cargo net that is stretched out and anchored between two telephone poles, and you climb up the wobbly thick web. It's fairly easy, but the only real concern is when you get to the top, because you have to throw one leg over the top, then the other one must follow, in order to get on the other side for the climb down. You know that one wrong move up there, and the 30-foot fall could kill you as the linked ropes sways back and forth. You're slightly comforted knowing that a drill sergeant is straddling the top line near you, and he'll grab you by the collar if you start to slip. However, you don't, and going down the other side is a big relief.

You then run fifty yards to a four-foot wooden wall and hoist yourself up and over it. Your landing is not perfect, and you stumble a foot or two to regain balance, but at least you didn't sprain your ankle. You keep moving.

You then come to a gravel pit that has horizontal telephone poles mounted on stubs three feet above the ground. There are four of them you must go over in sequential order. They're like track hurdles, but there's no way to clear them with a single leap. You run up to the first one, slap your hands on top of the first pole, and your forward momentum carries you over it sideways. The next telephone pole comes up just five strides later. By the last one your arms are getting tired, and you "cheat" by doing a little hop and plopping your abdomen on the top of the pole, which when done this way is called a "belly buster." You pivot your chest in a rearward direction, and your legs fly over it in the direction you need to go.

Twenty-five yards later you come up to an obstacle that reminds you of a Boot Camp movie scene. You hit the deck and low crawl under barbed wire that is inches above your back. Well, it's not actually barbed wire, because there are no barbs on it that would rip new uniforms, but it's metal wire nonetheless, and you don't want to snag yourself on it. The long crawl gets you all dusty, and you cough in your own dust cloud that you just created when coming to your feet at the end of it.

Next comes about 20-feet of monkey bars, the same type you used to play on in grade school. There are big thick green pads wrapped around the supporting poles, and you think to yourself, *How could anyone be that uncoordinated that they would fall and hit one of them?* You grab onto every bar above your head, and then drop to the ground after the last rung.

You sprint another 15 yards on the packed dirt to a small 2-foot-high wall, which is easy to go over, but it makes you realize that your strength is starting to get sapped. Some Soldiers try to "dog it," conserve their energy, but a drill sergeant can spot these individuals instantly, and then starts threatening them that they'll go back to the starting line if they don't "put everything you've got into it!" Fortunately, you're going at a good steady pace to blend in with the "hard chargers" in front of the pack.

The Balance Logs are a welcomed relief for you to slow down for a few seconds. All you have to do at this station is step up onto a flat board, place one foot in front of the other, walk the zigzag pattern that is elevated a foot off the ground, and not lose balance and fall off. The Soldier who fell off just in front of you had to run back to the beginning of it.

Those who have already crossed the finish of the obstacle course make their way to the boundary sides of the course and clap and yell, "Come on! You can do it! Go! Go!" to demonstrate the platoon's esprit du corps. You hear them, but you don't look at any of their faces. The cheers do seem to give you a boost of energy.

Next you come to a concrete sewer pipe, or Concrete Culvert as it's officially named, big enough for a person to crawl through with plenty of space to spare above your head. You're relieved that it's only about two body lengths long, and you make it through it in four seconds. Of course, that one moment that you planted your left elbow too hard on the curved concrete surface made you wince for a moment, but at least you made a mental note never to do that again.

By the time you cross the finish line, and at the acceptable time, you're rather proud of yourself that you went through all 18 obstacles, not to mention the short distance runs between each of them. Once you catch your breath you realize that you are stronger than you thought you were. You would have never pushed yourself this hard back home.

So, what would be the spiritual equivalent of a U.S. Army obstacle course? What's going to make you stronger and give you more endurance as a Christian Soldier? Obviously, it's a Christian Soldier obstacle course, and like every military obstacle course it has a name. Our obstacle course is named "Holy Bible."

Sometime during the Middle Ages, the Latin phrase *Biblia Sacra,* or in

English the *Holy Books,* was the first time the word "Holy" was attached to the word "Bible." Then in 1611 the English words "Holy Bible" appeared on the front cover. Ever since then, Christians have been calling it that.

Just as the Holy Bible is God's recruiting material, our Heaven & Earth Constitution, and our Field Manuals, it is also our obstacle course to build our spiritual strength and endurance. We don't need any other obstacle courses, because ours covers it all. Any other book or publication in the world is not God's Word.

Running through the whole obstacle course, the Holy Bible, is receiving the whole counsel of God, which should always be followed up with meditating on what you have read at each sitting.

"Christian civilians" read a verse here and there, like a spiritual form of Pin the Tail on the Donkey, by going to only those books in the Bible that they prefer, and randomly picking a verse. Most Christians know very little of the Old Testament, because that's "the God of War," a "harsh, strict God," or so they think. In fact, ask most Christians to explain to you in detail even New Testament stories, and they don't know all of the facts of the stories. They just give you a Children's Bible version of the stories.

Sadly, even most priests and pastors are what I call "topical teachers." They pick a different topic for each Sunday service, and then preach on it. Some topics, especially culturally controversial ones, never seem to come up, and that's because they are avoided on purpose.

On the other hand, a Christian Soldier starts the obstacle course, the Holy Bible, from point A (the Book of Genesis), negotiates every obstacle one by one (all the books of the Old and New Testament), and finishes at point B (the last verse in the Book of Revelation). That, Private, is what I mean by "the whole counsel of God."

To build endurance you must do it many times. You don't just read through the entire Bible once, you keep going through it, from start to finish, over and over. Yes, each time may take you a year or more, but that's how you receive the whole counsel of God and build your endurance at the same time. Obstacle courses are not designed to be easy.

Naturally, if you have difficulty on a particular obstacle on the obstacle course, then you'll have to work on it. For example, if you're weak on the Book of Leviticus, then that's the book you need to understand better by taking the extra time to learn it. However, you don't neglect going through the entire Bible while doing so. You still stick to your reading time set aside for going through the entire Bible, and the time for working on a single "obstacle" is in your spare time.

Great athletes don't just go through the physical motions of their sport, and then that's it. He or she thinks about every step and minute movement, even when not even physically doing it. As they are stretching before an event, they are imagining performing each technique from start to finish. When they're in the shower at the end of practice, they are mentally going through the competition again. It's the same concept I tell my students, "Combat is 90% mental, and 10% physical." Likewise, after reading any Scripture you need to meditate on it, and by "meditation" I don't mean the way Eastern religions do it, where you "empty yourself," for that is the enemy's (the demonic realm) technique, but in the Biblical sense, which is nothing more mysterious than "thinking hard about the things of God." You need to ponder the Scriptures that you read, asking yourself probing questions, such as, "What must it have been like to have actually been there?" "Why did God give those details and not others?" "What would I do if faced with the same situation today?" As you meditate on His Word you also pray, "God, what are you trying to teach me? Reveal more to me. Amen."

That is what a professional Christian Soldier does to be "Fit To Win."

THE GAS CHAMBER

Speaking of "mild forms of torture," the next experience you are going to go through after the Fit To Win obstacle course does not seem "mild" at all. In fact, the worst physical pain I have ever experienced in my life was in Basic Combat Training during the Nuclear Biological Chemical (NBC) warfare training. Today the U.S. Army calls it Chemical, Biological, Radiological, Nuclear (CBRN) training, but it's the same thing, the same pain.

About three weeks into BCT our drill sergeants sadistically prodded us emotionally, "You boys haven't experienced what real pain is yet," referring to the hard physical training that they had already forced upon our bodies, "but wait until you all go through the gas chamber."

The term "gas chamber" didn't sound good at all to me. In fact, these two words conjured up vivid images in my mind of the gas chambers in Nazi concentration camps scattered throughout Germany and Poland, and that's because back in my world history class in high school, along with watching the 1973-1974 T.V. mini-series *World At War,* I was familiar with the Holocaust of World War II. While watching some of the episodes I often asked myself, *How could millions of Jews, along with uncompromising Christians and political prisoners, let themselves be rounded up like cattle, transported to concentration camps in the container wagons of trains, and then go voluntarily into gas chambers that they believed were only hygiene showers?* As a young man I had a fighting mentality, because of my martial arts training that I had begun at 14 years old, and imagining myself in their shoes, had I lived at that time and place in history that they did, seemed like such an obvious choice – you simply escape when you see the telltale signs, or you fight to the bitter end if they try to take you.

That was my thinking as an eighteen-year-old, but since then one genocide after another have occurred upon this planet in my lifetime, and I now understand how such atrocities occur even among "civilized" cultures. Most people are not fighters, but rather obedient "sheep" that just desire tranquility. They simply can't imagine that their own neighbors or government could turn on them and would have a hand in their destruction. People generally have hope, and that hope often blinds them to the evil truths around them. We see this same blindness even today as the church is getting persecuted on all sides, even in the United States of America. It's the old proverbial "frogs in the boiling pot." It always starts with propaganda (the Bible is "hate speech"), then censorship (the Cancel Culture), and then... (use your imagination).

So, are you ready to go through the Gas Chamber in your own Basic Combat Training? Here it goes.

The dreadful day has finally arrived. It's autumn becoming winter. You're standing with your platoon in the morning dark as a mild cold rain shower comes down. It was the first time that you had to march in your rain poncho, and you marched the three muddy miles until the rising sun revealed the dark gray misty damp trees on both sides of the road.

"Platoon, Halt!" Sergeant Powell bellows out, and leaves you standing there in formation for ten minutes in the football field size clearing in the forest facing a tin shack with a single door and no windows. He didn't go through the door that you had your eyes fixed upon, but he went around to the other side of the garage size structure where you couldn't see him.

When he reappears several minutes later, he yells, "Platoon, attention!" and everyone snaps into position.

Just after that, a sergeant you had never seen before pokes his head out, and half his body, from the mystery door. He has on an olive drab green rubber suit that has a tight seal around his neck. The ensemble includes rubber booties and gloves. A gas mask is in his free hand that dangles by his side from the straps. He shouts out to Sergeant Powell, "We're popping them now!"

Sergeant Powell nods his head because he's in the know, and then he starts having everyone line up in front of the door according to squad numbers. You're in squad four, which means you're the last group to go in.

A few seconds later you hear POP! POP! POP! a short pause, and then POP! again.

After about a minute of just standing at attention, facing the shack without a word spoken by anyone, you noticed a ghostly light gray smoke pushing its way out through the many cracks of the tin building. You know that it's the horrible CS gas that they had been talking about for weeks. Your heart starts to race.

Sergeant Powell finally speaks up, "You will go in one squad at a time. Before you go in you will each don and clear your M50 Gas Mask, and I want it done in nine seconds, just like we taught you. When you go in you will form two lines inside, and then you will wait for further instructions from the NCOs inside. Do you understand?"

"Yes sergeant!" forty voices shout in unison.

It wasn't a very enthusiastic acknowledgement, but Sergeant Powell let it slide, "Oh, and if any of you drop your weapon or helmet you will be made to go back inside the gas chamber and retrieve it. That means two times in the gas chamber."

That was a good piece of advice he gave you. You don't know what it's like in there, but you imagined at that moment how you'll keep a hold of your M4 rifle, helmet, and gas mask when it comes time to pull the mask off. You're certain that everyone else is mentally running through the scenario as well.

Then, with a hearty chuckle before starting the "torture," Sergeant Powell tells the platoon, "You're lucky it is raining this morning and you have your ponchos on. That's good, because all your snot and vomit will just run down the front of them, and you won't have to worry about your uniforms getting soiled like the group that went through here before you."

Those words don't make you feel lucky at all, but quite the opposite. They just add to the building anxiety.

Then it comes. "Squad One! Forward, march!"

The first squad opens the thin wooden door and goes into the single room, single file. Gas comes swirling out of the open threshold until the door is quickly shut behind them. About twenty seconds later you heard muffled yelling and some moans. A minute later it is completely silent.

What happened to them? you think, since nobody came out. You were expecting the Soldiers from Squad One to come out the same door they went in by, but apparently there's a back door, and you will not see them until your squad is to be reunited on the other side. Of course, you can't help but think, *They're all dead, and that's why there is not even so much as a whimper now coming from that godforsaken shack,* but you know it can't possibly be true.

Squad Two goes in, then later Squad Three. It all goes the same way.

Then it is finally time for your Squad.

"Squad Four! Forward, march!"

Oh Lord, here we go.

The little room is so thick with gray CS gas that you could only make out human silhouettes inside, and nothing else. Three sergeants, all fitted with protective rubber suits and masks, wait for your squad to form two lines, one in front of the other. You're in the back line. You wonder if that is a blessing, or a curse.

You then hear one of the sergeants yell out from behind his mask, "First row, take off your masks!" which made his voice sound like he was yelling into an empty coffee can.

The Soldiers in front of you all removed their masks. At first nothing happens, and then about five seconds later the man in front of you starts hopping up and down. It's a weird form of panic you've never seen before, and it intensifies. One of the sergeants moves up to him, starts screaming at him with a muffled voice, and jerks him around a bit to get the Solider focused on him and not the sweeping pain. The sight of these grotesque movements makes you very much afraid.

Just about then you start feeling a burning sensation in your throat, and you start to cough. There is a strange odor in the mask.

Oh my God I have a leak! I have a leak!

You frantically look left and right, and your instincts tell you to run out of the room. *Just drop everything and run!*

You're just about to raise your hand to get the attention of one of the sergeants to inform him of your problem, and then you realize that they could care less about your problem, for they're about to do to you what they're now doing to those poor souls in the front row. So, you quickly take both hands and press your palms against the bottom edges of your gas mask to make the seal around your cheeks and chin tighter. It seems to work, and the burning sensation is not getting any worse.

By this time, you are in your own hell, and you're totally losing track of what is happening in front of you with the other Soldiers, but before you know it, the front row is not just escorted out of the room, but literally shoved out. The gas is so thick you can barely detect sunlight coming into the room when the door opened to let them out.

Just then a sergeant gets right in front of your face and yells out, "Group, take off your masks!"

You take in one long drag of mask filtered air, pull your helmet off with your left hand, and then with your right hand you strip the mask off from the bottom of the chin upwards, just like you were taught to do.

You hear one of the other sergeants standing in front of the Soldier to your left yelling at him, "Don't hold your breath! You had better suck in some air, or you will be here all day!"

You pretend to suck in air, hoping he believes it if he looks your way.

The Soldier to your left made no attempt to pretend to breathe, and the sergeant standing in front of him saw this and punched him in the chest. THUMP! This made him suck in a lung full of contaminated air. He starts crying out hysterically.

The sergeant in front of you, who was going to monitor you, decides to help his fellow NCO deal with the panicking Soldier who is now thrashing about trying to find the exit.

Five seconds into the ordeal it feels like someone had splashed acid in your face. Your nostrils start burning intensely. Then it feels like someone had taken a thin metal coat hanger, straightened it, sharpened the end to a fine point, heated this point over an open flame until it was white hot, and then punctured your eyeballs with the searing tip. The pain is intense, and you're sure you are going blind.

You have no choice. You just have to breathe. You can't hold it any longer. So, you suck in as little air as you can with tight puckered lips, but the little air that goes down your throat and into your lungs is painful. It is as if you just sucked in superheated air from an inferno. Involuntarily you take in more air, and more, and even more, and it feels like you're taking in air, but you can't seem to exhale. You start to panic as if someone is holding your head under water and won't let you up for air. You want to run out of the room, but you don't know where the door is. You are totally disoriented. A moment later you think you're going to collapse, and so you extend your left hand out and manage to hold yourself up by leaning against the corru-gated metal wall that's behind you. Somehow, in the agony of the moment, you're able to remind yourself not to drop your helmet, gas mask, or let your rifle sling slip off your shoulder. You have a tight grip on all of it.

At this very moment you actually think that you're going to die. You have never experienced anything like it before. The only comparison you can imagine it being like, is being stuck inside a burning house and choking on the toxic fumes before being overcome by them and dying.

Just as you're about to give up on life itself, you hear one of the silhouett-ed sergeants give the order, "Everybody out!"

Just where "out" is, you don't really know. You just grab onto the Sol-dier's poncho in front of you, who is grabbing the rifle sling of the Soldier in front of him, and somehow you all managed to file out of the gas cham-ber single file.

Through your closed eyes, with eyelids filled with uncontrollable tears, you can tell by the bright light that you are in the doorway, and then a moment later cold air is slapping your burning face. It is the first indication of relief, even though you are sputtering, snot is running down the front of your poncho involuntarily, and your face still feels like it is over the burners of a gas stove.

As you blindly walk away from the building you hear a few voices yell out to your group, "Don't rub your eyes!" and "Keep walking with your hands up!"

They were right, any rubbing of the eyes only contaminates them again, burning them intensely, and only fresh air will eventually cleanse the agent from your skin.

It took a while, a good twenty minutes before you could see and breathe properly again, but eventually you're back to normal with a slick poncho that must be rinsed off with a little water from your hydration system that you're wearing like a backpack. You notice that the rain had stopped while you are inside.

Ahhhh, it's good to be alive!

You're probably thinking, *Wow, Jim! You made me feel like I was actually inside that Gas Chamber, but why take so many words to describe it? What's the point? How does the Army's Gas Chamber have a connection to anything spiritual?*

The reason I went into such great detail, is for that very reason, I wanted to make you feel as if you were really inside the Gas Chamber. Short of you ever becoming a burn victim, God forbid, this Basic Combat Training experience is a fairly good model of what hell is going to be like for billions of people for eternity. If we truly understand how horrifying it's going to be in hell, then our mission here on earth is going to be that much more urgent. This is why we are in Believer's Combat Training in the first place, to keep people from going there.

I will try to describe eternity in hell with mere words, based on several descriptions found in the Bible. I will also personalize the experience the best I can, like I did with the Gas Chamber story, so that "you are there."

First of all, let me clarify something. There are actually two hells, yet because both places are referred to as "hell" in English, they are often confused with one another. They are not the same place.

ᾅδης (pronounced ay-dees in Greek), written "Hades" in English, is located in the center of the earth, and there were two compartments. One side **was for** the righteous souls after they physically died, and the other side, which is separated by a great abyss, **is for** the wicked after they die. Yes, I used the past tense and the present tense for the two different compartments on purpose. Jesus vividly described this place in Luke 16:1-27 using the experiences of two men living on the two separate sides of Hades. You should read it again.

When Jesus resurrected from the dead, He visited this place, the side containing the righteous souls, and freed them. Those souls are now in heaven waiting for that glorious day when Jesus resurrects their transformed physical bodies and unites them with their eternal souls. However, all the wicked souls who have died, including all those who just died today, are there now waiting for Judgment Day. Then, once they are condemned for refusing salvation, they will be sent to a permanent hell, and that's because *the heavens will pass away with a great noise, and the elements will melt with fervent heat; both the earth and the works that are in it will be burned up. 2 Peter 3:10* With earth gone Hades won't exist anymore.

The permanent hell is a location called γεέννη (a Greek word pronounced Geh-enna), and it's currently vacant awaiting the masses of condemned that will soon be there. Satan, the demons, the Antichrist, the false prophet, and all those people in history who did not believe in ישוע (the Hebrew name for Jesus, pronounced Yeh-shu-ah, which means *He saves*) will be thrown into this literal place. He saves you from what? From this awful place! Even death itself is thrown into γεέννῃ.

Since *God is not the author of confusion but of peace, 1 Corinthians 14:33* hell is the ultimate in confusion. You are floating in complete and utter darkness. There is no up, and no down. There are no references or anything solid at all. The darkness is so thick it feels like a heavy pressure on your suspended body. You are violently turning and twisting endlessly, and there is no place to rest your feet upon. Nothing to grab or to hold onto.

There are no sounds at all. It's "deadly" quiet, but not a peaceful quiet. It's no more peaceful than if you were drowning in turbulent boiling liquid. It's loud, but it's empty. It's empty because you are completely alone in the vast void. You will never hear a human voice again. You will never hear birds chirping, the sound of a forest stream, windchimes, or soothing music to the ears. That's because in hell there are great distances between each condemned person and spirit. Even if you were to bump into someone hurling in your direction, you'd never be able to hang onto them, and they'd drift off into the thick darkness making it impossible to locate him or her ever again. "Misery loves company," but you'll never have company again – ever. Hell is not going to be anything like the Medieval oil paintings depicting all the sinners huddled together as demons prod and poke them with pitchforks. In fact, those demons will be individually isolated somewhere in the void experiencing the same agony as you, but there is no comfort even in that thought.

The darkness and solitary confinement alone would make any person go completely mad. It's not like an earthly prison sentence, where you do your time for 20 years or more, and then you finally get released or die, hell is WITHOUT END. It's forever and ever. As such, Jesus spoke more about hell than He did about heaven, and that's because it is so terrible, and so awful there, that He didn't want anyone to end up there. He describes it as *the sons of the kingdom will be cast out into outer darkness. There will be weeping and gnashing of teeth. Matthew 8:12*

The weeping and gnashing of the teeth are because there is *the fire that shall never be quenched – Mark 9:43* It is a *lake of fire and brimstone, Revelation 20:10*

That's right, fire, and you know what fire feels like when you touch it. Now imagine being completely immersed in it, sinking and sinking, but there is no bottom. Imagine being locked inside a car completely engulfed in flames, except the fire in hell does not give off any light at all. It is black fire, and that is because Jesus is light. When describing Himself, Jesus said, *I am the light of the world. He who follows Me shall not walk in darkness, but have the light of life. John 8:12* You didn't want light? You wanted darkness, because you loved the darkness more than the light. Therefore, you'll get to keep the darkness you so longed for, even when it comes to the flames that endlessly lick your body. If that weren't bad enough, "brimstone" is burning sulfur. It's what is found in volcanic fissures, and it gives off an acrid odor. I imagine it will be like the U.S. Army's Gas Chamber, the real one that I experienced in 1980, where I stood in the shack filled with CS gas, which is an irritant. I could breathe the stuff in, which burned the throat intensely, but I felt like I could not exhale. The panic of suffocating made me want to panic all the more, but I didn't. The sergeant warned us beforehand that no permanent harm would occur. Oppps, I didn't give you that warning first when I took you verbally through the Gas Chamber. Well, not so with fire and brimstone. It's not an irritant, but harmful.

Oh yes, you will have your five senses in hell. They're not going away. In fact, even those who were missing one of the senses during their life on earth, due to being born that way or they lost it, will be given it back. You'll have your sight (although you won't be able to see a thing with your eyes), hearing (the sounds of the grinding of your teeth and your own screams), smell (of choking thick black smoke), taste (of flames and brimstone, probably like a bitter metallic taste mixed with hot gravel), and touch (I can't even endure a flame against my body for an instant, let alone for eternity).

There's not going to be any "we're going to party in hell," like many unbelievers flippantly said when they were warned about it. My earthly father, who was a deputy sheriff, tried to rescue a man and his wife who were trapped in a burning car. He couldn't get them out in time, and he told me that he will never forget, for the rest of his life, the screams coming from the fully engulfed car until they died. No, there are no parties for the wicked in γεέννη.

Jesus also gave a very interesting fact about hell. He said, *their worm does not die, and the fire is not quenched. Mark 9:45*

He used the Greek word σκώληξ (pronounced sko-lex, which is in the singular form). We still use this same Greek word today in English. Well, I don't, but others do. It refers to the anterior end of a tapeworm, bearing suckers and hooks for attachment to its host. Is this a literal worm you'll have inside of you? Most likely, because the darkness, fire and brimstone are certainly literal. If God can keep you "alive" as burning material for eternity, without destroying your nerve endings, then He certainly can keep a worm inside of you alive for eternity eating away at you from the inside. So, instead of the Holy Spirit dwelling in you, Whom you willingly rejected on earth, you'll have a nasty creature inside of you gnawing away instead. This is probably why you will be cursing Him for the rest of eternity, and still unable to "open your eyes" even in the torment of hell. You were "blind" then, and your sins keep you blind even now. Like all vicious criminals, you're not sorry for doing your crimes, nor for the victims you hurt, you're only sorry that you got caught and being punished.

Once again, this will be your existence, with no hope of ever changing it.

I don't know about you, but as a Bible believing Christian, just the thought of hell is enough for me to beg God for salvation again. Yes, I know, "once saved, always saved," but when I contemplate myself ending up in hell, even as I wrote the description of it for your benefit, I couldn't help but pray afterwards, "Lord, forgive me for all of my sins, my rebellion, and my flesh that wants to sin continually. I believe in your salvation plan. I believe that Jesus paid the full price for me on the cross. Please have mercy on my soul, I don't want to be thrown into the lake of fire. I want to be with You forever. Amen."

FIRST AID TRAINING

The sergeant holds up a small square camouflage canvas bag. He says, "This is an IFAK (pronounced eye-fak). Individual First Aid Kit. Those of you who will be going into combat will appreciate it when you get shot, when shrapnel rips through your body from an IED, or your battle buddy goes down next to you and is spurting blood out all over the place."

Whoa! Wait a second! you mentally hit the brake pedal. *My recruiter didn't say anything about getting shot or shrapnel or blood all over the place! All the posters on his wall showed guys doing cool stuff, not getting messed up.*

He opens up the kit and pulls out a C.A.T. tourniquet, and he begins to explain it, "The good thing about the C.A.T. (pronounced cat) is that you can put it on yourself if you're missing part of your arm or leg."

The sergeant grabs a "voluntold," and he slips the black tourniquet lasso over the Soldier's wrist and slides it up just above the elbow, and then pulls the red tab. He pulls it hard.

"Owwww!" the Soldier moans when the loop tightens to the point of cutting off the blood supply to his arm.

You start to feel a little woozy just watching it. Not because you sympathize with the Soldier being demonstrating on, for you're glad it's not you, but because it never occurred to you, up until now, that you could be horribly disfigured or even killed in a battle. Yeah, sure, you knew that it could happen intellectually, but the sergeant's words, and seeing a real tourniquet being put onto someone's arm, drives the reality home. It's the second moment in Basic Combat Training that you say to yourself, *What have I got myself into?*

Of course, several minutes later you eventually come to grips with the reality, and you actually start liking the course when you get to apply the tourniquet, and the field dressings, on simulated wounds on your training partner.

Just like U.S. Soldiers in BCT who come to the realization, not just intellectually, but in their hearts, that they could be wounded or killed serving the country, so too every Christian Soldier comes to a point in their walk with the Lord that fighting for His kingdom can be very costly: having friends or family members disown you, people at work disliking you because you're a Christian, or people even wanting to literally shoot you, such as an active shooter attacking your congregation during a church service. You can't help but think once in a while, *Is it worth speaking out against the sin of homosexuality or transgender? Should I tell my cousin, who calls himself a Christian, that it's wrong for him to be living with his girlfriend? Should I tell my boss that I do not like him using the Lord's name in vain around me?*

Then comes the moment, after you've given it some serious thought, when you accept your new reality, and say to yourself, *No matter what, I'll follow Him and speak His truth.* However, some people can't. They don't have the courage. That's the moment they call it quits.

Do you have your spiritual IFAK, *Individual Faith Always Kept*, on you?

Hopefully you're of the mindset that you're not going to abandon the God of the universe just because you could get wounded emotionally or physically by the people around you. And, if you are physically killed for your faith, then Amen – so be it. *And do not fear those who kill the body but cannot kill the soul. But rather fear Him who is able to destroy both soul and body in hell. Matthew 10:28*

BLUE PHASE

Blue Phase is the culmination, and also the most challenging part, of Basic Combat Training. It's done in the 8th week, and it starts with BIVOUAC, pronounced biv-wack. It's one of those French words that has carried over into the English language completely intact, and it means *to camp*. And, by camping I mean it's where you live in a tent community, eat food prepared out in the field, and practice all your combat skills in a simulated forward battle zone.

Of course, there's no transportation provided to get you and your platoon to the BIVOUAC site. Well, there is, for you see dozens of big trucks parked everywhere, but after all, it's the Army, and so you have to march there, some seven miles away, carrying your M4 rifle and a full pack: an extra uniform, four pairs of socks, two pairs of undergarments, a tent, a sleeping bag, and a sleeping bag mat.

Just before you are given the order to head out, there's a surprise inspection in the company area to see if anyone has contraband: a cell phone, snacks, energy drinks, or alcohol. Of course, there are several Soldiers who are caught with prohibited items after being shaken down, and it's all piled in front of the platoon on the cement. Those who were caught with contraband will be doing guard duty at the worst times of night and morning.

While you are out "camping" you also participate in Field Training Exercises (FTX) and Military Operations Urban Terrain (MOUT). In other words, "war games" of all sorts.

Everything is made to appear and feel like you are actually in a foreign country fighting a war. There's burnt out military vehicles scattered about the "battlefield," battle damaged buildings in a mock village, and even actors playing the part of the enemy. These guys are called OPFOR, *Opposing Force,* and they're all dressed in black uniforms toting M4 rifles that fire Man Marker Rounds (MMR), which are non-lethal projectiles made of a non-tox colored marking wax, thanks to the technology of a Close Combat

Mission Capability Kit (CCMCK) that converts real weapons into training weapons. Of course, everyone engaging in this type of force-on-force training must wear their ballistic vest and facemask with integrated goggles for safety.

As exciting as this type of training is, being out in the field for a few days also has a downside to it. There is no dining facility during these military exercises, and the two meals a day that are given out are in the form of MREs, Meal Ready to Eat, which Soldiers have nicknamed *Meals Rejected by Ethiopians.*

When you are trying to sleep, there is gunfire and explosions all night long to give it that "war" feel. Some are close by, but thankfully most are in the distance. The problem with loud noises that suddenly go off too close to the camp is that everyone has to jump out of their sleeping bags and defend the camp from an attack, a possible attack from OPFOR. Of course, if the Opposition Force does a surprise attack like this, they are only firing blanks from their weapons. However, the big fear is they'll toss in a CS gas grenade or two in the middle of the camp, and that is really miserable if you don't get your M50 mask on in time. It's the same stuff that riot police use to disperse an illegally assembled mob. Then after the attack you can forget about catching up on sleep until the next night.

YOU'RE A TRAINED SOLDIER NOW

It felt like it was never going to happen, but graduation day from Basic Combat Training has finally arrived, and it comes in a big way: parade flags, a military band, and a speech from a two-star general as you stand at parade rest on the "grinder." It's called that because all the marching done by Soldiers on that surface with their combat boots grinds little rocks into sand. Well, not really, but it's a cute description.

You feel good about yourself. It has galvanized a deeper pride for your country within you. When you hear the National Anthem played, while standing there on the parade ground saluting the Stars and Stripes, in your United States Army dress uniform no less, the song has more meaning to you than it did before you joined the Army. It's a feeling that 99% of the American people will never know. You now fully understand why all military personnel, and all veterans you have met over the years, had such deep emotions for the flag and the country. It's bigger than you. A lot of sacrifices had been made by millions of brave men and women before you, and you just contributed your first sacrifice for the United States of America, even though it was only ten weeks, it's a start.

I know, I know. When you first started reading this book you thought, When is he going to start talking about the whole armor of God? I thought that this is what the book was all about?

Well, now you appreciate how much goes into making a Soldier, at least when it comes to training, before he or she ever puts on body armor, picks up a weapon, and defends the nation. There's a lot that goes into it, and we're just getting started. It doesn't just happen overnight. Likewise, being a Christian Soldier does not happen overnight either. It's a lengthy process, and that's because Jesus knows, and says, *Behold, I send you out as sheep in the midst of wolves. Therefore be wise as serpents and harmless as doves. Matthew 10:16*

Hmmm, this is a good verse to start practicing your daily meditation, your meditating on God's Word, and there's no time like the present. Answer these six questions:

1. Why does Jesus call us Christians "sheep?"
2. Who are the wolves?
3. Am I a "fat sheep" that just wants to be fed, and not go out among the wolves?
4. Am I a shepherd? (those who protect the flock spiritually – pastors and teachers).
5. Am I a "sheepdog?" (those who protect the flock – church security).

Some churches don't even have one "sheepdog" for protection.

6. How are serpents wise? How do I use that wisdom for God?
7. What does a harmless dove symbolize? (Hint: Genesis 8:10-12 and Leviticus 1:14-17).

When trying to ponder the meaning of a Scripture, the Holy Spirit will speak to your heart about it. Sometimes the meaning will be understood immediately. Sometimes the meaning will come a little bit at a time, over a long period of time, or not until it is the right time for you. Some Scriptures will never be understood this side of heaven.

Rabbi Jason Sobel, the technical advisor for *The Chosen* (the multi-season TV show about the life of Jesus), said it best when he compared the Bible to an ocean. He said, "It's so shallow that even a child can wade in it, but it's so deep that you can never explore the depths of it."

This is me (second from the left) with my "band of brothers" during Basic Combat Training (BCT) at Fort Jackson, South Carolina, USA.

Just like BCT, many police academies train their recruits the same way as the military does. This is my class marching to Physical Training.

This is a C-130 Hercules that Airborne Soldiers jump out of. It' the same aircraft mentioned in so many of the U.S. Army cadence songs.

In Basic Combat Training, Soldiers are constantly punished with push-ups for their mistakes, to educate and to build up their strength.

Soldiers learn hand-to-hand combat, known as Combatives, if they become unarmed. I'm instructing two Army National Guard Soldiers.

This is the MOPP protective gear that instructors wear inside of the Gas Chamber to teach Soldiers what a chemical attack is like.

Hell is not going to be anything like this medieval relief sculpture that is located at the front entrance of the Bourges Cathedral in France.

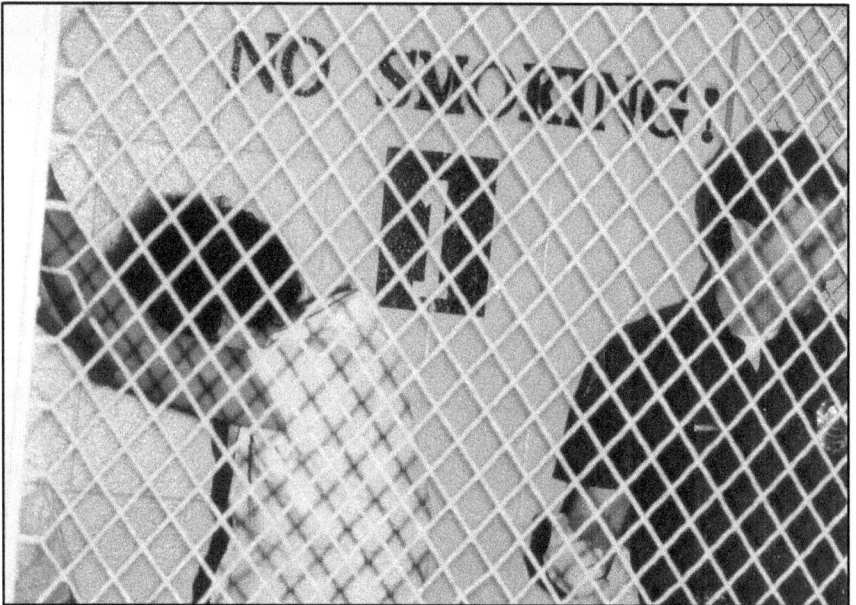

Those going to hell will be like the many prisoners I dealt with. They are not sorry for their crimes, but they are sorry that they got caught.

Soldiers learn to live out in the field at a camp site, which the Army calls "BIVOUAC." A tent city can be set up in just a matter of hours.

At 18 years old I had to live in a tent in BCT, and here I am in my 50s still enduring BIVOUAC with the military. "Embrace the Suck."

Injuries and death are a part of war. This is a photo that I took during a joint Los Angeles S.W.A.T. - U.S. Army first aid training at the base.

Toward the end of Basic Combat Training, Soldiers participate in training that simulates war, such as this 15-mile road march I was on.

Years later, when I went through a three-day U.S. Marine Corps Range Safety Officer (RSO) course, they too simulated combat conditions.

The day finally comes! Graduation from Basic Combat Training. That's me to the right of the BCT training certificate being held up.

Chapter 3

ADVANCED INDIVIDUAL TRAINING

YOUR ARMY JOB

Praying always with all prayer and supplication in the Spirit, being watchful to this end with all perseverance and supplication for all the saints - Ephesians 6:17-19

I know I'm jumping ahead with the above Scripture, but it has everything to do with your next step after graduating from Basic Combat Training, which is attending Advanced Individual Training (AIT), pronounced ay-eye-tee. The United States Army's tag line for this is BECOME AN EXPERT IN YOUR ARMY JOB.

Whatever Military Occupational Specialty (MOS) you selected during the recruiting phase, there is a school somewhere for that career. There is Infantry School, Air Defense Artillery School, Military Police School, the U.S. Army Armor Center, Aviation Logistics School, Ordnance Mechanical Maintenance School, Transportation School, and the list goes on.

For my AIT I was sent to Signal Corps School with the Latin motto PRO PATRIA VIGILANS, *Watchful for the Country.* According to the official U.S. Army website, *Signal Corps Soldiers develop the technical skills necessary to automate, transmit and receive voice and data information to keep the Army informed and ready to respond.*

After BCT I was placed on an olive drab green painted military bus, the only passenger, and the civilian contracted driver drove me the one hour and thirty-eight minutes from Fort Jackson, South Carolina to Fort Gordon,

Georgia located just outside of Augusta. This was a rather unique experience for me, because for the seven weeks that I attended the Radio Operator Course (201-05B10) I lived in a World War II Quonset hut. The roof and sides of this small building were corrugated steel sheets, bent to look like a metal cigar tube that had been cut in half, and then placed on the ground with the arch side up. The two ends of the half tube had walls made of plywood with doors and windows. The place was heated by two wood burning stoves, one on each end of the hut. The fires in those things were always going when I first got there, because my stay there started in the winter.

Although the living conditions were primitive, compared to Basic Combat Training, I welcomed the change of pace: less being yelled at, some free time, and I could sit and eat all my meals like a normal human being without having to devour them like a ravenous wolf.

To sum up my first military job in layman terms, my job was to set up various radio antennas in a combat environment, be able to go mobile with a variety of radio systems (be it in a vehicle or a radio on my back while on foot) and set up a radio network. This was back before the digital age, and so when we'd go out in the field, I had to hump a 14-pound Vietnam Era PRC-77, pronounced prick seventy-seven, on my back with a hand mic in my left hand and an M-16 rifle in the other. Whenever the company commander wanted to communicate with outside units, be it on a road march or BIVOUAC, he'd call me up to his position by simply shouting out, "Radio up!" There was no, "Hi, how are doing?" or any chit chat like that, but he'd just grab the mic out of my left hand as soon as I was next to him. I'd be like a dog on a leash staying by his side until he was finished.

Two hours after graduation from the United States Army Signal Center at Fort Gordon, I was put into the back seat of a government sedan and driven for three hours and fifty minutes to Fort Benning, Georgia, which was my permanent duty station. I was assigned to the HHC 43rd Engineer Battalion (Combat, Heavy). The motto was *POWER FOR SERVICE.*

During my service in the United States Army, Regular, there was not a "shooting war" at the time. However, it was the era of the Cold War. The closest I came to going to a shooting war was during President Ronald Reagan's first year in office.

February 17, 1981. It was 0430 in the morning when someone pounded three times on the door of our two-man room that immediately jolted Specialist Jones and me out of our sleep. A loud this-is-not-a-drill voice behind the door blared out, "Everybody up! Get dressed! Put on your full combat gear!"

The hallway went quiet for a few seconds after the rude awakening until the same wall shaking knock was heard at the next door down from our room. BAM! BAM! BAM! The same orders were given to those occupants.

Specialist Jones and I quickly got dressed, walked outside into the cold dark, and joined each groggy Soldier who shuffled to his position in the formation in front of the barracks. Everybody had on fatigues, jackets, web gear, combat helmets, and we waited for an NCO to show up to tell us what was going on. By the sounds of the humming engines of the C130 aircraft off in the distance on the airfield, it sounded like things were already well underway before we low ranking Soldiers were even aware of it.

About ten minutes later a sergeant, whom I had only seen once before and who belonged to another platoon within the company, came out and stood before us. Our own sergeant was nowhere to be seen, which made us all a little more apprehensive about what to expect. He called us to attention, and then under his breath said, "At ease."

Hmmm, that's weird, I thought. *He didn't bark out the orders like normal.*

Everyone dropped their stacked hands that were behind their backs down a little bit lower to relax the arms, and turned their attention to the sergeant.

"Gentlemen, the President of the United States has ordered us to be ready to go to El Salvador."

Someone spoke without permission from among the ranks, "Sarge, where is El Salvador?"

The sergeant snapped, "It's in Central America, dumb nuts!"

He went right to the business at hand, "Now, listen up, I don't want to repeat myself. The armory will be issuing you your weapons. You will sign them out right after breakfast. That doesn't mean you take your time eating and sipping your coffee. You will eat like you have a purpose this morning, and then go get your weapons and be back here in formation in one hour. Squad leaders, take charge of your squads."

The sergeant didn't even bother to get us back to the position of attention. He just walked off, which just added to the air of urgency stirring around us.

I was just an 18-year-old private, the lowest rung on the military hierarchy, and I had no clue that Secretary of State Alexander M. Haig had just briefed members of NATO only hours earlier on the nature of the problem facing the United States in El Salvador.

The Secretary of State had just presented a White Paper that gave definitive proof that the Soviet Union, Cuba, and their allies had been sponsoring the insurgent movement in El Salvador. As such, newly elected President Ronald Reagan was determined to stop all Third World revolutions and the expansion of communism, while at the same time maintaining his publicly stated position of preventing U.S. troops from entering into a ground war.

El Salvador had been embroiled in a civil war since October of 1979, eleven months before I joined the Army, and the United States was on the side of the military-led junta government that was brutally attempting to eradicate the Marxist guerilla organization Farabundo Marti National Liberation Front; better known by its Spanish acronym FMLN. A month after the civil war started the first American military advisors were flown into El Salvador.

Day One was a long day, and we just stood around for most of it waiting for more orders.

On Day Two we were assigned to load military Jeeps onto flatbed freight train cars. That was exhausting work getting them all up there and chaining them all down.

On Day Three my COMM, *communications*, unit had a Pre-Combat Inspection (PCI), and then we got in some trigger time on the rifle range. I always liked going to the range, and on this particular day I was wondering if soon I was going to have to use these lethal skills against real people.

On Day Four the 43rd Engineer Battalion was ordered to "stand down," without any explanation as to what was happening politically, and garrison life returned back to "normal," back to Cold War mode.

I found out the following year, when my stepbrother Johnny and I went to go play a newly invented game called "paintball gun," that he had been one of those U.S. military advisors in El Salvador, serving as a U.S. Army Ranger, at the time my Battalion was getting ready to deploy there.

Although I was ready to go into a shooting war for my country, even if it meant enforcing the interests of the United States of America in a faraway land, I'm glad that I at least had the privilege to serve during the Cold War.

I have a certificate, signed by the Secretary of Defense, that has the official American eagle seal centered at the top, the words CERTIFICATE OF RECOGNITION under the seal, my name, and the words:

In recognition of your service during the period of the
Cold War (2 September 1945 – 26 December 1991) in promoting
peace and stability for this Nation, the people of this Nation are
forever grateful.

This certificate is DD FORM 2774, 1 JUL 2001. That's right! I received it from the Department of Defense in the mail exactly 10 years after the Cold War had ended. That's because, unlike the shooting wars, no service medal was ever awarded to Cold War warriors, therefore the Department of Defense issued this Certificate of Recognition to all those who served at the time, and to this I say, "better late than never."

I'm bringing up this certificate for two reasons. First, serving the country is serving the country. It doesn't matter if you're facing off with the enemy to keep them from trying anything or you are shooting at the enemy. Second, during the 46 years of the Cold War many veterans, including me, did our part to defeat communism, and to keep it from becoming our country's own fate. Sadly, many Americans today not only want to usher in a communist system, the sister of socialism, but they're even willing to go as far as having a China-like form of communism rule over us. The trend towards this direction became evident during the 2020 riots that swept through many American cities when demonstrators and rioters spray painted the communist hammer and sickle symbol on national monuments and buildings.

The reason the United States of America had fought socialism and communism so fiercely for over 100 years, ever since Russia became the world's first communist state in 1917, is because both systems are sinful. That's right, they are systems that do not honor God.

Throughout mankind's history nations were ruled by kings, queens, or warlords. Some were good to their citizens, but most were oppressive and self-serving. The Roman Empire, the time in which Paul wrote Ephesians 6, was a period of heavy taxation and ruled with an iron fist. Our founding fathers were students of history, evident by many of their writings, and when they created our Republic, they created a system with a lot of safeguards in it to prevent the mistakes that other Western civilizations had made. This is why they referred to the newly formed government as "The Great American Experiment." Where ancient republics had failed before, the United States of America was determined to guarantee "Life, Liberty and the pursuit of Happiness," which they claimed were "unalienable Rights," that were "endowed (given) by their Creator." The Creator they were referring to is the God of the Bible. As such, they all believed in the

Ten Commandments, which at one time was in every public school in the land, with the First Commandment of God clearly stating, *You shall have no other gods before Me. Exodus 20:3* For this reason alone, although there are many more Scriptures that I could present to make my case, communism is a NO GO! To communists the government is their god, and they hate the God of the Bible. For those who don't believe this, all they need to do is take a trip to North Korea, China, or Cuba and start proclaiming the Gospel openly, and see what happens.

God tells us in His eighth commandment, *You shall not steal. Exodus 20:15* thereby making socialism a system completely contrary to the principles of the Bible. American socialists proudly admit their agenda of taking money from "the rich" or from the "corporations" in order to "redistribute the wealth" to others for "economic equality" or "social justice." That's stealing! It's not their wealth to redistribute, but that does not bother their conscience because they already broke God's tenth commandment leading up to the desire to confiscate, ***You shall not covet*** *your neighbor's house; you shall not covet your neighbor's wife, nor his male servant, nor his female servant, nor his ox, nor his donkey, nor **anything that is your neighbor's.*** This includes other people's money.

Yes, tax dollars are necessary for national defense, first responders, to facilitate commerce, and to provide a justice system that is "blind," and everyone is obligated to pay the same percentage as the Bible indicates, but the notion that the government should be in the position of picking and choosing the winners and losers, by dipping into some people's pockets more than others, is actually ending "The Great American Experiment." Founding father Benjamin Franklin knew this well, and he warned against it by stating, "When the people find out that they can vote themselves money, that will **herald the end** of the republic." The meaning of the word "herald" is one that gives a sign or indication of something to come.

As a Christian Soldier you should be communicating the importance of social justice to others. Not the world's concept of "social justice," but God's. *And just as you want men to do to you, you also do to them likewise. Luke 6:31* I don't want people coveting my things or stealing from me, and I will "do to them likewise."

As a former combat communications Soldier this is one of my favorite quotes:

Communication is everything.

This quote has proven equally true throughout my entire tactical career. My very survival as a law enforcement officer depended on good radio and MDT, *Mobile Data Terminal,* communications, especially when in hot pursuit of dangerous criminals. Even now, as an armed undercover church security officer and a bodyguard at various Christian conferences, I rely on good radio and cell phone communications to keep God's people safe.

So, what is the definition of military communication? It is *information from friendly units in contact with the enemy to be used by commanders to transmit messages, orders, and reports to their subordinates in order to defeat the enemy.*

So, what is prayer? It's not just a form of communication, but it's the most important form of communication in the entire universe. Prayer is literally talking to God, either through your thoughts or verbal speech. This is exactly why the Apostle Paul, after instructing us to *put on the full combat gear of God,* also wants us *Praying always with all **prayer and supplication in the Spirit.***

Praying how much? "Praying always."

The occasional prayer when someone only wants something from God, or prayers offered up only in times of trouble, is like flipping the selector switch of your *weapon of the Spirit,* which you'll be issued very soon, from SAFE to SEMI. Semi automatic fire, which is one trigger pull to fire one bullet, is a method to conserve ammunition. Yes, some prayers during a time of need or want is better than nothing, and God listens to those prayers, but God supplies us with unlimited "ammunition." He wants His Soldiers to go all the way by flipping the selector switch to AUTO and spray. Fully automatic means that the bullets come out nonstop from a single trigger pull, and lots of bullets going downrange means FIREPOWER! There is no need to conserve prayers, for we are encouraged to pray without ceasing, according to 1 Thessalonians 5:17

There is an actual military idiom, an amusing one at that, known as *spray and pray,* which is meant to poke fun at someone who is an amateur at using an automatic weapon. The idea is that the shooter in question is such a poor shot that he or she expends all their bullets all at once at the enemy and pray that at least one of the bullets hits the single target. Well, we Christian Soldiers don't *spray and pray,* but we *pray and spray.* First, we talk to God (pray) that His will be done, and then we ask Him to do things for us, others, and situations, thereby aiming at numerous targets (spray). If the prayers are "in the Spirit" then every single one of them will hit their target without fail. Perhaps the results will not always be as we'd like to see done, or according to our timing, but it will be 100% effective His way. Asking Him earnestly and humbly is **supplication.**

Jesus confirms this "military order" to **supplicate** by stating, *and whatever you ask in my name, that I will do, that the Father may be glorified in the Son. If you ask anything in My name, I will do it. John 14:13-14*

However, there's a hitch. *Yet you do not have because you do not ask. You ask and do not receive, because you ask **amiss**, that you may **spend it** on your pleasures. James 4:2*

The word "amiss" means, *in a mistaken way* or *in a faulty way.* However, to a Christian Soldier it means more than just that. Look at the word again. It's actually two words, **"a miss."** Your prayers will "miss" their targets if they're **"spent"** on your selfish pleasures. If that's the case, you had better collect your wasted "spent rounds," get the "brass" (the metal brass is the

Biblical symbol for judgement) cleaned up, and reloaded. Then fire those reloads (prayers) the right way.

As a Christian Soldier you need to earnestly and humbly approach God as the Commander in Chief, and not as Santa Claus. Too many Christians just want presents from God, but not His presence. Prayers should be asking for victory in battles over our enemies: the flesh, the world, and the devil.

What did Jesus pray just before he was arrested by the mob coming for Him in the Garden of Gethsemane? *"Father, if it is Your will, take this cup away from Me; nevertheless not My will, but Yours, be done." Luke 22:42*

Jesus knew God's war strategy, His strategy to save mankind, which was for The Lamb of God to be executed on a wooden cross (representing the *tree of life*). He prayed to the Father to take this military option, the cross, off the table, but only "if it is Your will."

Obviously, it was God's will for the cross to be the only path to total victory. A tree is the symbol of our downfall, and a tree is the symbol of our salvation. On *the tree of the knowledge of good and evil* were apples (sins), but on *the tree of life* was blood (God' own blood on the cross). *And according to the law almost all things are purified with blood, and without shedding of blood there is no remission. Hebrews 9:22*

Jesus' blood had to be shed, and we are blessed that God gave us insight to Jesus' prayer on that fateful night.

The wonderful thing about praying is that it is faster than instant. This is where my radio communications knowledge and real-world experience comes in handy in explaining what I mean.

A radio wave, which is rather instant, travels at the speed of light, which is 186,000 miles per second, and *yet there is not a word on my tongue, but behold, O Lord, You know it altogether. Psalm 139:4* It's a poetic way of describing "thoughts." Though a radio wave is extremely fast, God knows your thoughts, hence your prayers, before you even think or speak them.

Scientists estimate that the human brain sends signals through the nerves at 3,560 miles per second, and the human voice travels through air much slower than that at 1,125 feet per second. Therefore, God, who spoke light into existence, *"Let there be light,"* is always going to be faster than your electronic devices, your voice, or even your own thoughts.

Here's another interesting thing about radio waves. Those that leave the earth will travel forever until they hit something. Your prayers always hit God. He not only knows them all, but He knows the intent behind each one of them. In fact, He even knows the source of your prayers, your heart, better than you know yourself.

Electronic communications used by the United States Army originates from a transmitter and is sent, via electrical waves, to a receiver. So, when you pray to God, which direction do the prayers go?

They go up, up into heaven. They go through the atmosphere, through space, and to heaven before you even have completed the last word in your mind. How do I know this? Because it's in the Bible.

You may recall that Abraham sent his chief servant to Mesopotamia to find a wife for his son Isaac. When the servant arrived in the area, after a very long journey, the first thing he did was pray to God asking, "O Lord God of my master Abraham, please give me success this day," and he proceeded to describe a sign that he wanted God to give him to confirm who the right woman was. Then the next verse tells us, *and it happened,* **before he had finished speaking,** *that behold, Rebeka... Genesis 24:10-15* and it turns out that Rebeka was the woman that God chose for Isaac. Abraham's servant had not even finished the prayer yet, and God answered it. Wouldn't it be nice if we received the answer to all of our prayers before we even finished them?

King David, being a military man, could have described what prayer is like by giving a military metaphor, but he didn't. Although in his time, around 1000 BC, his army did not have electronic communications, they did have other means of communications: voice communication, written communication, signal flags and signal fires (smoke in the day and light at night), he chose to describe prayer to God in a beautiful poetic way. He wrote, *Let my prayer be set before You as incense, Psalm 141:2*

The mental picture that King David wishes for us to see is that of a sweet-smelling incense that is burning, with its sweet aromatic smoke continually floating upwards towards heaven. Incense smoke not only goes upwards, but it expands the higher it goes. So too your prayers should expand outward to cover more than just you, the source, but also include your family, your neighbors, your community, your nation, the world, and praising Him who made them all. The only way the "smoke," your prayers, will stop is if the fire is extinguished. Of course, **fire, the Holy Spirit, and communications** are directly linked together in the New Testament.

*When the Day of Pentecost had fully come, they were all with one accord in one place. And suddenly there came **a sound from heaven,** as of a rushing mighty wind, and it filled the whole house where they were sitting. Then there appeared to them divided tongues, **as of fire,** and one sat upon each of them. And they were all filled with **the Holy Spirit** and began to **speak with other tongues,** as the Spirit gave the utterance. Acts 2:1-4*

As a Christian Soldier, who now sees the great importance of prayer (communication), one of your favorite military quotes should now also include, *Communication is everything.*

What do you see when a group of teenagers are all sitting together? Most, if not all of them, are on their cell phones. Watch people standing in line at the Post Office or waiting to get in somewhere, and you'll see a bunch of heads looking down at a screen with their thumbs typing away, so they don't waste a single moment doing nothing. Everyone is communicating with someone or looking at something. Our society is obsessed with communications. God, the Creator of communication, desires for us to communicate with Him just as much, if not more, than the time we spend on our devices.

Are you keeping the Shema of Deuteronomy 6:4? *You shall love the Lord your God with **all your heart,** with **all your soul,** and with **all your strength,*** or is all your heart, soul, and strength spent on your device texting others, forwarding memes, watching videos, and playing games?

What's the one thing people do most when they love someone? They want to spend time with the person that they are in love with. They want to communicate; be it face to face or through a device. The greater the love, the more time the two participants set aside for one another.

How much time do you spend a day talking with God? Do you thank Him for each morning for another day of life He has given you? Do you ask Him to bless every meal? Are you praying for the persecuted church around the world? If you haven't been, then you need to. Yes, God is your Commander in Chief, but never forget that He is also your daddy, your lover, your groom, your shepherd, author and finisher of your faith, wonderful counselor, Head of the Church, the Truth, and everything you need Him to be, which is why He calls himself "I Am," not "I Was" or "I Will Be." I AM is present tense. Live in the moment, with Him. Therefore, when it comes to communicating, God needs to come first, because nobody, not your family, not your friends, nor coworkers or any associates, are to be placed before Him. In the Shema "all" means **all**.

Communication is everything. This is true in combat, business, and personal relationships. Why would it be any different with God?

Mission success depends on timely, accurate, communications. A Christian Soldier not leading people to the Lord is a *mission failure*.

The Cold War (1947-1991) was to stop godless communism. In this photo American troops face off with Soviet troops in East Germany.

As a young man I did my part to fight communism during the Cold War, and as an old man I enjoyed the fruits by visiting East Germany.

Chapter 4

FULL COMBAT GEAR

PUT ON AND TAKE UP

Put on *the whole armor of God, that you may be able to stand against the wiles of the devil. Ephesians 6:11*

Then, only two verses later, Paul repeats almost verbatim the same words,

Therefore *take up* *the whole armor of God, that you may be able to withstand in the evil day, Ephesians 6:13*

Why would He do that? Why the repetition?

Whenever a word, or a phrase, is repeated twice in the Bible it is to emphasize the importance of that word or phrase. For example, in the King James Bible (KJB), published in 1611 for the ever-expanding English-speaking world at the time, Jesus said on several occasions, "Verily, verily," (*Truly, truly*) before making His point. Unfortunately, the New King James Version (NKJV) published in 1982, which is the modern English version of the King James Bible (KJB), changed "Truly, truly" to "Most assuredly." Although I prefer reading modern English, I have to admit that in this particular case it "softens the blows" of the "double punch combination" that God intended.

Here's another example of the softening. In John 8:51 it reads *Most assuredly,* but it would have been better to keep the Old English *Verily, verily, I say to you, if anyone keeps My Word he shall never see death,* that's because legal testimonies, as described in the book of Deuteronomy, must be substantiated by at least two witnesses. Since Jesus is the one making the statement, and He is the third part of the Godhead, the first "verily" is acknowledging the Father as Witness number one, and the second "verily" is acknowledging the Holy Spirit as Witness number two, thus confirming Jesus' statement as legally established truth.

The most powerful example of Jesus repeating a word in order to call upon two divine Witnesses, and which absolutely confirms the Trinity (One God, yet three Persons), and that is when Jesus was hanging on a Roman execution cross, *and about the ninth hour Jesus cried out with a loud voice saying, "Eli, Eli, lama sabachthani?" that is "My God, My God, why have You forsaken Me?" Matthew 27:46*

The first cry out was to the Father, the second cry out to the Holy Spirit, and there was no third cry out "My God," because Jesus is the third part of the Godhead and He wouldn't be crying out to Himself. Jesus was forsaken by the Father and the Holy Spirit for you, so you wouldn't be the one forsaken on Judgement Day, and the penalty of sin that was paid through a blood sacrifice was legally confirmed by two divine Witnesses.

In the Old Testament we have another example of God speaking out His name twice. On Mount Sinai Moses asked God, *"Please show me Your Glory." Exodus 33:18*

Moses wanted to see God's face, but God said to him, *"You cannot see My face; for no man shall see Me, and live." Exodus 33:20* However, God made Moses stand in the cleft of a rock, and He covered him with His hand as He passed by. When God removed His hand, Moses saw His back. Just the glory of God passing by made the skin of Moses' face shine for weeks afterwards, and he had to wear a veil when talking to the Israelites at the camp. As God was passing Moses He (יהוה) proclaimed, *"The Lord (יהוה), the Lord (יהוה) God, merciful and gracious, longsuffering, and abounding in goodness and truth," Exodus 34:6*

He proclaimed His own name יהוה (possibly pronounced Ya-vay) twice, and not the title "Lord," as in the English translation. The Father was physically present with Moses, and thus He calls out to the Son, then to the Holy Spirit, as two Witnesses. Once again, this is a confirmation of the Trinity.

Now that we've established the importance of repetition in the Bible, it's crystal clear that God is emphasizing for all believers to *put on the full combat gear of God* by stating it twice in Ephesians 6:11 and 6:13. In fact, I'll repeat it in the modern vernacular so there is no misunderstanding as to its importance, "Put on the full combat gear of God" Christian Soldier, because we're about to go into the thick of things.

Before we move on, let me share something that may help you, as it has for me when it comes to which translation of the Bible to read. The "Spiritual Field Manual" that I read most often is the New King James Version (NKJV), despite a few modern English words and phrases that don't seem to have quite the same "punch" as the Old English. I prefer this translation because I highly value the original King James Bible (KJB), also referred to as the King James Version (KJV), but I just don't care for all the "Thys," "Thees," and "Thous," and the NKJV cleans all that up nicely. Try sharing the Gospel with someone on the street or in a living room proclaiming, "Thou shalt love the Lord thy God with all thine heart..." and they will think you're a Shakespearian actor that can't get out of character. Believe it or not, there are some older folks who actually pray out loud, or preachers who preach from the pulpit, using the Old English. That's because they grew up with the King James Bible, or they believe it to be more holy than modern English.

Speaking of "holy languages," and how people can get caught up in it, up until the mid-1960s, when I was a boy at the time, the Catholic Church, by authority of the Second Vatican Council, decreed that Mass (the liturgy of the Word, the Blessed Sacrament, and songs) no longer had to be given in Latin, but in the local languages. This was because most congregants did not understand this dead language (a language that is no longer spoken by the government or common people) very well, or even at all, and therefore the Word of God was not effectively reaching the hearts of most Catholics. The only reason Latin was used for so long by the Catholic Church was because in 600 AD it was declared "the only language for Scripture," and it was also one of the tools used to keep a separation between Catholicism and the Greek-speaking Byzantine Empire (the Eastern Orthodox Church), and then later in history from those within the Catholic Church, like John Wycliffe (1328-1384), a predecessor to Protestantism, who started the movement of defying the Church by believing that people should be permitted to read the Bible in their own language.

Imagine that. Somehow Latin was a "holy language," but their own language was not. Yet, Latin was not even the language of the Bible. If any language were to be holy it would be Hebrew, Greek, or Aramaic, since these were the original languages God used to record His Word.

Anytime you study the Bible in detail, which should be habitual, you should go online and compare the verses with the Hebrew Interlinear Bible for the Old Testament and the Greek Interlinear Bible for the New Testament; the two main original languages that the books of the Bible were written in. There are only 268 verses in the Bible written in Aramaic.

Seeing the original languages, with the English right under it, thus the term "interlinear," will increase your understanding of the Bible, and that's because you just click on the desired word, which is a link, and it will give you the definition and explanation of the word. You really don't have to read, write, or speak ancient Hebrew or Greek to understand the original writings.

Since I speak French, every evening I read the Louis Second French Bible, *la version Louis Segond de la Bible,* the 21st version, first published in 1910, *avec les mots d'aujourd'hui,* in today's words. I do this, not only to keep from getting rusty with the language that I first learned in college, and to effectively use it on a regular basis to teach my Reality-Based Personal Protection system in Francophone countries today, but the greatest reason is to use it to witness to French speakers. Yet, by reading the Bible in a different language I have found that some verses that I have read a hundred times before in English suddenly reveal something new that I overlooked before.

If you can read a second language, then give it a try.

*Therefore **take up** the whole armor of God, that you may be able to withstand in the evil day, and having done all, to stand. Ephesians 6:13*

The Greek word ἀναλάβετε (pronounced an-all-a-beh-tay) is "take up." Put on, take up, it's the same thing. Or is it?

Jesus said, *If anyone desires to come after Me, let him deny himself, and **take up** his cross daily, and follow Me. Luke 9:23* The root word "take up" in this passage is the same as Ephesians 6:13.

Anyone can "put on" a police uniform, and some do on Halloween for fun, but it does not make them a real police officer. Anyone can "put on" body armor and a helmet, but that does not mean they're going to do any fighting on behalf of the United States of America. However, to **take up** a police badge representing an actual police department, which is worn on a police uniform over the heart, is literally putting your life on the line every time you go out to serve the public. To **take up** arms for the United States of America after being sworn in as a Soldier is a true commitment that could cost you your life.

However, **put on** or **take up** does not only apply to military or paramilitary organizations, but civilians as well. An immoral pop singer, who has put on a cross around her neck or has it dangling as an earring from the left ear lobe, does not mean that she is a Christian – "Christ like." On the other hand, if a pop singer gets up on stage, or is on a talk show, while displaying the cross, and boldly states, "Jesus Christ is Lord," then that is not just "putting on" the cross as an accessory to her wardrobe, but actually "taking up" the cross.

As a Christian Soldier you are called to "take up" your cross daily, which means denying yourself and living for, or even dying for, Him.

KNOW YOUR ENEMY

that you may be able to stand against the wiles of the devil. Ephesians 6:11

that you may be able to withstand in the evil day, Ephesians 6:13

Essentially, the second half of verses 11 and 13 is a military WARNO, *Warning Order.* This WARNO has just been communicated by Paul (your commander) to you (the subordinate) to inform you that an OPORD, *Operation Order,* may be forthcoming.

A WARNO is issued to give you a head's up of a situation requiring military action, and your role in it should the order be given. A WARNO is also meant to give you a little time to make the necessary preparations.

There is no doubt that this particular WARNO issued by Paul is going to materialize for you, exactly when is not certain, warning you to prepare for battle soon against the devil *in the evil day*. Evil days are now upon us.

When an OPORD is given in the United States Army it is a five-paragraph, easy to understand, order containing: **Situation, Mission, Execution, Sustainment,** and **Command and Control.** This order not only serves to inform you, but it provides you with mission essential details on how to fight the enemy.

The **Situation** is that WE ARE AT WAR WITH THE DEVIL, THE UNBELIEVING WORLD, & OUR OWN FLESH (SIN). This war has been raging on for nearly 6,000 years, which began when our first ancestors, Adam and Eve, sinned in the Garden of Eden. This was a declaration of war against God. First, they disobeyed Him. Second, they stole from His tree. It was the beginning of mankind's rebellion. As a result, there have been mass casualties ever since, namely the death of every human being, animal, and plant that has lived before us. Somehow, even the very universe was ruined because of this action, *For we know that the whole creation groans and labors with birth pangs together until now. Romans 8:22*

The **Mission** is simple in its wording. STAND AGAINST THE WILES OF THE DEVIL. Notice, it does not say "destroy the devil." Wouldn't that solve the problem much faster than just standing against his plotting and planning? Why not just take him out?

The fact is, humans are flesh and blood, and Satan, and the fallen angels, exist in the spiritual realm. We simply don't have the ability, nor the equipment, to destroy them. We can destroy other human beings, but not them. Only God has that ability, and eventually He's going to do it. This is why our mission is only "to stand."

To understand the definition of "stand against" we must first go to America's "gold standard" for dictionaries since 1828, which is the Merriam-Webster Dictionary. The definition of the word "stand," as is intended by the Greek word στῆναι (pronounced stay-nay) means *to be in a position to gain or lose because of an action taken or a commitment made.*

Based upon the level of your commitment, and your actions as a Christian Soldier, God is going to place you into a position where you can win or lose on the battlefield. That's the reason for the sobering words, that you *may be able to stand.* This indicates that you *may not be able to stand* if you don't listen to instructions or if you go out there on the battlefield half-hearted or ill-equipped. However, let's not get ahead of ourselves. You haven't even been issued your body armor, equipment, or weapons yet.

The **Execution** phase of our order is, and will be, very difficult. "Standing" doesn't just mean, "Okay Lord, I'll just stand here and keep an eye on things for you," as you are out of harm's way. No, it means that you are to engage in the activities of spiritual sabotage, ambush, harass, push back, and hurt the forces of darkness. Of course, they're not going to take it lying down either. They're going to strike back whenever you come against them. Then if you retreat they're going to pursue you and try to shoot you in the back. The devil literally wants you dead. However, "difficult" does not mean impossible.

So, what's the meaning of "wiles," as in *that you may be able to stand against **the wiles** of the devil.* Until I came across this word in the Bible, I never used this word in my life, and I suspect you haven't either. It's one of those Old English words, used since the 12th century, that has fallen out of use.

μεθοδείας. Do you recognize this Greek word? Well, you may not be familiar with the Greek alphabet, but you'll definitely recognize the pronunciation, which is method-ay-as, from which we get the word "method." Synonyms for the word "wile" include *trick, ploy, ruse, scheme, gimmick,* and a fun one to say is *shenanigan,* as in, "I don't want any shenanigans from you." Therefore, let's read verse 6:11, the WARNO, in modern terms:

Put on the full combat gear of God, that you may be able to stand up against the military deceptions (MILDEC) of the HOSTILE forces. WARNO Ephesians 6:11

There's a new one for you, and that is MILDEC. The official definition of Military Deception (MILDEC) *is actions executed to deliberately mislead adversary military, paramilitary, or violent extremist organization decision makers, thereby causing the adversary to take specific actions (or inactions) that will contribute to the accomplishment of the friendly mission.* And yes, there is also a Field Manual all about MILDEC. It's FM 3-13.4

When describing the players of a battle we Christian Soldiers are also going to use the NATO (North Atlantic Treaty Organization, a military alliance between North American and 30 European countries) symbology. HOSTILE is an enemy force, represented by a red diamond on a tactical map, while FRIEND, or "friendly," are all Bible believing Christians, as opposed to the "I was born a Christian" or "I was baptized a Christian when I was a baby" types, who are represented by a blue rectangle. The HOS-

TILE in this WARNO is the devil (in Greek διαβόλου, pronounced dee-ah-bol-oo, meaning *slanderer* – a person who speaks false and malicious statements that damage the reputation of another).

The United States Armed Forces also uses deception, lying, and cheating to trip up our adversaries, and so does every military on earth. In fact, even law enforcement is authorized to deceive people, and lie directly to citizens, but only under certain circumstances. For example, when I was a police officer, a common trick was to separate partners in crime at the detention facility. We'd put one of the suspects in an interview room, like the ones you see in the movies: a small brightly lighted room, a simple metal table with a couple of office chairs on either side, while the other suspect would remain in a booking cage or a jail cell in another part of the facility.

I'd offer the suspect being interrogated a cup of water, a sandwich, or even a cigarette to make him feel relaxed. Then after a few simple questions I'd hit him up with, "Your partner has already told us everything. So, don't lie to me. I just want your side of the story. Why don't you just tell me the truth and save us all a lot of time."

That kind of lie was acceptable; telling him that his partner "sang like a canary," when he actually hadn't. However, there were restrictions when it came to deception and lying by the police. We were not allowed to use religion to deceive someone, such as, "Tell me where the body is. After all, the person you killed deserves a decent Christian burial." We also couldn't promise them less punishment if they cooperated, or promise them something we couldn't actually give them, like "Tell us what you know, and we'll set you free."

When I was a U.S. federal agent the authorized lies and deception went even further. I won't go into all the details here for OPSEC, *Operations Security,* reasons, but my official training included having a "cover story" if someone engaged me in conversation. In other words, I would assume the identity of a fictitious character, so my real identity would not be revealed nor ever discovered. My training also included stealing a car in a foreign country to get to a safe house, not allowing foreign authorities to arrest me under any circumstance (you can fill in the blank as to what exactly that meant), and then getting to the nearest U.S. Embassy or to a "friendly" embassy by any means possible to be exfiltrated from foreign soil.

Lying in the military was no different. One time I was teaching an advanced firearms and tactics course to a group of U.S. Marines at Camp Pendleton, all of whom were involved in Special Operations, and with them were some rough looking guys who were wearing civilian clothes, sporting long unkempt beards, and tribal-looking tattoos covering their arms. I was told that these men were "guests," and were authorized to take the course. Since Uncle Sam was paying me to train them, I didn't ask any questions.

Like any military course, the students had to fill out some mandatory paperwork, and since I was the instructor, I made sure it was done right.

One of the guys wearing "civies" forgot to fill out one of the boxes on the form, and I caught the mistake just as he was walking away from the table. I looked at the name he had just written down, and I called out to him, "Hey, Carlton!" but he ignored me and just kept walking away. After calling out to him twice, and he still did not respond, I ran after him, and I stopped him. I said to him, "I'm sorry, but you need to come back and complete a box on the form you just filled out."

When he came back to the table there were a couple of completed forms on the table face up. He looked a bit confused, and hesitated. I wondered why he wasn't picking up his form he had just filled out. Then he asked me, "What name did I give you?"

That question, matched by his non-caring demeanor, made me realize that he was either a "spook," someone in the Intelligence community, or a U.S. Navy SEAL. Either way, it was someone who would never reveal their true identity at a training course hosted by an outside agency.

Obviously, the form that "Carlton" completed had nothing but false information on it anyway, but as long as it was all filled out, and signed at the bottom, he could be whoever he wanted to be, as far as I was concerned. I did what I was supposed to do in case some Navy JAG lieutenant attorney ever questioned me.

During wartime the stakes are even higher, since national defense is at stake, and thus a lot of hours and resources are devoted to Military Deception. The means by which to conduct military deception include physical, technical, and administrative.

Technical MILDEC can be done through the "leaking" of false communications that leads the enemy to believe that there will be an attack at Point A, when in fact the actual attack will be at Point B.

A physical means of military deception is best illustrated by citing an actual mission to you that the U.S. Army conducted during the Iraq War in 2003.

The Americans wanted the Iraqi army, the enemy, to believe that a U.S. Special Forces team was going to hit a critical infrastructure target deep inside their own territory. If the ruse were to work properly, the Iraqi military command would have to pull soldiers away from the main objective and re-deploy them to guard the target that they thought was going to be attacked.

The Americans attached several large 150-pound blocks of ice to individual parachutes. Once over the drop zone, in the wee hours of the night, the blocks of ice were pushed off the end of the ramp of the C-130 aircraft, the parachutes opened by means of a static line as they fell out, and they all floated down to the desert floor behind enemy lines. When the morning sun came up the blocks of ice melted rapidly leaving the straps of the parachutes, which normally carried men in them, empty and dry. To any enemy military patrol stumbling upon these parachutes laying on the ground, it would look as if a Special Forces team had parachuted into their territory, got out of their harnesses and left the parachutes, and then went about their deadly mission to the nearest likely target. Needless to say, there would be quite a frantic search for these American "paratroopers," and this would tie up men and material.

The military deception worked, and the U.S. Army destroyed the target.

The good news is that God does not ever use deception. In fact, and I know that I am preaching to the choir here, God cannot lie. It's not His nature to lie.

God is not a man, that He should lie, *nor a son of man, that He should repent. Has He said, and will He not do? Or has He spoken, and will He not make good?* Numbers 23:19

in hope of eternal life, which **God, that cannot lie,** *promised before the world began, Titus 1:2*

When God tells you anything, either through His Word or by means of the Holy Spirit speaking directly to your heart, it's always the truth. However, the devil, who is not God's opposite as some may think, but is merely a created being, is infamously notorious for all manner of DEC (deception), *because there is no truth in him. John 8:44*

But, wait! you may be thinking. *Didn't God instruct judge-turned-general Gideon to have 300 warriors fool the enemy? Wasn't that deception?*

Well, let's take a look at the story of Gideon to glean its truths.

Somewhere between 1179 and 1154 BC the Midianites, a people from northwestern Arabia, oppressed the Israelites for six years. So brutal was their occupation that many Israelites were forced to seek refuge in caves and strongholds. They couldn't be out in the open in their own country.

The Angel of the Lord, an Old Testament term referring to Jesus before taking on human form, appeared to Gideon, and said to him, *"The Lord is with you, you mighty man of valor!" Judges 6:12*

This is somewhat ironic, because at that moment of the visitation Gideon was hiding in a winepress threshing wheat so he wouldn't be seen by any Midianites. Therefore, he didn't see himself as valiant, but God did.

There's that military word again that we've discussed – valor. The actual Hebrew is החיל (pronounced heh-kay-yil), and in its context החיל גבור it translates to "warrior of the mighty." Wow! What an awesome title to be given by the Creator of the universe, Warrior of the Mighty.

Gideon was given an Operation Order (OPORD) by God to muster up an army, and then go to war with the Midianites. Obeying the order, Gideon implemented a recruiting campaign. 32,000 men volunteered to join the newly formed army. However, shortly afterwards God gave Gideon a Fragmentary Order (FRAGORD), which is a military order that adds additional information and instructions to the original order. Here's the FRAGORD, spoken by God himself, *The people who are with you are too many for Me to give the Midianites into their hands, lest Israel claim glory for itself against Me, saying, 'My own hand has saved me.'" Judges 7:2*

That's an amazing statement from a human standpoint, because the Midianites were "as numerous as locus; and their camels (military vehicles) were without number, as the sand by the seashore in multitude." The Israelites were not just outnumbered by the enemy, but by overwhelming numbers. Even 32,000 would have not been enough to defeat such a force. At least not without God.

God gave an additional FRAGORD to General Gideon. It was to reduce the number of Gideon's troops even further. God ordered, *"Whoever is fearful and afraid, let him turn and depart at once from Mount Gilead." And 22,000 of the people returned, and 10,000 remained. Judges 7:3*

Imagine the Commander in Chief of the United States of America saying something like that today, just before starting a major war with China, our biggest foe, "Ah, whoever is afraid to fight, just go home."

God finally reduced Gideon's Army to just 300 brave men. No, this is not the same 300 Spartans who fought at the Battle of Thermopylae in 480 BC.

That's a great story, but that came about 670 years later.

In the Operation Order (OPORD), contained in the **Execution** paragraph, God's instruction to General Gideon was, *"Arise, go down against the camp, for I have delivered it into your hand." Judges 7:9*

Gideon wasn't given a **Sustainment** plan, which means maintaining and supporting the war effort, concerning the Midianites and Amalekites, and all the people of the East who were "as the sand by the seashore in multitude." God left that part out. Humanly speaking, 300 men against these massive armies was impossible. It was a suicide mission. However, Gideon believed that God would deliver his enemies into his hands.

Before briefing his troops, and launching the attack, General Gideon *worshiped. Judges 7:15*

This is the action every Christian Soldier should take before any battle – worship.

Are you going to face a child custody battle in court? Worship.

Are you having a problem at work, and you have been told by the boss, "I need to see you in my office?" Worship.

Are you having financial problems, and the bills are due? Worship.

God is either going to deliver your enemy into your hand, or He has another plan for you, but He's not going to let you be physically destroyed without a purpose. We know this, because Christians have turned to the following Scripture for two millennium when facing tough times, *For I know the thoughts that I think toward you, says the Lord, thoughts of peace and not evil, to give you a future and a hope. Jeremiah 29:11*

Worship Him no matter what the odds are against you. Worship Him no matter if you will physically survive or die during a battle. After all, *For to me, to live is Christ, and to die is gain. Philippians 1:21* It's a win-win situation when you're fighting in God's Army.

The final paragraph of General Gideon's OPORD, **Command & Control**, concluded with how he was going to exercise his authority over his men, and how he was going to direct them in battle. The battle plan was:

1. Divide the 300 troops into 3 companies.

2. Each soldier will have a trumpet in his right hand, and an empty clay pot with a burning torch down inside of it held by his left hand.

3. On the battlefield, upon arrival at the edge of the enemy camp at zero dark hundred hours, each soldier is to direct his attention to General Gideon, and do the same techniques and tactics as he does.

This Operation Order wouldn't make much sense today, and it didn't in ancient times either. "Trumpets, clay pots, and torches? What about archers, spears, or battle-tested maneuvers?" Yet, God gives us OPORDS we just don't understand at the time He gives them to us: A hurricane-like storm in the sea of Galilee when you told us to go to the other side? Our brothers and sisters being fed to the lions in colosseums? Imprisonment and execution for preaching the Gospel? Removed from a social media platform for quoting Scripture?

So, when it comes to OPORDs from God you're not always going to get battle-tested techniques and tactics, but methods that have you scratching your head sometimes. God explains it by saying, *"For My thoughts are not your thoughts, nor are your ways My ways," says the Lord. Isaiah 55:8* This is when the faith part comes in.

Let's finish the story.

So Gideon and the hundred men who were with him came to the outpost of the camp at the beginning of the middle watch (guard duty), just as they had posted the watch; and they blew the trumpets and broke the pitchers that were in their hands. Then the three companies blew the trumpets and broke their pitchers – they held the torches in their left hands and the trumpets in their right hands for blowing – and they cried, "The sword of the Lord and of Gideon!" And every man stood in his place all around the camp; and the whole army ran and cried out and fled. When the three hundred blew the trumpets, the Lord set every man's sword against his companion throughout the whole camp; and the army fled... Judges 7:19-22

Victory! Light pushes out darkness.

Your blood, sweat, and tears have paid off. You've been recruited. You joined the Army. You went through the rigorous processing. You endured Basic Combat Training. You sailed through Advanced Individual Training, and now it's the time you have been waiting for - being issued your *full combat gear.* HOOAH!

To win any battle you have to see "the big picture." Likewise, when you see things from God's perspective you'll always have the advantage.

To discover God's truths you don't just merely skim the surface, but you must go deeper into God's word. Read the Bible cover to cover.

Know your enemy. With approval, this is a "terrorist cell" that I formed and trained to test my department's S.W.A.T. team during training.

For Military Deception (MILDEC) Iraqi insurgents placed infants on the streets to ambush American convoys. I used a doll to train troops.

Before U.S. Army Soldiers go into battle an OPORD (Operations Order) is given. The entire chapter of Ephesians 6 is your OPORD.

You can never drop your guard. The enemy will try to slip through. I learned this on the U.S.-Mexican border with the U.S. Border Patrol.

FULL COMBAT GEAR OF GOD

Therefore put on the *whole armor of God*, that you may be able
to stand against the wiles of the devil.   Ephesians 6:11

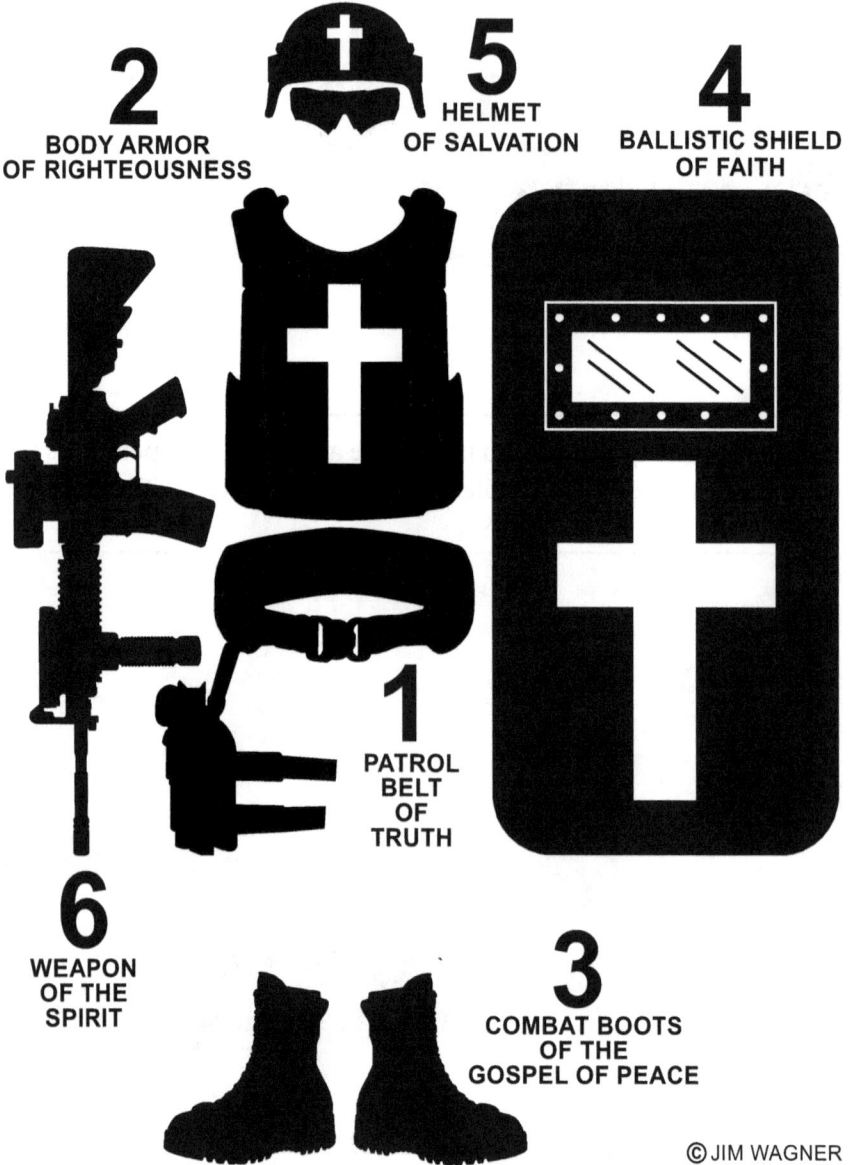

2
**BODY ARMOR
OF RIGHTEOUSNESS**

5
**HELMET
OF SALVATION**

4
**BALLISTIC SHIELD
OF FAITH**

1
**PATROL
BELT
OF
TRUTH**

6
**WEAPON
OF THE
SPIRIT**

3
**COMBAT BOOTS
OF THE
GOSPEL OF PEACE**

© JIM WAGNER

Chapter 5

PATROL BELT

THE WAY TO STAY CENTERED

Stand therefore, having girded your waist with truth. Ephesians 6:14

The word "stand" (in Greek στῆτε, pronounced stay-teh) is used a second time, and we know that a phrase or word repeated twice in the Bible means, in militaryspeak, *Listen up! This is extremely important to your survival and victory.*

In modern English we still use the word "stand," but to truly understand the essence of the meaning of this word today it would be best stated, "Stand up!" Examples used in a sentence would be, "Stand up, and be a man!" or "Stand up to him!" or even "Stand up for yourself!"

Using the Merriam-Webster dictionary definition of the term it means *to remain sound and intact under stress, attack, or close scrutiny.*

The Christian life is not a playground. The Christian life is a battleground. Therefore, the Christian Soldier prepares himself or herself physically, mentally, emotionally, and spiritually for the hardships, stress, attacks, and even scrutiny from peers and leadership that comes with this chosen "profession" of ours.

I know that this all sounds rather bleak, or even like "gloom and doom" to the non-believer "civilian," and that's because they just don't understand the extent of the love that a Christian has for God; a love that is self-sacrificing. It's very much like the 99% of the Americans who have never served in the military, nor will they ever. Even though many civilians may have respect for the military, just like many people may have respect for Judeo-Christian values, the general excuse for able bodied people not joining the United States Armed Forces is, "I don't want to risk my life for the country," or "I could make more money in the civilian sector than I would in the military," or "The military is just too rigid and controlling for my liking."

Of course, there are also those individuals who have zero respect for anyone who has served in the military, or who is serving now. Many of these hostile types are the ones who are found taking a knee in disrespect at a sporting event as the U.S. National Anthem is played, or who may even go out of his or her way to yell at an active-duty soldier or veteran, "Murderer!" or some other vulgarity. They just can't comprehend how someone could love their country to the point of possibly losing their life, making less money, or living under uncomfortable conditions for it.

Yes, we Christian Soldiers stand up for what we believe. Yet, from our perspective, how could we not? After all, Jesus explains exactly how the sacrifice works, *For whoever desires to save his life will lose it, but whoever loses his life for My sake will find it. For what profit is it to a man if he gains the whole world, and loses his own soul? Or what will a man give in exchange for his soul? For the Son of Man will come in the glory of His Father with His angels, and then He will reward each according to his works. Matthew 16:25-27*

Once you have found the courage to "stand up," the first piece of combat gear that God instructs you to put on, or *gird*, which wraps around your waist, is the *patrol belt*.

The verb gird means *to prepare oneself for action.* However, when talking about a belt it means *to make something, such as clothing or a sword, fast or secure.* In other words, the *patrol belt* that you've secured to your waste is not going to be loose or come off.

When it comes to any physical conflict, the waist is the most critical part of the body, and I'll explain why.

If a criminal is about to attack you, even if you are not familiar with the Criminal Assault Cycle, statistically 90% of all concealed weapons are carried in the waist area. This area includes the waistband of the pants, the belt, and the front and back pockets. Therefore, this is the area you should focus on when an unknown, a suspicious person, is approaching you. That, and watch the hands. As the law enforcement expression goes, *It's the hands that kill.*

Speaking from experience as a former law enforcement officer, I have recovered most concealed weapons from the waistband area of criminals when doing pat down searches. This is exactly why on felony stops, conducted at gunpoint, suspects are told to raise their hands "to the sky." This is also why anyone being arrested, be it for a misdemeanor or felony, is told to interlace their fingers behind their neck before being handcuffed, which is the old Los Angeles Police Department arrest and control position. If the suspect suddenly reaches for a concealed weapon from this position, which the odds are 90% they'll have a concealed weapon somewhere around the waistband area, at least it's a long reach for the hand that is up in the air, or from the back of the neck, to get to. The distance that must be covered to get to the weapon gives the law enforcement officer a little more reaction time than if the hands were lower near the waist area.

Before I move on, it's important that you know the Criminal Assault Cycle that I mentioned in the beginning of this chapter.

Criminals are not ghosts. They don't just suddenly appear out of thin air, and then attack you. If you are the intended victim of a criminal, there is a pattern that a criminal will take, in sequential order, which you should be aware of for your own safety. If you know the indicators, then you may be able to extract yourself out of the situation before it happens, or at least have some advance warning if there is no way out of it:

1. Selection (the criminal selects you for a reason: money, property, or physical harm).

2. Contact or Positioning (the criminal moves toward you or waits to ambush you as you walk into the "fatal funnel").
3. Assault (the unarmed or armed physical attack against you).
4. Getaway (no criminal wants to be arrested, and so he or she flees the crime scene on foot or by a vehicle - a "getaway car").

Just as most criminals carry concealed weapons in the waistband area, so too 90% of all weapons carried by American law enforcement officers, both concealed and exposed weapons, are also around the waistband area.

Think about it. Where do you see the pistol of a uniformed police officer? It is in a holster on his or her duty belt, either on their right hip or their left hip (8% to 10% of the population is left-handed). The same is true for the less-lethal weapons that law enforcement officers routinely carry on the job: Taser, baton, and pepper spray. They're somewhere on the duty belt as well – the waist area. Duty belts are also referred to by some departments and agencies as "Sam Browne belt" or "utility belt."

There are two belts that a uniformed law enforcement officer wears while on duty. I already mentioned the duty belt that accommodates the sidearm and less-lethal weapons, but there is another belt underneath it that holds up the uniform pants. This belt, called a uniform belt, is made of leather or nylon. The uniform belt is not only for comfort, but it is critical for safety since the duty belt is secured to the uniform belt with four belt keepers. Belt keepers are straps, made of leather or nylon to match the material of the duty belt, that "keep" the duty belt firmly attached to the uniform belt at four anchor points: two in the front, two in the back, and all evenly spaced. Belt keepers keep the duty belt from sagging down on the hip, due to the weight of the weapons, and it also keeps the duty belt from shifting to one side or the other after an activity such as hopping a wall or during a physical confrontation. The last thing a law enforcement officer needs when attempting to draw his or her gun, after rolling around on the ground with a suspect in a struggle, is having the duty belt shift to a different position and the pistol is not where it is supposed to be. Nothing is worse than reaching for a weapon when you need it, and it is not there.

Many law enforcement officers also carry a backup firearm in case the primary pistol malfunctions, such as with a Class 3 malfunction, which is also known as a "double feed" (two bullets that get jammed together trying to occupy the same feeding chamber). This "mother of all malfunctions" takes too much time to clear during a gunfight, and thus the need for a backup pistol for survival. The backup pistol is carried in one of three places: in a back pocket, on the ballistic vest in a special pocket, or in an ankle holster. I always preferred to carry my five-shot .38 caliber Smith & Wesson Airweight Model 642 in my back left pocket, the waistband area, while on duty as a police officer, and then when I was a deputy sheriff. Unfortunately, the feds wouldn't allow us Federal Air Marshals to carry a backup firearm, which was a rather problematic restriction considering we were all trained counterterrorists. At 32,000 feet above the ground, one does not have time to clear a Class 3 malfunction.

When I was on my police department's S.W.A.T. team I, along with my fellow officers, wore two belts during a call out. The first one was the uniform belt, which went through the belt loops of the Battle Dress Uniform (BDU) pants. However, the belt I wore was a far superior uniform belt than the ones worn by street cops. The belt I wore was called a Rigger's Belt. It was developed by the military and adopted by civilian tactical teams in the 1990s.

A rigger's belt is more than just a sturdy belt to hold up one's pants, but it's a versatile belt for three specific purposes. The first use is for training. When full tactical gear is not required, a holster or holster rig can be attached to the rigger's belt. The second use is for rappelling. There is a metal D-ring just to the side of the military-grade metal buckle that can flip outward after pulling a Velcro tab, and a carabiner is then attached to it. Once a rope is laced through the carabiner the S.W.A.T officer is able to descend the side of a cliff, building, or down an elevator shaft. A rigger's belt has the tensile strength between 5,000 to 7,000 pounds, which is more than enough to hold the weight of a couple of people suspended, or even absorb the sudden tug of a fall. The third use of a rigger's belt is as a tourniquet. Loop it over a limb above the severed artery, slip in a windlass and twist, and a life can be saved by effectively cutting off the blood supply to the injured limb.

When I became a Reserve Soldier in 2006, in a Military Police unit, I immediately began wearing a rigger's belt instead of the U.S. Army's standard issue uniform belt. That was my own decision. The issued belt was fine for those Soldiers with desk jobs or mechanics while in garrison, but not for tactical occupations. Surprisingly, very few Soldiers in my unit wore a rigger's belt for that very reason, because they were not issued to us. Most Soldiers, like cops, are notorious for not getting or improving their equipment if the money has to come out of their own pocket. On the other hand, the "hard chargers," those who are most concerned about safety and tactics, are constantly acquiring gear or replacing inferior pieces with better ones, even if they have to pay for it themselves.

Since I was a Military Police (MP) Soldier for seven years, and then transferred over to the Security Forces (SECFOR) for three, I wore a law enforcement duty belt over my rigger's belt while on duty, and the two belts were connected by means of four belt keepers. On my nylon duty belt, starting from the gig line and then going clockwise from there, was my holster that contained a M9 pistol with a 15-round magazine inserted inside the magazine well, a handcuff case containing Smith & Wesson Peerless handcuffs (the standard for American law enforcement), and two ammunition pouches on my front left side that held a total of 30 rounds of 9mm, 115 grain, full metal jacket, ball, ammunition. At that time in history my unit didn't authorize less-lethal weapons. The use of force continuum went right from a verbal warning to lethal force. We did have access to riot batons, but those were only authorized for one situation – riots.

American combat Soldiers wear a patrol belt. This belt is not generally held in place by Belt Keepers, although it can be, but fits snug around the waist. It can even be "enhanced" with padding, thus making it a Padded Patrol Belt.

The Padded Patrol Belt was designed by the United States Special Operations Command (SOCOM) to carry combat loads comfortably. It has two rows of MOLLE (Modular Lightweight Load-carrying Equipment), which is a series of heavy-duty nylon loops stitched into the belt for attaching various equipment, and the front of the Padded Patrol Belt has a quick-release buckle for fast and easy ditching.

The Patrol Belt is the first essential piece of equipment for warfare. From it hangs the tactical holster that contains the M17 pistol. The pistol is the secondary weapon of a Soldier, and the first being the rifle for modern warfare. Depending upon the unit, and the individual Soldier's preferences, various gear can be attached to the MOLLE system of the patrol belt: a combat knife, which serves as a weapon or survival tool, an Individual First Aid Kit (IFAK), ammunition pouches, hand grenades, et cetera.

The belt worn around the waist of a Roman soldier in Paul's day, from which we get our metaphor, served the same purpose 2,000 years ago as it does today. It had a sheath attached to it, which contained their secondary weapon - the sword. The primary weapon was the spear (the pilum).

The Bible equates the belt worn in battle as "truth." And of course, that is where our faith must begin, and be solely based upon – TRUTH. Just as the belt is located at the center of the body, truth must be at the center of our spirit. A human spirit guided by truth, eventually leads the soul home.

The opposite of truth is a lie; something which is not true. Paul stated it best.

And if Christ is not risen, then our preaching is empty, and your faith is

*also empty. Yes, and we are found false witnesses of God, because we have testified of God that He raised up Christ, whom He did not raise up—if in fact the dead do not rise. For if the dead do not rise, then Christ is not risen. And if Christ is not risen, your faith is futile; you are still in your sins! Then also those who have fallen asleep in Christ have perished. If in this life only we have hope in Christ, **we are of all men the most pitiable.***
1 Corinthians 15:14-19

If Jesus did not rise from the dead then Christianity is a lie, and we are "most pitiable" for wasting another minute believing anything the Bible has to say. Yet, we know that everything contained in the Holy Scriptures is divinely inspired based upon the historical records and archeological artifacts discovered so far, scientific statements that have only been confirmed in the last couple hundred years, hundreds of prophecies that have been accurately fulfilled from ancient times all the way up to this present year, and the Holy Spirit dwelling inside us that bears witness that our faith is not a "waste," but truth wrapped around our "waists." Therefore, taking a Biblical worldview keeps us centered.

Whoa! What does that mean? "Taking a Biblical worldview keeps us centered?" because that would also imply that those people who do not take a Biblical worldview are not "centered."

Well, let me ask you this, "Where is the Center of Gravity (COG) located on the human body?"

If you answer anatomically that it is where the vertical and horizontal centerline, while standing erect directly over the Base of Support (BOS), intersecting anterior to the second sacral vertebra, then you're correct. In layman's terms, the Center of Gravity is located at the upper hips, in the center of the body, exactly on the same line where the belt is worn. Depending upon which way a person leans or shifts their body weight, the COG moves within the circle of the belt line known as the transverse plane.

So important is understanding the Center of Gravity of the human body in combat that biomechanics research is conducted by the U.S. Army Combat Capabilities Development Command (DEVCOM) Army Research Laboratory, for what's known as Weapons and Materials Research (WMRD), to develop the best possible equipment to be worn by combat troops. The research is also incorporated by professional athletes to improve performance and minimize the risk of injury, and even large corporations utilize the knowledge to keep their employees from hurting themselves doing daily movements incorrectly. For example, when I was working for The Walt Disney Company, twice for Disneyland Resort Security & Emergency Services, part of the onboarding process, called *Disney Traditions*, was a mandatory program called SIM-plicity™ Module developed by the vendor Safety In Motion®. It is an education process to reduce strain, pain and musculoskeletal injuries. Of course, it includes making one acutely aware of one's own Center of Gravity when doing routine tasks safely such as turning movements, pushing and pulling items, and lifting and setting down items. I found this course extremely helpful in my own daily life to prevent even minor soft tissue injuries, and the program was all based on the Center of Gravity.

And, speaking of gravity, here's my next question to you, "What is gravity?"

According to our government's top experts at NASA (National Aeronautics and Space Administration) *gravity is the force by which a planet or other body draws objects toward the center. The force of gravity keeps all of the planets in orbit around the sun.* In other words, they don't know what gravity is, they only know how it functions. That's why they called it a "force." Not surprisingly, the same goes for magnetism. It's also called a "force." Even the atoms, of which everything in the universe is made of, is called "the strong force." Of course, we Christians don't know what these forces are either, but we do know with certainty, *And He is before all things, and in Him all things consist. Colossians 1:17* The "force" is God's handiwork.

Just as being aware of one's own Center of Gravity prevents avoidable injuries, and likewise wearing a patrol belt that is located on the transverse plane of the body where weapons and equipment are "centered" for easy and rapid access, so too a Biblical worldview, following God's truths, will keep a Christian Soldier from avoidable physical, emotional, and spiritual injuries. When we know the Scriptures well, the "spiritual equipment" on the *patrol belt of truth* are easily and rapidly accessible, making us indeed "centered." Being centered simply means not being confused. *For God is not the author of confusion but of peace, as in all the churches of the saints. 1 Corinthians 14:33* On the other hand, the world is becoming increasingly confused. So much so, that they are becoming delusional. Many of those in the enemy's camp don't even know when life begins in the womb. They don't know how many sexes there are. They don't know how the universe came about. They don't know why there are so many different languages spoken. They don't know why there's sea life fossils at the summit of Mount Everest, which is the tallest mountain in the world. They don't know a lot of things that we who are "centered" do.

Just as a good U.S. Army patrol belt makes a combat load easier to carry, the *patrol belt of truth* eases the stress from those things that can weigh you down. Circumstances that may be intolerable to the unbeliever, are easier for a believer to handle, such as marriage, a family, ministry, or even a prison sentence.

The interesting thing about the "belt of truth" is that it is located just below the navel and above the genitals. Your patrol belt happens to be evenly spaced between the two.

The navel, or "belly button" as it is most often referred to as, is an undeniable symbol of every person's birth, although most people don't give it much thought. Besides life itself, the belly button is the only physical evidence that every human being was once inside their mother's womb, because the belly button marks exactly where the umbilical cord was once attached to the body from the placenta, both of which were inside the liquid space of the uterus.

The genitalia represent procreation – new life. It takes a man and a woman to make a baby.

When a Christian Soldier goes into battle, be it physical or spiritual, both symbols also go along with him or her wherever they go. Therefore, a Biblical worldview, which keeps one centered and balanced, can only lead God's warriors to the conclusion that all innocent life, those who are already here (represented by the belly button), and those who are yet to come (represented by the genitalia), are to be respected and protected. After all, In the day that God created man, *He made him in the likeness of God. Genesis 5:1*

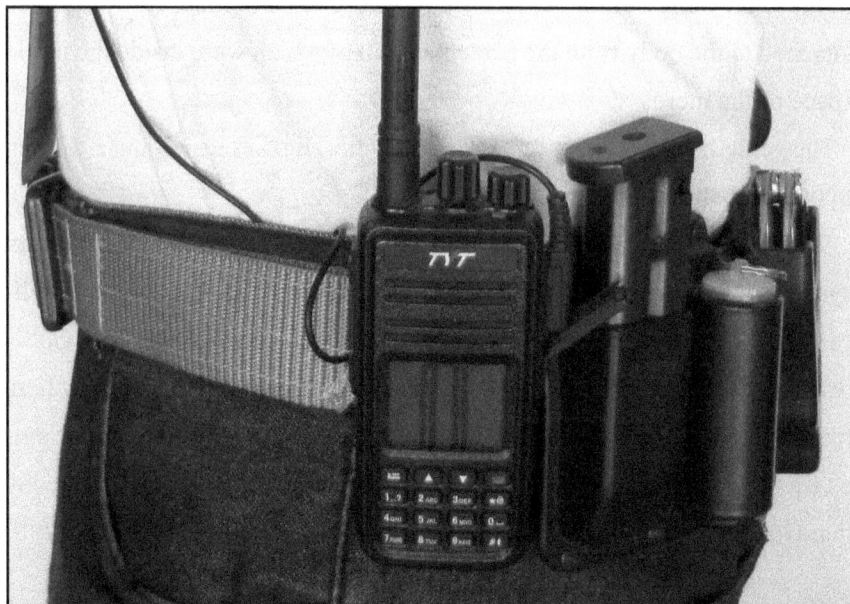

This is the side view (left side) of a rigger's belt. I wear it while doing undercover work for my armed church security team when on duty.

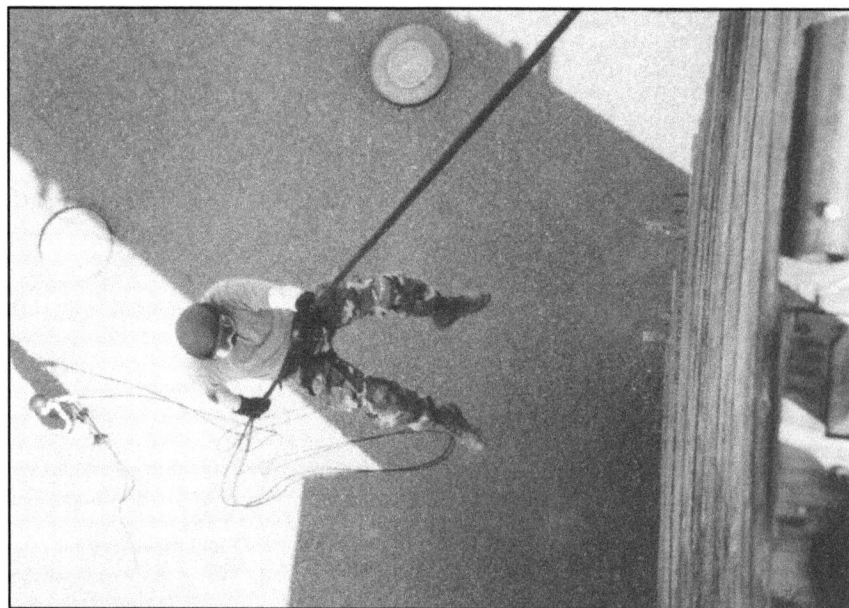

A rigger's belt has a D-ring on it so a carabiner can be attached to it, and the wearer can rappel down. That's me rappelling from a tower.

The military rigger's belt can also be used for Special Patrol Insertion/Extraction (SPIE). I'm the last one on the rope under the helicopter.

I (on the right) am wearing my patrol belt that has my M9 pistol, ammunition pouches, handcuffs, and tactical flashlight attached to it.

Chapter 6

BODY ARMOR

STRONGER THAN STEEL

having put on the breastplate of righteousness, Ephesians 6:14

Above the patrol belt an American Soldier wears a combination of soft body armor and armor plates, also known as a "ballistic vest." This is the modern descendant of the breastplate.

Although Paul listed the θώρακα (pronounced thor-aka, breastplate) as an essential piece of battle gear for warfare over 2,000 years ago, it serves the exact same purpose today. Body armor protects the rib cage, heart, lungs, digestive system, kidneys, and even most of the spinal cord on the backside. Although the materials have changed over time, the general shape of body armor remains the same.

In ancient times breastplates were made of leather, bronze or iron. Depending upon the century and the culture, breastplates were made of either chain mail, which were interconnecting links of metal rings to form a mesh, while other designs were small overlapping rectangular plates of metal (scale armor), or even single sheets of hammered metal. Such metal breastplates were bulky, heavy, and difficult to move around in. More primitive cultures had breastplates made of bone, bamboo, or other hard materials that could prevent the penetration of a sharp object or projectile. They were lighter than their metal counterparts, but also less effective.

The most common material used today for soft body armor is Kevlar, which is flexible like a thick cloth, and reinforced with hard body armor made of steel, ceramic, or Polyethylene plates.

Kevlar (Poly-paraphenylene terephthalamide), manufactured by DuPont since 1971, is a heat-resistant synthetic fiber that has an incredibly high tensile strength-to-weight ratio, five times stronger than steel. That's because the molecules are unidirectional (parallel) to each other. Not only is Kevlar woven into sheets, and can be layered to make it even stronger, but it is lightweight, corrosion resistant, rust free, and it effectively absorbs vibrations.

Although Kevlar fibers can stop various bullet calibers from penetrating the vest, the blunt trauma from a bullet alone can seriously injure or kill the wearer since the energy is transferred from the fibers to the body; enough to break bones or stop the heart. Therefore, a harder material needs to be placed over the Kevlar in critical areas.

When I first went to the streets as a police officer in 1991, after graduating from the police academy, I wore a Kevlar vest, and on the front of the vest was a pocket to insert a convex shaped steel plate that covered my entire sternum. Should a bullet have struck me at "center mass," the center of my chest, the Kevlar would have prevented the bullet from entering my body, and the steel plate would have prevented the blunt trauma from damaging my sternum or stopping my heart from beating.

Some hard body armor is made of ceramic. The most common materials are alumina, boron carbide, silicon carbide, and titanium diboride, all of which are lighter than metal alloys. However, the drawback is that ceramic plates are also thicker than steel plates. Yet, it is because of this important feature that many militaries around the world use it for the protection of their military personnel – less weight. The United States Armed Forces refer to ballistic ceramic plates as Enhanced Small Arms Protective Inserts (ESAPI). Remember what I told you in the beginning of the book? Everything has an acronym, even ceramic plates.

Believe it or not, plastic is used to stop bullets. That's right, the same stuff for making grocery plastic bags is also used to protect our Soldiers. The material is called Polyethylene (PE), with some other ingredients added to make its chemical structure stronger than a grocery bag.

Much like Kevlar, PE has unidirectional fibers, but it is a thermoplastic material. This means that when a bullet strikes a plate made of PE, which is spinning at thousands of revolutions per minute, the friction caused by the rotating impact makes the Polyethylene material melt instantly, which "holds" the bullet in place as the material cools down and re-hardens.

Ask me any more information about soft and hard body armor than what I've already explained here, such as the molecular structure of the various materials or the physics behind the ballistics testing, and I'm at a loss. It's like electricity. I know how to flip on a light switch, and the various products that light up when I turn them on or off, but I couldn't tell you in any great detail how the electricity actually works, and so I rely on people who can. What I know about ballistic vests comes from actually being educated on them and wearing them for my entire adult life. In fact, I'll be slipping on one this week. I currently own two of them for two different types of mission profiles and for firearms training. That stated, just the little information that I've provided should make you realize that there is a lot of scientific research, and a lot of intelligent minds involved, who make our Soldiers, Airmen, Sailors, Marines, and Guardians (those in the U.S. Space Force) safer by supplying them with soft and hard body armor. One could spend an entire lifetime just learning all there is about how to keep a bullet from entering a human body. Likewise, I can't possibly know the infinite wisdom and ways of God, but I know enough that when He tells me that I need to put on the "breastplate (body armor) of righteousness," then that is exactly what I must do, even if I don't understand everything about this piece of "equipment."

Now let's make some comparisons between physical body armor and spiritual body armor.

The definition of righteousness, δικαιοσύνης (pronounced di-kay-os-eeness), is *being right with God.* Let me repeat it – BEING RIGHT WITH GOD. I'm emphasizing this very important point, because Christians often confuse righteousness with self-righteousness, which is defined as *being convinced of one's own righteousness, especially in contrast with the actions and beliefs of others.*

There is no additional room "in the body" for Christian Soldiers to also put on the *body armor of self-righteousness,* and yet many have done just that throughout history, which resulted in countless *blue on blue* situations. "Blue on blue" means *Soldiers injured or killed by their own army or by Soldiers on the same side as them.*

Most American Christians know very little of church history, if any at all, and that's because of laziness to study it. That, and the United States of America is truly an "exceptional" country, having been given by our founding fathers the very First Amendment of the Bill of Rights that uniquely proclaims *Congress shall make no law respecting an establishment of religion, or prohibiting the free exercise thereof.* As such, we just naturally assume that everyone in the world has been free to believe or not believe what they want, like us. However, this has rarely been the case, and believers over the ages have wasted a lot of their ammo shooting at each other, literally, because of *self-righteousness*: violence over icons in the eight century, the Lombard attack on Ravenna in 751, the Frankish attack on the Lombard king in 756, Charlemagne defeating the Lombards in 774, the German state church in 962, the clash between Pope Gregory VII and Henry IV in 1073, the beginning of the Inquisition by Pope Lucius III in 1184, Pope Innocent III in 1198 bringing peasants and princes to their knees with excommunication and interdict, the Venetians persuading the crusaders to capture the Christian town of Zara on the Adriatic coast in 1202 leading to the conquest of Constantinople in 1204, the slaughter of the Albigeneses in southern France, and the authorization of torture by Pope Innocent IV in 1252. Then came the Reformation (1517-1648) further dividing Christians between Catholics and Protestants, which led to many bloody wars. Then came centuries of much bloodshed between Protestant groups. It would take an entire book to list all of the infighting that has taken place.

So, when unbelievers say that "religion is the cause of all the wars in history" they are absolutely right. Almost every war in history has been over religion, even among Christendom. However, none of this should surprise us, because Jesus warned us from the very beginning that the church was going to grow very large, and all kinds of evil would find its way into it, *The kingdom of heaven is like a mustard seed, which a man took and sowed in his field, which is the least of all the seeds, but when it is grown it is greater than the herbs and becomes a tree, **so that the birds of the air come and nest in its branches.**" Matthew 13:31-32* The birds represent evil.

With over two thousand years of history in mind, you can see why we must put on *the body armor of God*, and avoid the temptation of the *body armor of self-righteousness*, so that we don't repeat the same *blue on blue* incidents that have continually plagued Christianity. Not only are we to love our enemies, but *all will know that you are My disciples, if you have love for one another. John 13:35* It's a bit hard to do this if you are self-righteous.

In other New Testament passages this Greek word δικαιοσύνης is also used to mean being *right before others,* and a third meaning is *justice.* Therefore, the modern English translation "righteousness" is perfect. It originates from the 16th Century Old English word *rihtwis,* which is a combination of two words, *riht* (right) plus *wis* (condition) with the ending of *ness,* to mean *a state, condition, or degree of.*

So, what does it mean exactly to "be right with God?" Well, that's simple. It means the same thing as being a Christian, and the word "Christian" means "follower of Christ." We must "be" like Jesus Christ. A good verse to explain it all, is this one:

*Therefore, **gird up the loins of your mind,** be sober, and rest your hope fully upon the grace that is to be brought to you at the revelation of Jesus Christ; as obedient children, **not conforming yourselves to the former lusts,** as in your ignorance, but as He who called you is holy, you also **be holy in all your conduct,** because it is written, 'Be holy, for I am holy.'"*
1 Peter 1:13-16

The first sentence of this verse is really weird to a modern person reading it, but the Apostle Peter uses a military term that everyone would understand in the 1st Century. It's basically referring to the region of the genitals, and the patrol belt. That's right, we're revisiting the *patrol belt of truth* for a moment to better understand body armor.

The term *gird up the loins* refers to a technique that a Roman soldier would do to protect his "loins," which we call today "groin." A man who gets struck there, especially with a forceful strike, ends up getting the fight taken out of him, because it is extremely painful. However, "girding up" is more than just protecting the private parts.

Most ancient people didn't wear underwear like we do today. Yes, it existed in such places as Egypt and Mesopotamia, but even then, it was a luxury item for the ruling classes. Roman citizens didn't wear undergarments, which meant that they "hung loose" under their robes called chitons. Chitons for warm climates extended down to just above the knees, and chitons for cooler climates extended all the way down to the ankles. Think of it as a long robe for a man and women, although there were different cuts for each sex to distinguish the difference.

Roman soldiers, especially enlisted personnel, couldn't afford more than a garment or two, for clothing in the ancient times was extremely expensive. Soldiers were also limited to what they could carry during a campaign or redeployment. Therefore, the clothing they wore into battle had to have multiple purposes, and be worn during the day and night.

Before going into battle a Roman soldier, or foreign mercenary who augmented the force, would pull up the hem of his chiton all the way up to his thighs with both hands. He would then grab the handful of cloth in front of him and bunch it up into a phallic shape. The soldier would then shove that cloth bundle between his legs, and then bring up the end as high as to the back of the waist. Pulling up the cloth up between the legs would keep the scrotum and penis firmly pressed against the pelvic. Then, there would be just enough material in the back to have a set of "wings," one to the left side and the other to the right, to be pulled around to the front of the waist, and then the two loose ends were crisscrossed and shoved down into the battle belt so it wouldn't come undone. The technique is very similar to how cloth diapers are wrapped around babies in Third World countries, except they tie the two loose ends together instead of shoving into a thick leather belt.

Not only did *girding up the loins* give better protection to the genitals, by having an extra layer of cloth protecting the organ, but it also allowed the soldier to run better, because one could easily trip while running in a robe. I know, because a few years ago one of my friends, Debbie, ran out the door of her work during a fire drill, and she was wearing a dress that extended down to almost her ankles, and she did a faceplant when the cloth wrapped around her leg and tripped her. She almost lost her two front teeth because of the fall, but the dentist was able to save them.

Oh, and by the way, women do have loins, but today we also call this area of the female body "groin," just the same as we do for males. Therefore, the Biblical term *gird up the loins* also applies equally to women. And, on a side note, when I teach my Women's Survival course, which I have been doing since 1986, I also teach them how to block an incoming kick or knee strike to the same area from the attacker. Every self-defense instructor teaches women how to "kick him in the balls," in hopes of a successful hit-and-run tactic to escape, but what many self-defense instructors fail to teach that it is a two-way street. If a woman gets kicked in the groin area, she too can sustain a minor or serious injury as well. Obviously, it is not exactly the same, due to anatomical differences, but flesh is flesh, and pain is pain. Therefore, a woman needs extra protection there as well, be it from a protective "cup" or blocking the strike with her arm or leg.

The loins, for both men and women, not only need protection against pain and injury in a physical fight, but they are the center of procreative power. From the loins comes new life. Even some modern soft body armor and hard body armor extends down to cover the groin area. This piece is used by civilian S.W.A.T. officers or military combat personnel. It looks like a thick inverted pyramid apron hanging down below the patrol belt line. So, when God tells us to *gird up the loins of your mind,* He's talking about our thoughts. As the genitals bring forth life, babies, so the mind brings forth thoughts, and thoughts often lead to actions. Therefore, we Christians, we Christian Soldiers in particular, must protect our minds from corruption. *For as he thinks in his heart, so is he. Proverbs 23:7*

Now, going back to the torso, *the body armor of righteousness,* which we now know means being Christ-like, includes being *sober,* believing that you are saved by *grace* and not by The Law or works. The *body armor of righteousness* that you wear also protects you from *former lusts, as in your ignorance.* Lust, of course, is a strong desire for something which God does not want you to have or do, because it will destroy you emotionally, physically, spiritually or all three. Just like a bullet that will penetrate your body without body armor covering you, so too will sins penetrate your very soul if you're not obedient to Him. If you didn't need the *body armor of righteousness,* then God wouldn't tell you to put it on. The fact is, we must have it on. Especially now, as the days wax worse and worse.

I know that some of you reading this may be thinking, *Yeah, but body armor is uncomfortable, and it restricts movement. Body armor is really hot in warm weather, and even sweaty in cool weather. Body armor drives you crazy if you have an ich underneath it that you can't reach, and when worn long enough you can't help but feel the weight of it upon your shoulders; it*

*really starts to dig in. Plus, when first putting it on, it was really great look-
ing the part, 'Hey, look at me, I'm a warrior,' but now comes the realization
that it makes me a legitimate target for the enemy. It's like walking with a
big bullseye painted on my chest and back. When I was just a Christian
civilian, I could just slip away into a nice quiet place when I wanted to or
offer only a little moral support here and there to my brothers and sisters
when I pleased. However, now I'm in the thick of things.*

My answer to all of those concerns is, "No kidding! Nobody said that it
was going to be easy. Embrace the suck!" In other words, deal with it.

In the physical world, I have worn body armor as a Soldier, as a law enforcement officer, serving on my church security team, and even when I am
teaching firearms courses on live-fire gun ranges in the hot sun, and I can
tell you first-hand that it is not comfortable wearing it. I'd prefer a loose-fit-
ting comfortable shirt in the summer or a cozy well-worn sweatshirt in
the winter any day or night of the week over a ballistic vest, but not when
facing the enemy. As an American Soldier and law enforcement officer I've
made the tradeoff of protection over comfort, security over sensual, and life
over death many a time. Likewise, sin can feel good, even rather comfortable over God's ways, but, then again, by wearing my *breastplate of righteousness* as a Christian Soldier the tradeoff is protection of my thoughts
over this world's corruption, security in His strong tower over destructive
sin for a season, and eternal life over the second death. And, let me tell you
Soldier, eternity is a long, long, time. So, suck it up, and *Be holy.* This war
ain't going to last forever.

There are some other interesting things I'd like to bring up about the
breastplate, body armor, before we go grab the other pieces of war equipment Paul tells us that we need to have to go into battle with.

As you know, many law enforcement officers wear body armor today.
When I was a police officer for the Costa Mesa Police Department in Southern California, just an hour south of Los Angeles, an agency I served for

10 years, I wore body armor every day on patrol, and even when assigned bicycle patrol. I wore a Level IIIA ballistic armor vest. A Level IIIA vest can stop handgun bullets up to a .44 Magnum. I also served on the department's S.W.A.T. team, *Special Weapons And Tactics,* for three years. In this capacity I had a Level III ballistic armor vest that could stop 5.56 mm and 7.62 mm rifle rounds. Those are bullets used in warfare.

When the requests from law enforcement agencies and military units became too many for me to teach all of them in my free time, I decided to leave full time law enforcement and become a Reserve deputy sheriff. It was an easy transition, because a lieutenant with the Orange County Sheriff's Department, America's fifth largest Sheriff's Department in the United States, had been trying for a year to recruit me to join the Search & Rescue Reserve Team (SRRT), because I already had some of the training and experience having been on the civilian Saddleback Search & Rescue Team.

My Search & Rescue career lasted no more than a month after I was sworn into the department, because the sergeant of the Reserve Division voluntold (asked to volunteer, but actually told) me, "Jim, you want to be on the newly formed Dignitary Protection Unit, don't you," as he shook his head up and down in the affirmative.

I got the hint immediately, and I said, "Ah, yes. I do."

"Good, I thought you would say that," he said with a big smile across his face, for he wanted to impress the sheriff, and I was one of the pawns on his side of the chessboard.

That very month I was promoted to the rank of sergeant, and I was made the team leader of the Dignitary Protection Unit (DPU). During this two-year assignment I again wore Level IIIA body armor while protecting the Sheriff, visiting dignitaries, and celebrities.

On September 11, 2001 Al-Qaeda terrorists attacked the United States of America using passenger aircraft to take down the World Trade Center in New York City. That same day another plane slammed into the Pentagon, and a fourth plane went down in Shanksville, Pennsylvania. Over 3,000 innocent people were murdered in the name of the Islamic god Allah. After these tragic events the federal government launched The Global War on Terrorism and were recruiting anyone with Special Operations training and experience to increase the ranks of the United States Federal Air Marshal Service, which was only a handful at the time. I applied, they stamped my file HIGHLY QUALIFIED, and a few months later I found myself in New Mexico attending counterterrorism school. However, when I was sent to the FAM Los Angeles Field Office to fight terrorism, I was not issued body armor, nor were any of the other agents across the country. That's because ballistic vests at the time, even the thinnest ones, would reveal a "vest signature" under normal street clothes. In other words, someone who was tactically inclined, the "bad guys," would see the telltale signs, or "signature, and be able to spot the undercover agent aboard an airplane or in the airport terminal. That's not a good situation for a counterterrorist who needs to get the jump on a terrorist cell wanting to take down a passenger aircraft or cause carnage in an airport. Therefore, I had to accept the fact that I was vulnerable in a gunfight without ballistic protection.

Fast forward to 2006, and I again raised my right hand, swore an oath to protect the United States of America against all enemies foreign and domestic, and began a 10-year career as a Military Police (MP) Soldier and finishing out my military career in the Security Forces (SECFOR). For these armed duties I wore a Level IV ballistic armor vest. This vest weighed 25 pounds, which included a radio, extra magazines, and a few medical supplies that were packed in the pouches sewn to the body armor carrier. This vest was able to stop a military-grade armor-piercing round. Such a bullet striking the plate would knock me off my feet, just from the kinetic energy alone, but at least it was survivable. But, let me tell you, it is the most uncomfortable thing I ever wore on my body. My biggest fear was getting knocked down and being like a turtle on its back. Yes, I could upright myself, but it wasn't easy. That, or ending up getting pushed into a body of water, like the Olympic size pool that was on base or into a pond at the private golf course, because with that vest on I'd sink immediately to the bottom like a rock.

So, why did I take the time to explain to you the different body armor levels for Soldiers and cops? It's because the devil, and his minions, have a wide variety of spiritual ammunition that they fire at us. Who is us? "Us," are those in uniform, – Christian Soldiers. However, if you're a "luke-warm" or backslidden Christian, you're not a high priority target of the enemy. You're not much of a threat to the enemy. You're too much like the world to cause much damage. However, if you're wearing the *body armor of righteousness* on the battlefield, you can count on being fired upon continuously. That's because you are a *clear and present danger* to the enemy. The Bible refers to these spiritual projectiles as "fiery darts." Just as there are different levels of ballistic vests that can stop various caliber projectiles or fragmentation, and not others, so too there are "fiery darts" that even a *body armor of righteousness* cannot stop. But, not to worry. You're going to be issued some more equipment that can stop the heavy stuff.

While we are still on the topic of law enforcement officers, when I was a police officer I wore a police badge, which is referred to as a "shield." When I was a deputy sheriff, I wore a six-pointed "star" on the left side of my chest, just like the ones you see in the old Western movies. I joking-ly-seriously called myself a "lawman" back then to identify with the histor-ical taming of "the wild west." After all, California is the West Coast of the United States, and I love historical connections. When I became a federal agent, I carried a federal "shield," but because I was always working under-cover it was a "flat badge" pinned in a leather black wallet along with my credentials. So, how did law enforcement badges come about? What's the history? Why are some badges called "shields?"

Well, believe it or not, the origins of law enforcement badges evolved from the military breastplate. That's right, the metal badges you see today on the uniforms of American law enforcement officers are the last remaining articles of ancient metal armor that survived the centuries.

Breastplates protected warriors from sharp projectiles (spears and arrows) ever since the fall of mankind, and right up until the invention of firearms in the 14th century. Once firearms, using gunpowder as a propellant, took to the European battlefields, the days of traditional breastplates started to decline, and that's because bullets were able to easily penetrate metal armor, which meant nasty gunshot wounds.

Thicker metal breastplates became the only logical solution to the low velocity bullet threat, based on the available technology at that time. Yet, these metal breastplates were extremely heavy, and were too difficult to carry and fight in.

By the time the 18th century had rolled around, body armor had all but disappeared. However, a remnant of it still remained, although in a miniature form, and it was to identify officers. The "armor" was a gorget (pronounced gor-jut), which was worn about the neck of military officers. It's a crescent outward convex shaped plate of silver, that looks like the letter "U" upon the chest suspended by a cord attached at the two upper points, and it indicates the rank of the wearer. When viewed close up, the metal was engraved with the owner's regimental affiliation.

There is a famous 1772 portrait, painted by Charles Willson Peale, of Colonel George Washington serving in the British Army at that time, wearing a gorget on his uniform, and it bears the Virginia Regiment that he fought with during the French and Indian War.

During the American Revolutionary War (1775-1783) George Washington, the General and Commander in Chief of the Continental Army, presented Lieutenant Alexander Hume, of the Second South Carolina Regiment, a silver gorget that has the date 1776 engraved upon it, the Latin motto LIBERTAS PORTIOR VITA, *Liberty is more important than life,* and an illustration of the liberty pole, crossed flags, and crossed muskets.

The first modern police uniform dates back to 1829, from our mother country no less, England, established by the London Metropolitan Police. They wore dark blue uniforms, and upon their tall pickelhaube style helmets, the famous "Bobby hat," was a large metal badge in the center. Emulating the British, the New York City Police Department, America's first official police force founded in 1845, issued navy blue uniforms that were surplus United States Army uniforms. In fact, the Los Angeles Police Department, formed in 1869, actually used surplus Union Civil War uniforms for their police officers, as did other police departments nationwide. This is why even today American law enforcement agencies are referred to as "paramilitary" organizations. However, instead of the badge on the top hat, like the Brits had, the Americans had the metal police badge placed on the chest instead, much like a gorget, except it was pinned on the left side of the chest and not in the center of the chest hanging from a cord. Wearing the badge on the left side of the chest symbolizes the heart, because the commitment to protect and serve the community comes from the heart.

When I was with the Costa Mesa Police Department there was a 16" x 14" photograph of our police badge in a gold metal frame hanging on the wall of the stairwell leading down to the basement where the lockers, briefing room, and gun range were located. Underneath the photo of the badge were the words THIS IS THE SYMBOL OF YOUR INTEGRITY. The definition of "integrity" is *a firm adherence to a code of especially moral or artistic values, incorruptibility.* In other words, "righteousness."

Whenever I saw that police badge photograph, while going up or down the stairs, it reminded me of the oath that I took, and whenever I pinned on the badge to my navy blue uniform in the locker room before a shift, I knew that it was a symbol going all the way back to Medieval knighthood, and it was a routine that only a very select few people ever get the privilege of doing. This is why back then, and even today, I can't tolerate crooked cops: cops that lie, steel, or abuse their power. Integrity is everything to a true police officer.

During my career, I was also issued a Disneyland Resort Security badge, much like the shape of a police shield, in 2016 and then again in 2019, but it did not have the same symbolic meaning nor the symbol of authority as those issued to me by government entities. You're not exactly protecting freedom and liberty with the silhouette of Mickey Mouse in the center of the badge. Although I took my role of protecting cast members and guests seriously, my service there was not the same as being a sworn law enforcement officer or an American Soldier. Yes, I had a "badge" at "The happiest place on earth," and there is indeed a Medieval castle in the center of the park, and even some characters wearing breastplates, but they are not authentic. They are a fairytale come to life to entertain kids and adults. Likewise, there are some so-called "Christians" who are not authentic either. They may look and act the part, and even boast that they are wearing a *breastplate of righteousness,* but it has neither real power nor authority.

For those who have worked uniformed or plainclothes private security for a corporation, I'm not implying that private security is not important. Used correctly, private security is definitely valuable, and that is why I have worked for some of the biggest private security corporations in the world: Disneyland Resort Security & Emergency Services (they have their own security company, and I've already mentioned them), Contemporary Services Corporation (also known as CSC, which is the largest crowd management service in the United States), Allied Universal (the largest private security company in the United States), Blizzard Entertainment Global Security (the largest gaming company in the world), and SECURITAS (the largest private security company in the world).

Just as the Roman army had mercenaries (individuals with combat skills who take part in a military conflict for personal profit, but who are not official members of the host military), and the United States paid Private Military Contractors (PMC) in both the Iraqi and Afghanistan wars to augment the U.S. Armed Forces, so too private security is an unofficial augmentation of law enforcement. If a private security officer screws up, then the governmental law enforcement is not liable, and if a security officer does his or her job well, then they are another set of eyes, a deterrent to crime, or even a witness to crime, which greatly helps law enforcement keep the community safer.

This brings up the question, "Are there spiritual 'mercenaries or PMCs' that augment Christian Soldiers?" The answer is, "Yes."

The Bible gives several examples of unbelievers in the past that assisted in military operations. Some of them are very unlikely people, like Rahab the prostitute.

General Joshua, in 1406 BC, was ready to begin the invasion of the land of Canaan, but before doing so he sent two military spies to the city of Jericho.

The two spies didn't know anybody in the city, but where is the one place anyone can go and not draw attention when spending the night? That's right, a brothel. The criminal element in the "Red Light District" rarely cooperates with the authorities. However, in this particular situation the spies did not go unnoticed. Apparently, some town folks saw the strangers visit Rahab the prostitute, and they informed the king.

So, the king of Jericho sent to Rahab, saying, "Bring out the men who have come to you, who have entered your house, for they have come to search out all the country."

Then the woman took the two men and hid them. So, she said, "Yes, the men came to me, but I did not know where they were from. And it happened as the gate was being shut, when it was dark, that the men went out. Where the men went, I do not know; pursue them quickly, for you may overtake them." But she had brought them up to the roof and hidden them with the stalks of flax, which she had laid in order on the roof. Joshua 2:3-7

The scriptures do not state whether she was paid with money or not to keep their presence a secret, but she certainly requested something of great value – her life, and the life of her family, to be spared. The entire city was terrified that the Israelites were going to take the city, for they had heard what happened to the Egyptians and the Amorites, and she wanted no part of that. Therefore, she was willing to side with the enemy of her country.

Rahab, whose house was located on the city's defensive wall, let them down by a rope through her window, and they made it back to friendly lines. When the Israelites finally did conquer the city, Rahab and her family were spared as the spies had promised.

Even a person who gives a cup of cold water to a Christian will get rewarded, according to Matthew 10:42

Now that you have been properly fitted for your *body armor of righteousness,* let's get the next piece.

Law enforcement badges are remnants of ancient metal breastplates. I'm receiving my police "shield" (above), then my deputy sheriff's star.

Body armor protects internal organs from bullets and fragmentation. I wore Level III body armor when I was a police S.W.A.T. officer.

I (second on the left) had thinner, lighter, Level IIIA body armor for Executive Protection with the Orange County Sheriff's Department.

When I went back into the military I wore Level IV body armor, which is designed to stop military-grade armor-piercing rifle rounds.

Chapter 7

COMBAT BOOTS

BURY ME IN MY BOOTS

and having shod your feet with the preparation of the gospel of peace;
Ephesians 6:15

When was the last time you shod your feet?

I have to admit, I have never used the word "shod" in my life, nor did my mother ever say to me, "Jimmy, shod your feet before you go outside to play."

Okay, I'll admit that even the New King James translation of the Bible can have a few outdated words that we don't use any more, but since such words are few and far between, I still like the accuracy of the translation.

The word "shod" simply means "shoe," but in context it means a specific kind of shoe. Therefore, in the context of Ephesians 6:15, which is a list of military gear for a Soldier, it means footwear for combat, or in today's vernacular, "combat boots." So, let's read Ephesians 6:15 as if it had been written today:

, and having put on your combat boots in preparation (a solid knowledge of something) to deliver, in person, propaganda to convince the enemy to surrender, and if they do, they will not be harmed.

Propaganda sounds so negative. It brings up mental images of former Soviet pamphlets, posters, and protagonists. However, let's first get the official definition from Merriam-Webster, and there are three of them.

Definition of propaganda

1. *A congregation of the Roman curia having jurisdiction over missionary territories and related institutions.*

No, that's definitely not it.

2. *The spreading of ideas, information, or rumor for the purpose of helping or injuring an institution, a cause, or a person.*

That's the one! This is the definition we're after. However, let's look at the third definition for scholarly reasons.

3. *Ideas, facts, or allegations spread deliberately to further one's cause or to damage an opposing cause.*

Wait! We'll also include this definition as well, in order to better explain why Christian Soldiers wear the *combat boots of the Gospel of peace.*

During a war, propaganda is always used to persuade people's opinion. The propaganda can be directed to one's own people by the government to arouse hatred for the enemy, as a military recruiting tool, or even warning the citizens of the consequences of defeat if everybody does not do their part to support the war effort. Propaganda can also be directed at the enemy to demoralize them or warn them of their inevitable defeat. This can be done by dropping leaflets on them from an airplane or by sending radio signals or Internet messages into their own country. Depending upon the combatants, the propaganda can either be truthful or lies.

The Gospel, which in Greek means "Good News," is our side's propaganda, and it is 100% true. When we Christians Soldiers leave Gospel tracts in a public place, quote the Scriptures on social media, or give copies of the New Testament to people who are asking us questions about God, then we are literally walking onto these battlefields in our "combat boots," or taking the time to walk to our device to send out the messages.

The purpose of spreading our propaganda, the Gospel, during the war is for all of the traditional reasons:

1. To arouse hatred for sin and the kingdom of darkness. *You who love the Lord, hate evil! Psalm 97:10* and *He has delivered us from the power of darkness, and has translated us into the kingdom of his dear Son: Colossians 1:13*

2. To plant the seed of salvation into peoples' hearts, and then it's up to the Holy Spirit to save their souls. Once this is accomplished, we then have more Christian Soldiers in God's Army. The Commander in Chief orders each one of us, *"Go into all the world and preach the gospel to every creature. He who believes and is baptized will be saved; but he who does not believe will be condemned." Mark 16:15-16*

3. To encourage fellow believers to support the war effort. *Therefore com fort each other and edify one another, just as you also are doing. 1 Thessalonians 5:11* and *Iron sharpens iron, so one person sharpens another. Proverbs 27:17*

A good question is, "Do we also have propaganda that is directed towards the enemy?" The answer is, "Most definitely."

First, let's determine who the enemy is. We don't just have one enemy that we're fighting, but we actually have three. Just as the United States of America was fighting three enemies at once during World War II (Nazi Germany, Fascist Italy, and Imperial Japan), so too we are waring with *the flesh, the world, and the devil.*

When it comes to *the flesh,* the mortal body which Paul refers to as the "old man," it's not going to be allowed to enter into heaven. It can't. It's completely corrupt, and it must be completely renewed. However, until that glorious day comes, and it will come, we are each stuck living in our cursed

163

bodies. However, the born-again spirit is able to rule over this evil *flesh* of ours. *But God be thanked that though you were slaves of sin, yet you obeyed from the heart that form of doctrine to which you were delivered. And having been set free from sin, you became slaves of righteousness. Romans 6:17-18* Hallelujah!

Our enemies are indeed the unbelievers of *the world.* However, it is not their bodies we seek to destroy, but it's their sin nature that we must destroy. The devil and his demons will eventually be destroyed by God, but the unsaved are not who we are commanded to destroy. In fact, quite the opposite. Our Commander in Chief, Jesus, commands us, *But I say to you, love your enemies, bless those who curse you, do good to those to hate you, and pray for those who spitefully use and persecute you, Matthew 5:44*

Yes, I agree, this is probably the most difficult scripture in the Bible to agree with. Why? Because it goes back to *the flesh* issue. Our own *flesh,* we just determined, is our first enemy, because it's always there. Our *flesh,* which is corrupt to the core, does not want to love our enemies, it wants to get even with them. It wants revenge. It sometimes even wants to see them wiped out physically. Yet, after hours of being beaten and scourged by Jews and Gentiles alike, Jesus hung upon a Roman cross, which was cruelly designed to inflict maximum pain on the human body, He said to His Father concerning His enemies that were gawking and mocking Him at the foot of His cross, *"Father, forgive them, for they do not know what they do." Luke 23:34*

You may not like God's command to "love your enemies," and your *flesh* may not agree with it either, but orders are orders. You don't have to like it Christian Soldier, you just have to do it. Amen. There's no room in His Army for insubordination.

Finally, God's propaganda is not just a threat to Satan, and a third of the angels who rebelled with him in heaven, but it's a promise. There's not going to be any prisoners taken by the Lord when the war is over. *And fire came down from God out of heaven and devoured them. Revelation 20:9* That's right, the fire devoured men. In the near future there is going to be a time when forgiveness is no longer offered from our Warrior King. *The devil, who deceived them, was cast into the lake of fire and brimstone where the beast and the false prophet are. And they will be tormented day and night forever and ever. Revelation 20:9-10*

What are the practical aspects of American combat boots? First of all, a good sturdy pair of boots protect a Soldier's feet from rough terrain. Imagine trying to run on a battlefield barefoot. You wouldn't last long. There are sharp items all over the ground. Shrapnel, broken glass, debris, and expended casings are typical items littered about a battlefield. Then there are potholes, both small and large. Without combat boots, which extend firmly above the ankles for support, the wearer is at greater risk of getting a sprained or broken ankle. One could not even walk on such ground safely, let alone run on it. In addition, the ground can also be covered in spots with slippery blood or mud. Therefore, the soles of modern combat boots have deep and angular oil-and slip-resistant multi-tread for traction in wet conditions.

Just as a lot of technology goes into soft and hard body armor, so too with modern combat boots: fabrics that are resistant to abrasions and tears, innovative rapid-dry technology, heat and flame-resistant materials, fence-climbing toes and steel toe composites, and even various cupsole platforms for comfort and stability.

Having the right footwear for the battlefield goes all the way back to Paul's day, which he observed with his own eyes. Roman military sandals, although more like a sandal-boot called *caligae* (pronounced cal-eh-guy), were heavy-soled layers of leather with iron hobnails on the bottom of the soles. They were very much like today's sport cleats in function, so that a soldier would have good traction when advancing on the enemy and maintain good stability while fighting. The caligae was worn by all ranks of

Roman legionnaires, from auxiliaries all the way up to top ranking officers, until the end of the 2nd Century. After that came the closed boot that we'd recognize today.

Just as the 1st Century church was just starting to spread the "Good News," shortly after the ascension of the Lord, from 37 to 41 AD the evil Emperor Gaius ruled the Roman Empire. The reason I bring him up is because this man is better known by his nickname Caligula. The word "caligula" (pronounced calig-you-lah) is the singular form of *caligae,* which means "little boot." The emperor was affectionately given this nickname from his father's bodyguard soldiers when he was three years old, and it stuck. Ever since then, 2,000 years later, the boot represents government totalitarianism.

We get the more recent term *jack booted thug,* which is synonymous with militarism and totalitarianism, from the Jackboots that German soldiers made infamous in the 1930s Nazi propaganda films, and by humiliating the conquered peoples in occupied territories in the 1940s, by goose-stepping on pavement in unison in large columns.

When English novelist George Orwell (1903 – 1950) described what he thought the world would be like in the future, in his classic book *1984,* he wrote, "There will be no curiosity, no enjoyment of the process of life. All competing pleasures will be destroyed. But always – do not forget this, Winston – always there will be the intoxication of power, constantly increasing and constantly growing subtler. Always, at every moment, there will be the thrill of victory, the sensation of trampling on an enemy who is helpless. If you want a picture of the future, **imagine a boot stamping on a human face – forever."**

The widely used term "boot on neck," which means government pressure or oppression, has been around for decades, and as we have learned from the examples I have mentioned, the military boot is a very powerful symbol.

So, here's another question for you. "What did Adam and Eve wear in the Garden of Eden before they sinned, and were kicked out?" That's an easy one. The answer is, "Nothing. They were naked," which also means that they were barefoot.

Now, keep in mind that when man was placed in the garden it was a perfect environment. There were no thorns or thistles to step on. Those came later when God cursed the earth. All the plants were watered in a unique way, *but a mist went up from the earth and watered the whole face of the ground. Genesis 2:6* Therefore, there was no mud, ice, or snow to slip on. Precipitation did not exist until Noah's day when *the rain fell on the earth forty days and forty nights. Genesis 7:12* There was no need for shoes in the beginning just after creation.

The first thing God did for Adam and Eve after the fall was to cloth them with "garments of skin." The symbolism is that of a blood sacrifice, the first creatures to physically die, and for them no less, and it was most likely a lamb for each of them. It's also fair to assume that shoes were included with the new garments. After all, it was a rough world outside the borders of the garden that they were forced to walk on, and they needed to protect their feet. However, there were no provisions, coverings, made for Satan. His fate had already been sealed prior to the garden incident.

Inside the garden our original parents had no need for *breastplates of righteousness,* because before the fall they were already righteous, and there was no warfare on the earth at the time, and they were unaware of the spiritual warfare. This also means that there was no physical death, not even for the plants and animals. God's original design was, as He put it, "very good." And, since they did not need breastplates there, they also had no need to gird up their loins. There was nothing to gird them up with. They were naked before the fall. And, if they didn't need breastplates or girding up, they also had no need to shod their feet to spread the Good News, for there were no other people on the planet to share the "Good News" with.

The population was two. They themselves would not even be given the Good News until God sentenced them for their sins. Remember, they were living during the time of "very good," which was good enough.

The day that the first man and the first woman were evicted from paradise, some five thousand and something years ago, the physical and spiritual warfare on earth began. The warfare was just as brutal back then as it is today. In fact, their very first son, Cain, who they thought was going to be their "savior" based upon their own interpretation of God's words during the sentencing process, murdered his younger brother Abel. Who taught Cain how to hate and murder? He was the first human to be born on earth, and his parents, who were created and placed there, certainly didn't teach him how to hate his brother or commit homicide. Can you imagine their horror and heartbreak having once been perfect? This was all new to them, and it was an agonizing way to begin human history. Yet, God is very clear how the physical and spiritual war started, and He pins it directly on Adam.

Therefore, just as through one man sin entered the world, and death through sin, and thus death spread to all men, because all sinned - "
Romans 5:12

Don't let this confuse you. Adam and Eve were both guilty of insurrection, but God saw them as "one person" due to their marriage. *Therefore a man shall leave his father and mother and be joined to his wife, and they shall become **one flesh.** Genesis 2:24*

From that "one flesh," that fallen corrupted flesh, came forth Cain. The first person born during the war, and the first person to wage physical war. Yes, there was war between God and Lucifer before the fall of mankind, but that is a different conflict on an entirely different level. He'll deal with that later. The point is that the world was for man, and he, she, blew it.

After the fall, Adam and Eve needed the *body armor of righteousness,* which was symbolized by the animal skins they both wore upon their

PUT ON THE FULL COMBAT GEAR OF GOD

chests. Sadly, the first-born man, Cain, chose not to have this protection for himself, and he committed murder against his brother, who did choose to clothe himself with the *breastplate of righteousness,* for the Bible makes it perfectly clear that Abel presented a blood sacrifice to God, *of the first-born of his flock. Genesis 4:4* Jesus the Christ is referred to as both "the last Adam," and "the firstborn over all creation," (1 Corinthians 15:45 and Colossians 1:15). In other words, He's a picture of Adam, both male and female, before the fall, and the firstborn blood sacrifice to restore the re-lationship that was once enjoyed in the Garden of Eden. The *tree of life* is replanted in the new garden, but the *tree of the knowledge of good and evil* is never mentioned again. That thing is going to be firewood in hell. Not that we would ever be tempted again by that awful tree if God chose to have it remain, but we who already "ate his body and drank His blood" will live forever. That's why Adam and Eve were given the mercy of expulsion from the Garden of Eden and given the curse of physical death, *lest he put out his hand and take also of the tree of life, and eat, and live forever"* in his fallen state. Our tree of life is the cross.

Later in history, Moses' brother Aaron would become the first high priest under the old covenant. God required him to wear a "holy garment" (Exo-dus 28:2) that included a specially crafted *breastplate of judgment,* which had twelve stones upon it representing the twelve tribes of Israel. This was the first time that the symbols of warfare and religion came together, and blood sacrifices were the temporary solution to man's eternal problem.

Interestingly enough, the Bible does not mention shoes being worn on the feet of Aaron, or any other high priest after him when they did their duties in the Tabernacle in the wilderness, Gilgal, and Shiloh, and then afterwards in the two Temples in Jerusalem when they were built. Although in the Book of Exodus, God meticulously tells Moses how he wants the priestly garments to be made, and how they are to be worn, nothing is said about what was to be on the feet. In fact, when Moses first encountered God "in flames of fire from within a thorn bush" on Mount Horeb, God said to Moses, *"Do not draw near this place. Take your sandals off your feet, for the place where you stand is holy ground." Exodus 3:5*

Hmmmm. Adam and Eve didn't have any sandals on in the Garden of Eden either. So, does that mean that the Garden of Eden was also "holy ground?" It would appear so, because just after disobeying God's command not to eat of the *tree of the knowledge of good and evil "they heard the sound of the Lord walking in the garden in the cool of the day, and Adam and his wife hid themselves from the presence of the Lord God among the trees in the garden. Genesis 3:8* Wherever God is "physically," that is holy ground.

When Jesus was nailed to the cross his feet were bare.

So, what does that mean? It means that He took our place to be executed for our crimes. He didn't have on boots, which is the symbol of a Warrior King, which He has every right to wear. He didn't have on sandals either, because bare feet are a symbol of recognizing God's physical presence, yet the Father and Holy Spirit turned away from Jesus while on the cross. If this were not enough for us to recognize Him as the sacrificial Lamb spoken about in the Old Testament, Jesus also wore a crown of thorns that some Roman soldiers had fashioned and placed upon His head. Of course, thorns and thistles (Genesis 3:18) were placed upon the earth as one of the curses due to the fall of mankind, and God appeared to Moses as a burning thorn bush that was not consumed. Therefore, Jesus was not just cursed by being hung on a tree, but He was the "King of the cursed." A king is responsible for all of His subjects.

You may be thinking, *Aren't you stretching this 'combat boots' metaphor a bit too much?*

I don't think so, and I can prove it by having you answer a question. "When Jesus and His disciples were coming down into Jerusalem for the Passover, what type of animal was the Lord riding upon?"

That's right, he rode upon a colt – a donkey (Luke 19:28-40), and as He did the people lining the street were saying, *"Blessed is the King who comes in the name of the Lord!"* and Jesus accepted the title. Not only did he accept the title of King, but when the Pharisees told Him to forbid the crowds from proclaiming it, *He said to them, "I tell you that if these should keep silent, the stones would immediately cry out." Luke 19:40* The stones would cry out that He was the King. However, He was not there as a Warrior King, and He was certainly not there to take down the existing Roman Empire. He was there as the Sacrificial Lamb, to die and resurrect for the sins of man, and as such he rode upon a donkey, which in those days was the symbol of humility and peace. Had Jesus come riding into Jerusalem upon the back of a horse, that act would have been proclaiming Himself a military conqueror, for that was the symbol of military conquest throughout the entire ancient world. Rome would have seen such an action as a direct threat to their authority, but Him coming in on a donkey was not lost on Roman governor Pontius Pilate. Jesus of Nazareth was entering the Jewish capital in peace, but His followers were indicating something entirely different – replacement of Roman authority.

The Roman justice system required that the crime of any prisoner to be executed on a cross, a punishment reserved solely for non-citizens, was to be written on a wooden board that was nailed to the cross above the prisoner's head for all to see. Pontius Pilate ordered that Jesus' crime be written in Latin (the official language for government affairs across the Empire), Greek (the language of most foreigners and the educated class), and Hebrew (the language of the Jewish religious leaders), THIS IS JESUS THE KING OF THE JEWS. The citizens and foreigners got the message loud and clear. The crime of insurrection was indeed a Roman crime punishable by death, and Romans were not happy that only hours earlier they were proclaiming Jesus as their "king."

Not only did the Romans attempt to put down any insurrection that was forming, but they did what Romans often did with defeated kings, and that was to strip them naked and parade them through the streets before executing them. It was the ultimate in humiliation before permanently removing them as a threat to the Empire. Jesus was paraded through the streets of Jerusalem, and then stripped naked before being nailed to a cross. It was Rome's way of saying, "You want to be a king? Then be a defeated king. Does anyone want to follow Him now?"

As such, Jesus was not wearing the boots of a victorious king upon the cross, nor even sandals, but He was naked and barefoot – the "last Adam" before the fall - naked and barefoot.

How do you know this, Jim?

Because, the Scripture tells us that the Roman soldiers *divided His garments* (ἱμάτια, pronounced him-ah-tee-ah), *casting lots, that it might be fulfilled which was spoken by the prophet: Matthew 27:35*

There is no mention of Jesus' sandals. Although the garments Jesus had been wearing were completely covered in blood, garments were so expensive in those days that it was worth taking them and washing the blood out. Today we wouldn't even give it a second thought to throw away someone's bloody clothes, especially that of a condemned prisoner. Plus, the fact that the soldiers did not want to divide up the garments by tearing them, proves that it was cloth that they were talking about, and not leather sandals.

I mentioned "holy ground" before. Wherever God is "physically" on the ground, then that ground is holy ground, and shoes must be removed from peoples' feet whenever they are in His presence. However, when the price was paid for the sins of anyone who would believe in Him, Jesus' feet were not touching the ground. They were suspended above the earth nailed to a cross. During those hours there was no longer a single square inch on the earth that was holy, not even the Holy of Holies in the Temple that was within eye shot of Golgotha.

Then, behold, the veil of the temple was torn in two from top to bottom, and the earth quaked, and the rocks were split, Matthew 27:51

The Old Covenant, the Law, was finished. Jesus even said upon the cross before giving up the Holy Ghost, "It is finished!" Then, approximately 40 years later, there was not even the physical structure of the Holy of Holies left on the planet. There was nothing left for future generations to falsely worship, because in 70 AD the Roman Army, under General Titus, scraped the site clean, just as Jesus prophesied, *"Do you not see all these things? Assuredly, I say to you, not one stone shall be left here upon another, that shall not be thrown down." Matthew 24:2*

I've actually seen some of the massive stones that the Romans threw down off of the Temple Mount, for they are still there, and there is not a Third Temple standing there now. Not yet anyway. Therefore, the ground we all stand upon is not holy ground, but it is in fact a battleground, and souls are being lost and saved every day. This is exactly why we need the *combat boots of the Gospel of peace* on our feet now, and why we are commanded by the Lord to, *"Go into all the world and preach the gospel to every creature." Mark 16:16*

The Gospel, the Good News, in a nutshell, is contained in the most quoted verse of the Bible:

For God so loved the world that He gave His only begotten Son, that whoever believes in Him should not perish but have everlasting life. John 3:16

I suspect that after the Second World War, and I'm not talking about World War II that ended in 1945, but the brief war that occurs after the Thousand Year Reign of Jesus Christ upon the earth, that in heaven we will all have sandals on, even though we'll be standing on holy ground before God's presence. My supporting text is the story of The Prodigal Son.

A man had two sons. The younger one asked his father for his share of his inheritance, left home, and wasted all his money on prodigal living. There

173

was a severe famine in the land where he was living, and he ended up with a menial job feeding pigs. To feed himself he ate the same slop that was given to the pigs to eat. When the young man finally realized that he was going to starve to death, he went back to his father's house in hopes of his father taking him back as a servant, for he knew that he was no longer worthy to be treated as a son. However, when the father saw his youngest son approaching, he had compassion for him, and ran to embrace and kiss him. The father said to his servants, *Bring out the best robe and put it on him, and put a ring on his hand **and sandals on his feet.** Luke 15:22*

When Jesus told this parable to quite a mixed group (tax collectors, sinners, Pharisees and scribes), He purposely included this seemingly obscure detail of "sandals on his feet." Why? Because they, we, **you,** are that prodigal son, and don't deserve being His servant. As a son, or a daughter, you spent your inheritance (giving the world over to Satan, forfeiting your own soul to death), and you lived among the swine (the world) eating their slop (sin). Then, at some point you realized you were starving to death (spiritually) and decided to return back to Him (in repentance). You were willing to take anything from God, knowing that He treats all those who serve Him good (for even the unbelievers know instinctively that He and His ways are good). The Father did not turn you away (when you surrendered your life to Him), but He restored you (salvation) to your former position as a member of the family (who will be living in His home forever with all the rights associated with being His child). Therefore, you will be given the privilege of wearing shoes in His presence, a symbol of your status.

You may want to "die in your boots" here on earth, an idiom that means to "die while fighting" or to "never give up," but in eternity you're not going to need your combat boots anymore. That's because things are going to be "very good" again, and your footing will always be firm, not to mention that it's going to be pretty nice walking on the streets of gold in heaven in those new shoes.

SNAP OUT OF IT! You're not there yet! It was nice thinking about the future, but at this moment we're still at war. Let's get focused.

Jesus' First Coming was as a baby born in a manger where donkeys ate out of, and the angels rightly proclaimed, *Glory to God in the highest, and on earth peace, good will toward men. Luke 2:14* Then as an adult He rode into Jerusalem on a donkey, which was the symbolism confirming that He came as the King of Peace. However, His Second Coming is the opposite? He comes riding on a white horse, a war horse.

Now I saw heaven opened, and behold, **a white horse.** *And He who sat on him was called Faithful and True, and in righteousness* **He judges and makes war.** *Revelation 19:11*

Did you catch the last sentence, especially the part in bold type? "He judges and makes war." He's coming soon as a Warrior King, and probably wearing combat boots. This same verse also includes three other pieces of the *full combat gear of God* described in Ephesians 6:11 – the *body armor of righteousness,* the *patrol belt of truth,* and the *ballistic shield of faith.* Go back and find them in the verse to confirm this.

Coincidence? I think not. Not with God.

Speaking of the *ballistic shield of faith,* it's now time to issue you one.

The floor of this battle damaged room has broken glass and debris all over it, and this is exactly why good combat boots are essential.

Soldiering is harder on footwear than with most occupations. This Soldier is digging a fighting hole in dirt mixed with a lot of rocks.

When I teach my tactical courses I always emphasis the need for good footware for traction, support for kicking, and preventing injuries.

JIM WAGNER

Chapter 8

BALLISTIC SHIELD

MOBILE COVER & CLOSE COMBAT

above all, taking the shield of faith, which you will be able to quench all the fiery darts of the wicked one. Ephesians 6:16

The image that you may have in your mind is that of Roman soldiers in a Testudo, "tortoise," formation all carrying their heavy oblong shields on their left arms, armed with short swords in their right hands, isn't an accurate image for today's Army. Get that image out of your mind. Today's American combat Soldiers do not carry shields into battle. The technology has changed dramatically since Paul wrote this Scripture. The "shields" of today that protect troops in battle are M1 Abrams main battle tanks, M3 Bradley Fighting Vehicles, M1117 Armored Security Vehicles kicking up dust and diesel exhaust, along with the armored Apache Longbow attack helicopters swooping in from above. These metal war machines can get the soldiers safely to the target by "shielding" them.

However, when it comes to the traditional rectangular hand-held shield, the United States Army does have them. Of course, they're not made of layers of leather overlapped on wood like the Romans had, or sheets of hammered metal like in the Middle Ages, but today they are transparent shatter resistant plastic shields that the public is familiar with - riot shields used by the Army National Guard. These types of shields protect the users from the top of the head to the knees, and they will stop thrown rocks, bottles, and other small projectiles. And yes, sometimes the "Weekend Warriors" will get into a Tortoise formation if the projectiles are raining down on them. The front row of police officers have their shields facing the rioters, while the following rows of police officers have their shields above their heads to create a protective "roof." This technique is still taught to riot units world-wide, along with other ancient battle formations.

I expressed to you earlier that I am always intrigued with military equipment or traditions that are directly linked to the past. Shields are one of those, and I have spent a lot of time training and using them during my tactical career.

The very first time I was requested to teach a S.W.A.T. (Special Weapons and Tactics) team, outside of my own department that is, was in 1994 for the Housing Authority Police Department of the City of Los Angeles. The team leader, Lieutenant Robert Piernas, wanted me to teach his operators a course on how to deal with hostile subjects by using controlling force and impact force during police raids. In policespeak we call this type of training "defensive tactics," which is the term used for self-defense for law enforcement officers. More specifically, I was asked to teach his officers how to use their shields in "don't shoot" situations, and that's because there was no training available for using shields in this manner anywhere in the United States at the time. Keep in mind that the first S.W.A.T. team in the world was formed by the Los Angeles Police Department in 1967, and although they were the "gold standard" for S.W.A.T. teams across the nation, things were still developing. Therefore, twenty-seven years later, I had the opportunity to develop a comprehensive program for shield work, which I named *Shield Defense*. Yes, officers were trained at the time how to use shields for ballistic protection, which are what the non-riot shields are designed for, but not for hand-to-hand combat. I had to fill in the gaps with the techniques, tactics, and training methods that S.W.A.T. officers needed to know if a suspect tried to kick their shield, used martial arts style tripping techniques, grabbed the top of the shield and tried to pull it down, et cetera.

Some of the shield techniques and tactics that I taught to the Housing Authority Police, which eventually spread worldwide to other military units and agencies, were based upon the research I had done on ancient shield methods, which also included information I found on the Roman Army's use of them. Other techniques and tactics in my course were based upon my original teachings for modern hand-to-hand combat situations that law enforcement officers typically faced on the job. I just knew how to blend it all together. To God goes the glory!

I bring up the training I provided to the Housing Authority Police, because it illustrates that some things are lost over time, like the comprehensive use of war shields. Ancient warriors used shields to protect themselves from projectiles, just as the police and military did in 1994, but the ancients also used a broader spectrum of techniques and tactics for shields simply because they relied on them more as a secondary weapon. If they dropped their sword, or it was knocked out of their hand, they used their shield to push, strike, or bring the edge of it down violently onto the opponent's head or body like a blunt blade. When shields made their comeback among modern warriors, such as S.W.A.T. officers, they didn't rely on shields as secondary weapons until more and more unarmed combative situations required it.

Just as many fighting techniques and tactics have faded away into the backdrop of history, like fighting with a war shield did for a while, so does the faith of Christians individually or collectively. The old saying, *use it or lose it,* is never more true than with the *ballistic shield of faith.* You may never completely lose your faith in Jesus Christ, but if you haven't been in the fight for a while then some things that once made you, or a congregation, strong are lost. As such, few Christians want to engage in hand-to-hand combat by pushing back with the *ballistic shield of faith* against the public schools teaching children evolution. Many Christians won't even make a negative comment to anyone, let alone striking the agenda with their *ballistic shield of faith,* as employers require mandatory Critical Race Theory seminars, which is nothing more than godless Marxist teachings that have substituted the workers' consciousness of their plight, that was never embraced by Americans, with blaming white Christian males for all the ills of American society in order to divide people along racial and socio-economic lines. Most disturbing of all, many Christians have not wielded the *ballistic shield of faith* in such a long time that they no longer bring it down hard and crush the false doctrines that has crept into so many churches. They had relied so much on the shield for defense that they forgot how to use it for offense.

When I re-enlisted into the military as a Reserve Soldier I was placed in a Military Police unit at Joint Forces Training Base in Southern California, and since I had served as a civilian police officer, deputy sheriff, and a U.S. federal agent, the commander of the Provost Marshal Office (PMO) tapped into my training and experience by assigning me to the instructor cadre, which is exactly what I had prayed for. In this capacity I taught law enforcement and military skills to National Guard, Army Reserve, and State Guard Soldiers, and my duties also included teaching Combatives, which is the military term for hand-to-hand combat. And, yes, you guessed it, I also had the opportunity to teach riot control, which included the use of riot shields; the transparent shatter resistant plastic shields I mentioned earlier.

The training I gave to the Military Police, in addition to the past training I had given to S.W.A.T. teams in previous years, turned out to be needed in the country of Holland.

For a couple of years, I had been teaching the instructors at the Academie Politie Amsterdam-Amstelland, which was the tactical training academy for the Amsterdam Police Department. This particular academy was strictly for firearms, defensive tactics (remember, this is the term for law enforcement self-defense), and sports training. Whatever was taught at this academy was then taught to other police departments throughout the Netherlands.

To prepare for the 2011 training year the instructor cadre had me teach them a course I designed called Police Baton & Riot Control. My Dutch police students were armed with long riot batons and round shields. In their various team formations, they reminded me of Spartans. I not only taught them all the techniques and tactics I thought that they needed, but I also ran them through several realistic scenarios using role players.

When the training had been completed the Academy surprised me during the course graduation ceremony, where the officers are presented their instructor training certificates, and by the order of the commander I was made an honorary police officer and honorary member of the instructor cadre. They had a ceremony, on top of the ceremony, where they presented me with an actual Amsterdam Police Department badge, a "shield," and their shoulder patch. And to think, part of what led to this great honor was that I taught them how to effectively use a shield. Of course, I'm convinced that God had me there for reasons beyond just teaching police officers how to use their equipment more effectively in riots.

Did you notice a common theme in my personal stories about shields? S.W.A.T. teams use ballistic shields in their line of work to protect against bullets, and they also use them against unarmed combative subjects. Military police and National Guard units use riot shields against hand thrown projectiles and Molotov cocktails (a wine bottle filled with gasoline with a burning cloth wick stuffed into the mouth of the bottle as the ignition source), and also to push, strike, and hammer rioters with an edge who will not disburse. Of course, civilian law enforcement riot police do exactly the same thing when dealing with an unlawful assembly. The spiritual parallel is that the *ballistic shield of faith* is the same wherever you go also, whether it's in your own backyard or internationally. Not only do you have to be proficient with your *shield* to keep the firery darts of the devil from hitting you, but your *faith* has to also be used offensively for hand-to-hand combat as well: push the enemies back, strike the enemies, and hammer the enemies with it. It's a war after all!

I don't think I would have ever learned these spiritual truths if it had not been for me working with shields for so many years. I also know that this book would have never been written, not from me anyway, if God had not set me on a lifelong path that had me personally use every piece of war equipment on Paul's Ephesians 6 list. After all, how many Christians are there in the world who use shields today? I'd venture to say, "Not many."

Now I want to teach you a physical shield technique that you can train at home with, provided you have a couple of willing training partners, which will also directly link you to the *shield of faith* metaphor.

Not only do I teach military personnel and law enforcement officers, but I'm also a self-defense instructor for civilians teaching my own international system *Jim Wagner Reality-Based Personal Protection*, and one of the techniques that I have taught all over the world, in my Crime Survival course, is my original technique I named *Flexible Shield.* I came up with this civilian technique having seen first-hand how peaceful demonstrations can turn ugly, and knowing how volatile the "mob mentality" can be. It's not just at a political rally where things can turn violent, but a brawl can happen inside a bar, at an amusement park, or anywhere there is a group of hostile people. When tensions increase, it doesn't take long before objects start flying through the air.

The name *Flexible Shield* implies exactly what it means. A coat, jacket, pullover, or beach towel can be used as an improvised shield to protect yourself or someone you're with. That's right, you too can use ancient shield techniques if you ever find yourself caught in the middle of an angry mob throwing small objects in your direction. You can also find this technique in my book *Warrior Wisdom in One Month,* but I'll give a brief description on how it works.

Once projectiles start flying, you need to get that flexible shield up just above the top of your head and stretch the material tight with the FRONT TOWARD ENEMY. In essence you are creating a net that will stop the airborne object upon contact, causing it either to bounce off the flexible shield or fall straight to the floor once it loses energy upon contact with the cloth. You'll be behind the shield of course, and the person you are protecting will be behind you, as you both make your way to an exit, and then to safety. Yes, you may get hit on a finger or two along the escape route, but it's better than getting struck in the head or torso. Once a rock, frozen plastic water bottle, or a chunk of concrete hits you there, then it's "game over."

I have my students practice the technique, as role players throw boxing gloves at them. Then on the next go around they move up to tennis balls being thrown at them, of course with face protection on. For those brave enough to try, they have real glass bottles thrown at them, and that requires wearing face protection and a hard-shell helmet for safety.

Granted, the odds of the average person ever having to use my *Flexible Shield* technique is probably one in a million, but when it is needed it will be the only option. That, or get hurt.

Should you ever have to use the *Flexible Shield* technique, you will be physically connected to Ephesians 6:16, which means that it will no longer be just theory, but reality.

Using a flexible shield is obviously not the best shield in the world, as you can imagine, but it is better than nothing when bottles and rocks are being thrown at you. Having a little *faith* is not only better than no faith at all, but in God's economy it's actually more powerful than you realize. That's not my opinion, but it's the Lord's. *So, Jesus said to them, "Because of your unbelief; for assuredly, I say to you, if you have faith as a mustard seed, you will say to this mountain, 'Move from here to there,' and it will move; and nothing will be impossible for you." Matthew 17:20*

A mustard seed is a tiny seed, yet it can grow into a large tree. Now, let's go even deeper into the spiritual aspects of a shield.

above all, taking the shield of faith, Let's stop there.

ἐν πᾶσιν (pronounced en pasin) in Greek transliterates *in all.* However, the English translation *above all* that is used in this sentence is exactly as it would be said, and mean, today.

Patrol belt, check. *Body armor,* check. *Combat boots,* check. ***Above all, taking the shield of faith.***

Above all, having taken up (ἀναλαβόντες, pronounced ana-la-bont-es) *the shield.* In other words, more importance is placed on this piece of equipment, the shield, than the previous pieces of *battle rattle* (slang for *full combat gear*) mentioned before it. And, as you have just learned from my military and law enforcement examples, the shield is to protect the entire body. It can be raised up to stop projectiles or strikes coming downward. It can be placed in front of the head and torso to stop straight incoming projectiles or blows, and it can even be lowered to protect the legs and feet from skip rounds, which are projectiles that skim the surface like a smooth rock that is skipped across a glassy pond or lake. Go to a kneeling position, and the shield serves as a temporary bunker. However, with all of the benefits that a shield provides it cannot stop everything.

In the days of Paul, from which we get the Ephesians 6:16 metaphor, Roman soldiers carried the *scutum* (pronounced skoo-tum), which is an oblong and convex shield measuring two and a half feet wide and four feet long. It was great for stopping spears, arrows, and edged weapons, but it would not stop a bolder flung from an enemy catapult some distance away, or a very large bolt (an oversized arrow) shot from a *ballista* (a large machine that has many of the same features as a crossbow). Of course, we get our modern word "ballistic" from this war machine that dates back to the Greek Empire, and then perfected by the Romans.

So, why did I bring up the catapult and the ballista? It's because a Roman infantry soldier could not stand against such heavy weaponry out on the open battlefield. Likewise, an American Soldier today, despite all of the personal body armor and weapons he or she may carry, cannot survive against a direct hit from an artillery shell, a cruise missile, or a nuclear bomb out in the open. Therefore, Paul is telling us Christian Soldiers that the military equipment issued to us, the ones we have covered so far (truth, righteousness, spreading the Gospel, and faith) are for Close Quarters Battle (CQB), which means fighting multiple combatants with small arms at a short range. Yes, we also have access to crew-served weapons (the assembly of the saints, meaning church, Bible study, or other fellowship) if we don't forsake it as stated in Hebrews 10:25, or heavy weapons (fasting and prayer) if we're willing to use them, and we may even be able to sabotage some "big stuff" by getting behind enemy lines, but we'll address these three things a little bit later. But, for now, let's stay on topic – the shield.

Ballistic shields, like body armor, are made of different materials depending on what type of mission they are to be used for. The most protective personal shield is Level IV, which will stop an armor piercing rifle .308 bullet. So, what is a spiritual shield made of? The answer is – *faith.*

Above all, taking the shield of faith, Ephesians 6:16

Hebrews 11:1 tells us, *Now **faith** is the substance of things hoped for, the evidence of things not seen.*

When I drive to church every Sunday morning, I drive on a bridge that takes me over the 405 Freeway. The bridge is quite high, so much so that I can see for miles when I have reached the summit. I have faith that the bridge will not collapse as I drive over it. When I turned on the computer each day, the very one that I wrote this book on, I had faith that all of the words I typed would be saved each time I pressed the SAVE icon. When I fired my pistol on duty as a police officer, I had faith that the hammer would hit the primer, which in turn would ignite the gunpowder inside the cartridge, trusting that the expanding gases would propel the bullet through the barrel at the correct velocity.

For all three of these real-world examples, I knew in the back of my mind that my *faith* could have been tested or even shattered. Sometimes the atmospheric elements corrode bridges, and parts of the bridge, or even all of it, could fail and collapse. Sometimes computers crash, and Lord knows that it has happened to me umpteen million times in the past. Some bullets can be duds, even those manufactured by the best companies in the world, and it's possible to have a Class I malfunction, a Failure to Fire, on my hands. However, God never fails. I know this, because the Bible tells me so.

The problem with *faith* is not on His end, the problem is always on our end. It's our *faith* that sometimes wavers. It's our *faith* that is sometimes weak. It's our *faith* that God tests, and not for His benefit, but for ours. If you already had ample *faith*, then He would not have told you to take up the *shield of faith.*

You may be thinking, *Yes, I get it. I know what a shield is, and I know that I must have faith that God will protect me like a shield, but what specifically is the 'shield?'*

That's an easy question to answer. God is the *shield.*

Most Christians know Psalm 3:3, *But You, O Lord, are a **shield** about me, My glory, and the One who lifts my head.* That's because they are also the words of a beautiful contemporary worship song by the title *A Shield About Me,* by songwriters Donn Thomas and Charles Williams. Go to a search engine and look it up. It's inspirational!

There are many passages in the Bible where God is referred to as "a shield," and here are two examples:

*The Lord is my rock and my fortress and my deliverer, My God, my rock, in whom I take refuge; **He is a shield** to those who walk in integrity, Psalm 18:2*

He stores up sound wisdom for the upright; **He is a shield** *to those who walk in integrity. Proverbs 2:7*

No wonder Paul tells you and me to take up the *shield of faith,* which essentially means "take up God, and He'll protect you. Don't take up God, and you're unprotected."

Now that you know what the war shield is, it's important to know what level of protection it provides. What are the specifications? What type of weapons of the enemy will it protect you against? Let's re-read Ephesians 6:16 to find out. After all, repetition is how you develop muscle memory.

Above all, taking the shield of faith, which you will be able to quench all the **fiery darts** *of the wicked one. Ephesians 6:16*

Not some of the *fiery darts,* but "all" the *fiery darts.*

Wait a second! The only "darts" that come to mind is the game darts, a game found in English pubs, American bars, and some people's game room or garage. Well, if you thought of an official throwing dart, when you first read this Scripture, then you're not too far off the mark.

The word "darz" is an Old French word, which originated from the West Germanic word "dars," which in Middle English means "spear or lance," which is a projectile quite a bit bigger than the darts one pinches between two or three fingers.

When the Romans laid siege to fortified enemy positions, such as a wooden fort or a walled city, they used archers who shot flaming arrows or bolts into them. If they landed on a flammable material, then they would burn the structure down. These were the earliest forms of thermal weapons, thus the name "fiery darts." Therefore, get the game of darts out of your head, and think in modern terms – bullets being fired at you, or even a hand grenade lobbed at you. A good ballistic shield will provide adequate protection.

So, what kind of spiritual "fiery darts" will the wicked one, Satan, fire at

189

you? Well, he has a lot of different calibers in his arsenal. Sometimes he'll fire small caliber rounds at you: flattering people, name callers, or gossipers. If that doesn't work then there are medium sized calibers: envious people, jealous people, flirty people, or thieves. Nothing gets your flesh all worked up more than someone who has stolen something valuable from you. If none of those fiery darts takes you down, then out come the big guns: abusive people, alcohol, drugs, sex, the love of money, or the temptation of power. Satan doesn't always know what will hit you, but he'll keep trying until something does. Then, once he makes you bleed, he won't give up. The wicked one is ruthless and relentless. In fact, if given the opportunity he'd even lob literal hand grenades at you if God allows him. Yes, that's right! Satan literally wants to kill you every day. Oh sure, he may not be personally after you, because you may be small potatoes to him, and Satan is not omnipresent. Meaning, he can only be at one place at one time. He is not the opposite of God. He is a created being with limited abilities. Yet, he has a lot of fallen angels, and wicked humans, in his army of darkness. So, unless you are a "high value target," he'll have one of his demons or spiritually blinded human followers try to *take you out* (kill you). Hence, the need for the *shield of faith.*

Faith is the heaviest piece of spiritual personal protective equipment you'll have to use in battle and during the lulls, but when you use it all the time your strength increases, thereby making it easier to handle over time. Also, when you use your *shield,* your *faith,* more and more, you also get faster at blocking. After all, *fiery darts* come in fast.

Don't ever make the mistake of thinking that you're out of range of the enemy. He does not always hit you head on with a phalanx (a formation of heavily armed infantry standing shoulder to shoulder coming at you), but he may use sniper tactics. Meaning, sometimes you're ready for the big battles, but a small thing could be your undoing if you don't stop it. Therefore, to be successful on the battlefield against massive attacks or tiny skirmishes, the *shield of faith* has to be with you at all times. Even if you have to back out of a bad situation, what's called a "tactical retreat," you had better keep the *shield* facing the enemy as you move away from the situation so that you don't catch a *fiery dart* or two in the back.

This relief shows Roman soldiers with large oval shields. I studied their tactics, and other cultures, to develop my Shield Defense course.

The Los Angeles Housing Authority Police had me teach their S.W.A.T. team how to use ballistic shields against unarmed combative subjects.

These Los Angeles Sheriff's Department deputies do a "tactical retreat" during a victim rescue. The shield continues to face the threat.

These Dutch police officers are armed with riot batons and light round wicker shields, and they work as a team so that everyone is safer.

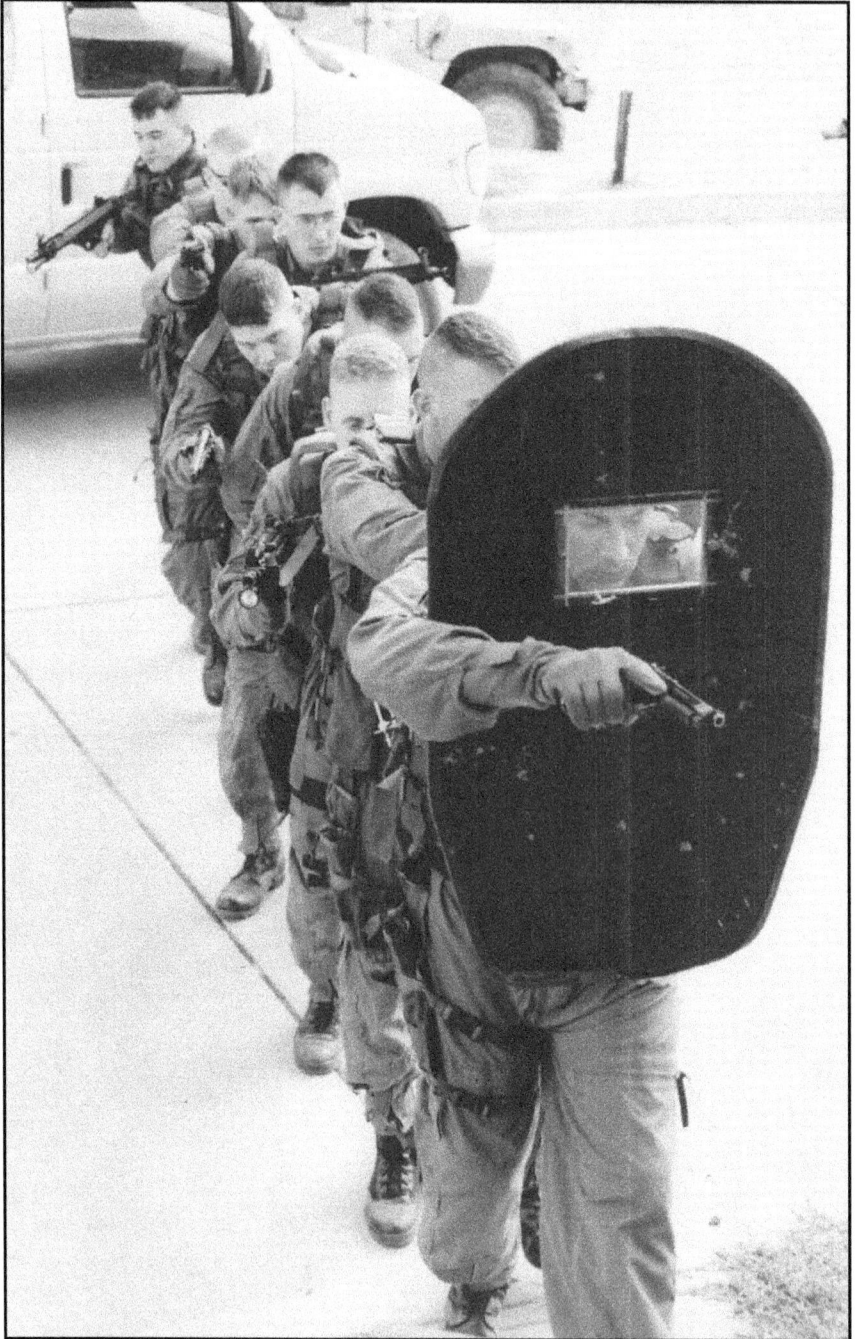

This U.S. Marine team is about to enter into a building of hostiles that are inside. The point man leads with a ballistic shield, weapon up.

To teach my civilian students aggression and endurance I created a drill called Shield Fighting. Contact is made with soft kicking shields.

This Flexible Shield is a jacket that is held up as a "hostile" throws an empty plastic water bottle at the "victim" who is trying to escape.

Chapter 9

HELMET

THINK TACTICALLY

And take the helmet of salvation, Ephesians 6:17

The swells were bigger than I thought, which isn't a problem in the open sea, but when you're under a Gas & Oil Platform, a "GOPLAT" as they call it, the sudden upward thrust of thousands of cubic feet of water could send your head crashing into a steel support beam and knock you out, or worse. Neither option is good while in dark frigid ocean water at 4 a.m. in the morning, several miles off the coast of California, and especially when it happens to be during feeding time for Great White Sharks. That's why it was crucial that I kept paddling as hard as I could against the strong current with my swim fins in order to stay centered underneath the massive structure that towered above me as I struggled in the black ink Pacific Ocean. That, and getting the grappling hook, that was attached to the caving ladder and painter's pole, up and over the railing of the catwalk as soon as possible. If I didn't, I, and the entire team, faced the possibility of getting crushed or drifting out to sea – away from the objective, which was to get onto the GOPLAT and neutralize the terrorists who had seized it, before they blew it up and caused an ecological disaster for the Golden State.

It sounds like an action movie, doesn't it? It certainly had the elements of one, except the terrorists on the "skyscraper of the seas" were role players, and I was in the water to fulfill my yearly waterborne operations training with *high speed, low drag* Special Operations men from around the world.

In the year 2000, just on my team alone, were Honolulu S.W.A.T. team members, a Swiss infantry soldier, an Australian federal agent, and a couple deputies from the Los Angeles Sheriff's Office. This particular year of training was the Tactical Swimmer Course taught by two U.S. Marines instructors, "quiet professionals," from Marine Corps Base Camp Pendleton.

Training or no training, there were some serious risks doing that Gas & Oil Platform takedown training, and it was one of those rare moments when I was very conscious of the helmet upon my head, and the protection it afforded me.

The helmet I was wearing during the GOPLAT training was manufactured by Pro-Tec®, and it was a quality black, Acrylonitrile Butadiene Styrene (ABS) hard shell, professional skateboard helmet, which were also worn by U.S. Navy SEALs and Marine Force Recon operators at the time for waterborne operations. Ballistic helmets were just too heavy to add to all the other gear that had to be in the water with the swimmers. Weapons and ammunition were a higher priority.

In 2005 Special Operations units replaced the skateboard helmets with the FAST, Future Assault Shell Technology, helmet. The average weight was only 2.28 pounds, and that's because it was made of ultra-high-molecular-weight polyethylene.

Of course, once my team managed to climb up the mammoth structure, there were even more hazards to threaten my noggin. There were low hanging pipes everywhere, and some of the decks were slick with oil, because that's what these structures do – they pump oil from underneath the sea floor. One good slip on the metal surface on the lower decks, which were covered in a thin layer of congealed oil with a film of sea water on top of that, and a head injury was almost certain.

When I was 18 years old in the United States Army, I was issued the M1 helmet, which was nicknamed the "steel pot," because that is what they were made of, a thin layer of stamped sheet metal. In fact, they could even be used to cook in if need be. It was 1980 when I joined the Service, and so it was a Vietnam Era helmet. They were useless against a direct bullet strike, but effective against ricochets, some fragmentation, and bumping into hard objects.

By the time I was on my police department's S.W.A.T. team I was given a PASGT (pronounced paz-get), helmet, which is, of course, an acronym for Personal Armor System for Ground Troops. That's right, American S.W.A.T. teams used surplus military equipment.

The nickname for the PASGT helmet was "Kevlar," because that is what it was made of; layers of Kevlar with a type of resin to make it hard.

Even though I was a civilian police S.W.A.T. officer, I mentioned to you before that I taught a lot of courses at Marine Corps Base Camp Pendleton, and in return I was allowed to "piggyback" onto a lot of Marine courses. One of those courses I was privileged to attend, and to be certified in, was the Military Operations Urban Terrain Assault Course Range Safety Officer, which you guessed it, is shortened with the acronym M.O.U.T. Assault Course RSO. It consisted of one day in the classroom, and then three days of learn-by-doing intense firearms instructions, which included the use of fragmentation hand grenades. Obviously, law enforcement doesn't use such deadly devices, but my Marine students certainly did, and that's why I was required to learn all the techniques and safety procedures associated with them. The bonus was that I got to blow things up.

Anyway, why am I bringing up this Range Safety Officer training? It's because I learned something valuable from the U.S. Marines that I practice to this day, and it's something you should know as well.

When I was going through the police academy none of the firearms instructors wore a ballistics vest. At the time that didn't seem odd to me, because when I was an 18-year-old Soldier in the U.S. Army, years earlier, the drill sergeants didn't wear any ballistic protection either.

By the time I was on my police department's S.W.A.T. team, and teaching other S.W.A.T. teams, more and more firearms instructors were wearing ballistic vests. Then, when I started attending U.S. Marine Corps firearms courses the Standard Operating Procedure (SOP) for firearms ranges was for there to always be a Corpsman (a U.S. Navy medic) present at the training, and for all firearms instructors to wear a ballistic vest and ballistic helmet. Of course, the "lightbulb" went on in my head, and I thought, *Well, yes. That makes sense. Why protect the torso and not the head?* So, whenever I teach a live-fire course, be it beginners or a national counterterrorist team, I always have on my ballistic vest and helmet. That's because I'm not only concerned about some student having a Negligent Discharge (ND), but I'm keenly aware of what I coined the "Chris Kyle Syndrome."

Chris Kyle was a U.S. Navy SEAL sniper who served four combat tours in the Iraq War. In 2012 he had written the book *American Sniper,* which became a bestseller autobiography, and it was even made into a movie, a movie I recommend that you watch. A year later Chris Kyle was teaching a firearms course to veterans. Then one of his students, Eddie Ray Routh, a former Marine suffering from Post-traumatic Stress Disorder (PTSD), turned his weapon on his instructor Chris Kyle, for no reason, and murdered him along with fellow instructor Chad Littlefield.

The murder of Chris Kyle was the most infamous shooting of its kind, and that was due to his notoriety, but many military firearms instructors have met the same fate when their students turned on them, mostly in Islamic countries. As such, I wrote an article about this emerging phenomenon not long after Chris Kyle was murdered, and I named it the Chris Kyle Syndrome. One, to honor his name, and two, to make instructors aware of this demonic phenomenon. As such, I'm always prepared if one of my students turns on me with a live firearm, and so I always wear a ballistic vest and ballistic helmet as a precaution, plus I am always armed to defend myself.

So, what's the spiritual take away from the Chris Kyle Syndrome? It's this. Sometimes Christians turn on each other. Therefore, you can never completely trust people. Oh, I'm not saying that they're literally going to shoot you by surprise, although some certainly can and do, but you're going to find out sometime in life, and you may have already, that the people you thought you could trust will "fire" at you in other ways: gossip, hurtful comments, or just not being there for you when you need them. That's why God warns us *Do not put your trust in princes, nor in man, in whom there is no help. Psalm 146:3* We are to continually love our Christian brothers and sisters, but if for some reason one of them turns on us, thankfully we're wearing our *body armor of righteousness* and *our helmet of salvation,* which keeps us from blaming God for their actions. We recognize it for what it is - they may be saved but they still live in fleshly bodies. It's the same wisdom that keeps us from badmouthing all Catholics because of the Inquisition or sexual abuse by many priests, or calling the Crusades evil because some soldiers went rogue and massacred Jews, or looking down on fellow believers because they worship differently than we do.

THE DANGER OF CHERRY-PICKING

Although I take the necessary precautions at the gun range when I teach, virtually no other civilian firearms instructors I know wear a helmet. Sure, they almost always have their vests on, but not the helmet. I just don't get it. It's not like I don't remind them. That's why I understand Paul when he tells us twice to "put on the full armor of God," because Christians are notorious for not listening, or just cherry-picking Scriptures. In other words, they have no problem obeying the Scriptures they like, but tend to ignore others that make them uncomfortable or disagree with altogether. Therefore, Paul has to make the point *take the helmet of salvation,* and that's because many don't, or won't, just like the civilian firearms instructors I see all of the time who won't put on a ballistic helmet at the live-fire gun range. Somehow, they think that an unintentional, or on purpose, bullet won't be coming their way. It's a classic case of denial, which means someone who does not see reality clearly.

If people don't see physical reality clearly, then how are they going to see spiritual reality clearly?

PHYLACTERY & HELMET

A νομικὸς (pronounced nomikos), which is a lawyer, asked Jesus, in order to test Him, *"Teacher, which is the great commandment in the law?"* *Matthew 22:36*

Jesus said to him, "'You shall love the Lord your God with all your heart, with all your soul, and with all your mind.' This is the first and great commandment. And the second is like it: 'You shall love your neighbor as yourself.' On these two commandments hang all the Law and the prophets.'" *Matthew 22:37-40*

For first part of Jesus' answer to the lawyer He recited the Shema Yisrael, "Hear, O Israel."

You may know, or you may have noticed, that on the door post of a Jewish house, business, or even on a gate is attached a decorative vertical rectangular case, sometimes placed straight up and down or sometimes slightly tilted, with the Hebrew letter "ש," (pronounced shin for Shema) on it. This case is called a *mezuzah,* and inside of it is a piece of parchment called a *klaf,* which is the Old Testament scripture Deuteronomy 6:4-9 written only by a qualified scribe, a *sofer stam.*

As I sit here this very moment typing this very page for you, I am in my office at home, and on the doorpost of my office I too have a mezuzah that I bought in Jerusalem. I'm not Jewish, but it serves the same purpose for me as it does devout Jews, and that is to remind me of the Shema. If it's important enough for Jesus to quote it, then it is important enough for me to be reminded of it also. That, and I like the tradition. This is how the Shema reads,

Hear, O Israel: The Lord our God, the Lord is one! You shall love the Lord your God with all your heart, with all your soul, and with all of your strength.

*And these words which I command you today shall be in your heart. You shall teach them diligently to your children, and shall talk of them when you sit in your house, when you walk by the way, when you lie down, and when you rise up. You shall bind them as a sign on your hand, **and they shall be as frontlets between your eyes.***

You shall write them on the doorposts of your house and on your gates. Deuteronomy 6:4-9

The second scripture that Jesus quoted to the lawyer was Leviticus 19:18 *You shall not take vengeance, nor bear any grudge against the children of your people, but you shall love your neighbor as yourself: I am the Lord.*

So, there you have it. Jesus said, "on these two commandments hang all the Law and the prophets."

Orthodox Jewish men, when they are doing their morning prayer, wear phylacteries. These are small black leather boxes, called *tefillin,* containing the inscribed parchment that is wrapped around the upper left arm by means of a leather strap. A second leather strap around the head keeps the other box centered on the forehead.

As Orthodox Jews wear the phylacteries, so we Christian Soldiers wear the *helmet of salvation* upon our heads, and we are to keep it on during the duration of the war.

We know that a helmet protects the head, but we have yet to define "salvation" in our study verse, *And take the helmet of **salvation**, Ephesians 6:17*

Salvation means *to be saved from the consequences of sin,* and the consequence of sin is eternal separation from God in a literal location named hell, which I described to you after your Gas Chamber experience. However, to recap, it's a horrible place of floating in solitude, writhing in flames that

203

give off no light, and tormenting memories of all of the missed opportunities of salvation that had been presented, but were all passed over.

For all have sinned and fall short of the glory of God, Romans 3:23

This means that everyone, without exception, is on death row (the area of the prison for those prisoners sentenced to death); "death" as in "the second death." The only way to not just commute (reduce) your dreadful sentence, but have it dismissed completely, *is by grace you have been **saved** through faith, and that **not of yourselves,** it is the gift from God, not of works, **lest anyone should boast.** Ephesians 2:8-9*

By simply believing that Jesus Christ paid the price on the cross for your sins, you are saved, because God gifted mercy (grace) to you, and nothing you could have done, or can do now, or will ever do in this life, is enough to secure your place in His eternal presence, lest you **should boast.**

SALVATION. You don't have to "wrap your head around it," but the *helmet of salvation* wraps around your head.

When victory comes, and we're finally home with the Lord, we'll have our helmets replaced with something better upon our heads, and that is five royal crowns. I have them listed in the order that the New Testament lists them:

Crown 1: *And everyone who competes for the prize is temperate in all things. Now they do it to obtain a perishable crown, but we for an **imperishable crown.** 1 Corinthians 9:25*

Crown 2: *For what is our hope, or joy, or **crown of rejoicing?** Is it not even you in the presence of our Lord Jesus Christ at His coming? 1 Thessalonians 2:19*

Crown 3: *Finally, there is laid up for me the **crown of righteousness,** which the Lord, the righteous Judge will give me on that Day, and not to* *me only but also to all who have loved His appearing. 2 Timothy 4:8*

Crown 4: *Blessed is the man who endures temptation; for when he has been approved, he will receive the **crown of life** which the Lord has promised to those who love Him. James 1:12*

Crown 5: *and when the Chief Shepherd appears, you will receive the **crown of glory** that does not fade away. 1 Peter 5:4*

Imperishable, rejoicing, righteousness, life, and glory. Those are not just our war medals that we'll receive after the war, but it will also be our existence: never growing old or dying, rejoicing in His righteousness, with an eternal life filled with glory. I'd say that the combat tour we did on earth makes it all worth it. Therefore, if you keep your head about you, buy wearing your *helmet of salvation* for protection during this war, you'll have that new life that is promised to those *who have loved His appearing* and *who endured temptation.*

It's time now to go over to the armory.

This was the target: Gas & Oil Platform (GOPLAT) Esther located offshore of Southern California, which was taken over by "terrorists."

Although I took off my helmet for this photo (top center), four of my teammates have theirs on as we pose on the helicopter landing pad.

I (on the right), and two fellow U.S. Federal Air Marshals, wait to go inside the live-fire Shoot House with our PASGT ballistic helmets on.

These are the riot helmets that my military police unit was issued. They have shatter resistant face shields to stop thrown projectiles.

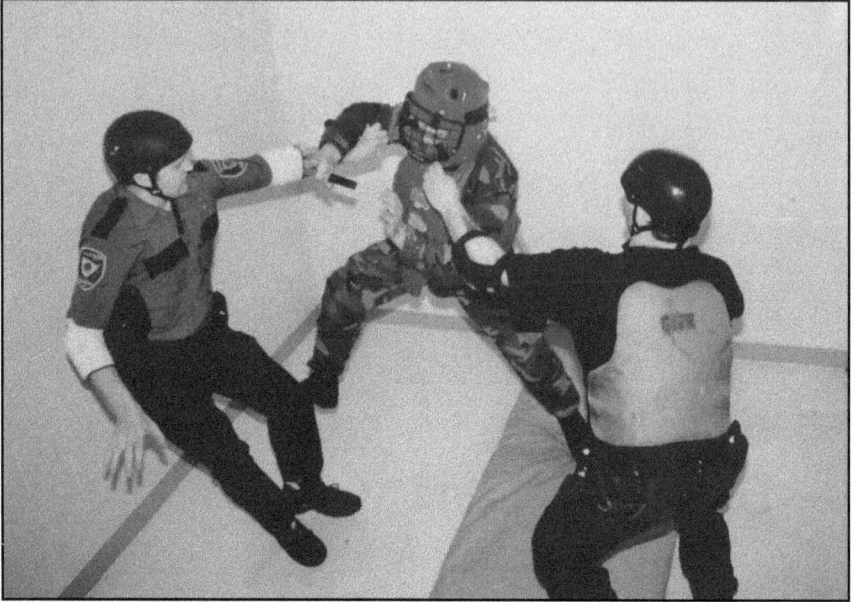

These corrections officers of the Quinault Tribal Police Department wear helmets when doing training and actual Cell Extractions.

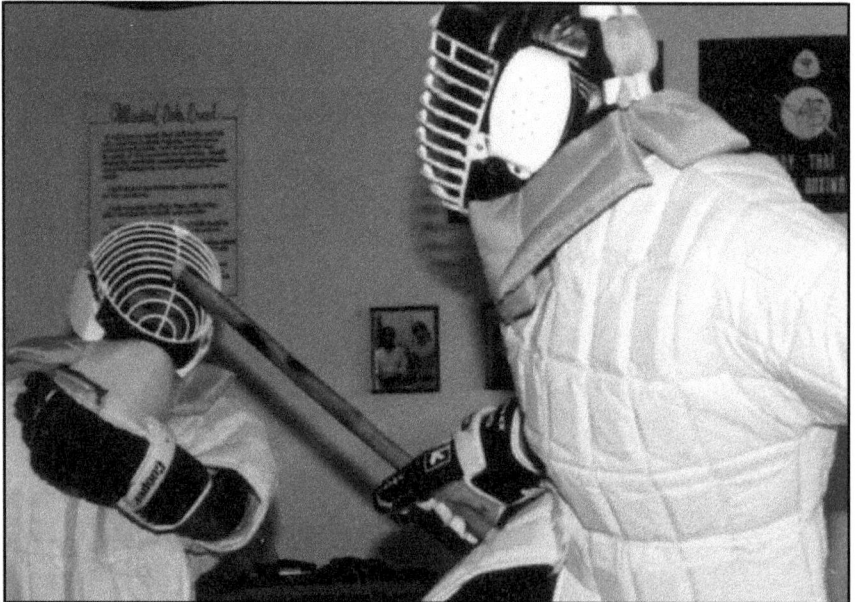

For full contact stick fighting, in the Filipino martial art of Kali, the students must wear helmets with face cages to avoid impact injuries.

This is me on an Easter morning service, out of public view, as part of the Counter Assault Team (CAT). I am wearing my ballistic helmet.

JIM WAGNER

Chapter 10

WEAPON

LOCK & LOAD

And the sword of the Spirit, which is the word of God; Ephesians 6:17

The sword was the primary weapon of a Roman infantry soldier, and as such many Christians read this passage and think that the "whole armor thing" is an antiquated notion. It's the same exact mistake that Christians make when reading the following Bible Scripture:

Nor do they light a lamp and put it under a basket, but on a lampstand, and it gives light to all who are in the house. Let your light so shine before men, that they may see your good works and glorify your Father in heaven. Matthew 5:15-16

Obviously, this passage describes the technology of that day. A lamp in the 1st Century, over 2,000 years ago, was a small metal or terracotta covered dish-like container, no bigger than the palm of a hand with a protrusion at the front of the lamp for the wick and flame. The design of the lamp included a larger hole on top to pour vegetable oil into (the fuel), and a handle at the end so it could be carried from room to room. The bottom of the oil lamp was flat in order for it to be placed on a shelf or table.

Most oil lamps used in homes throughout the Roman Empire had just one wick per lamp inserted into a small hole of the protrusion, with larger lamps having up to three wicks resembling three-fingers spread apart. Think of a single wick oil lamp as one burning candle today, and a lamp with three wicks giving off the same amount of light as three candles. One candle has

211

enough illumination for a small bathroom, and three flames could light up a living room enough for evening activities. Place a big basket over an ancient oil lamp with a single flame, or even three flames, and it is very easy to hide the light, and yet still not burn the basket.

For Americans candles are no longer necessary for daily life. Today they are merely items to create a relaxing or romantic ambiance. Even simple candles are being replaced more and more with replica electric ones. The "flame" of an electric candle is nothing more than a moving piece of reflective metal, cut to the shape of a flame, with small LED lights shining on it.

A single candle flame puts out 1 lumen, but if you think of Matthew 5:15-16 in terms of modern technology, then the metaphor becomes even more powerful - literally. The average living room lighting today, which is approximately 100 square feet, puts out 1,000 to 2,000 lumens. That would be a lot of candle flames burning all at once. Therefore, having a circuit breaker go out, which kills the power to the electric lights, is a big deal. Just as ancient people depended on oil lamps and candles made of bees' wax or animal fat, we're dependent on electricity. Take away electricity in a modern society, and we are in a world of hurt.

Just as you need to update your thinking to a blackout instead of a basket over a candle, you must also update your thinking of a sword to a rifle. After all, the primary weapon of today's American combat Soldier is a rifle. Yes, swords still exist in the U.S. Army, just as candles still exist for homes, but swords are only used by officers and noncommissioned officers for a few formal military ceremonies. During my entire military career, I only used a sword once, and that was as a noncommissioned officer at a fellow sergeant's wedding, yet I had a rifle with me countless times.

Now let's make some comparisons between the sword and the rifle to bring you up to speed. A sword is a weapon designed to wound and kill. It is an offensive weapon. If a sword was merely for defense, then an ancient soldier could have just as easily blocked incoming blows with an iron staff or rod instead. There would have been no need for a point or sharp edges of a sword.

So, let me state it again, "a sword is a weapon designed to wound and kill." The tip of a sword has a point so it can be thrust into a human body. Shove that tip into the chest cavity and it's going to puncture an internal organ: the heart, lungs, liver, intestines, or something. Slash at the enemy's throat and it is going to cut open that fleshly tube called the esophagus, or rip open the carotid artery, spurting blood all over the place. A sword can divide a head in half or even decapitate it from the body. A sword can also chop off fingers and limbs.

What does a modern rifle do? It does the same thing as a sword. It is designed to wound and kill. Fire a bullet into someone's body, and it will not just penetrate the body, but it's "messier" than a blade penetration. Not only does a bullet create a puncture site, but a rifle bullet (the 5.56 x 45mm NATO for example), which exceeds supersonic speed at 500 yards, rotates at 3000 revolutions per second (rps). Once this spinning bullet hits a bone inside the body it can veer off into any direction, ripping everything along its path. A bullet entering the shoulder (the entrance wound) can hit a bone, instantly change direction, travel the length of the body, and go out of the heel of the foot (exit wound). Just hitting soft tissue alone can strip the full metal jacket from the lead core, causing fragmentation inside the body where the tiny shrapnel goes into separate directions.

I mentioned that rifle bullets travel at supersonic speed, and as such rifle bullets are more powerful than handgun bullets. Handgun bullets, traveling at subsonic speeds, have a lot of power, but nothing compared to a rifle bullet. The rifle bullet is literally creating a vacuum behind it as it travels through the air. When the bullet goes inside the body, so does a large volume of air with it. When the bullet exits the body, if it exits, then the air that was sucked into the body must go somewhere, and so it follows the bullet out. The result is a small entrance wound, and a huge exit wound. Whereas a handgun has a small entrance wound, and relatively the same size exit wound, provided the bullet did not enter at point blank range. However, if the rifle bullet is a hollow point (a bullet that opens up like an umbrella once it hits flesh), then you have a really nasty wound. Basically, you now have a circular saw ripping through the body at an extremely fast RPS.

There's one more thing that I'd like to add concerning ballistic wounds. Since a bullet has such a tremendous amount of energy when it penetrates the body, there is a temporary cavity that is formed in the body. In other words, all the tissue is instantly turned to mush, due to the sudden expansion and compression, then a permanent cavity remains, which is the actual channel made by the bullet.

During my career I have seen my share of knife wounds and bullet wounds on many people, and both are grisly and equally deadly. Therefore, in my mind, there is no difference between the lethality of a sword or a rifle. This is the reason I have no problem at all comparing the *sword of the Spirit* to the U.S. Army weapon.

Why did I use the word "weapon" instead of rifle? That's because in 1980 my drill sergeants drilled it into my head that the M16 A1 air-cooled, gas operated, magazine fed, cyclic rate of 900 rounds a minute, rifle with the effective range of 400 meters, was not a "gun," but a "weapon." Call it anything other than that, and the wrath of a drill sergeant would come down upon you.

When I trained U.S. Marine units for 9 years, the "Devil Dogs" also referred to the pistol and rifle as a "weapon." When I reenlisted in the military, serving just over 10 years the second time around, the pistol and rifle still were still referred to as a "weapon." So, for that span of 36 years I've referred to firearms as "weapons." It was deeply ingrained into me.

When I began my training to be a National Rifle Association (NRA) instructor, every one of my instructors said, "You can't use the word 'weapon.'"

Apparently, the word "weapon" had been deemed politically incorrect some time ago, as a result of the National Rifle Association having been under attack from the radical left for decades. Therefore, in order to better protect the Second Amendment of the United States Constitution, and not give the radical left any more ammunition (pun intended) than they already had, even vocabulary use by the organization is strictly enforced. One instructor charged me one dollar every time I said the word "weapon." By the end of every class, he'd always have enough for a good dinner.

For the NRA pistols, shotguns, and rifles are just that, pistols, shotguns, and rifles. That's because they teach a variety of ways to use them: target practice, sport shooting, hunting, and self-defense. Whereas a "weapon" is purely for self-defense.

For me personally, I revert back to the word "weapon," and that's because I use firearms for one purpose only – self-defense. As such, I also overlay the word "weapon" over the word "sword." Yet, I dare not actually change the Scripture, for that would be blasphemous.

So, a rifle is the modern version of a sword, and as such the *sword of the Spirit* should now have more meaning for you, because the comparison removes it from a purely historical context and puts it into practical use for today.

Yes, we staunch Christians all like the symbolism of the Medieval Crusader lifting his sword upside down in front of him with his gauntlet, having the sword appear in the shape of the cross. We're also fond of the chivalrous children's stories about knights in shining armor, thereby giving swords a certain nostalgia, but in a modern context, the lethal combat rifle helps us see the spiritual reality that we are facing today.

To complete Paul's metaphor we must now find the meaning of "Spirit," and its connection to the weapon.

The *sword of the Spirit* (Πνεύματος, pronounced pneu-matos) is none other than the Holy Spirit.

When the Old Testament was translated into Greek in the 3rd Century BC, known as the Septuagint, the word used for God's Spirit is Πνεῦμα (pneuma), which means "breath." In English we have the word "pneumatic," that means *operated by air.*

My lovely wife is Armenian, the country where Noah's ark came to rest on Mount Ararat after the Great Flood, and in the Armenian language the word for "Bible" is "Breath of God."

Do you remember how Adam was made, and how he came to life?

*And the Lord God formed man of the dust of the ground, and **breathed into his nostrils the breath of life;** and man became a living being. Genesis 2:7*

Fast forward to the beginning of the Christian church.

Then, the same day at evening, being the first day of the week, when the doors were shut where the disciples were assembled, for fear of the Jews, Jesus came and stood in the midst, and said to them, "Peace be with you." When He had said this, He showed them His hands and His side. Then the disciples were glad when they saw the Lord.

*So Jesus said to them again, "Peace to you! As the Father has sent Me, I also send you." And when He had said this, **He breathed on them, and said to them, "Receive the Holy Spirit.** If you forgive the sins of any, they are forgiven them; if you retain the sins of any, they are retained." John 20:19-23*

These two verses make it clear that God breathes the Holy Spirit into people who believe, and that the Bible, His Word, is God.

*In the beginning was the Word, and the Word was with God, and **the Word was God. He** was in the beginning with God. John 1:1-2*

Did you notice that? The Word is called a "He." The Word and the Holy Spirit are one in the same.

Whoa! That's incredible, because that means God is telling us to take up the most powerful weapon available to man – the *weapon of the Spirit.* The Holy Spirit is inside of us, and His power is locked and loaded in the Word – the Bible. *Heaven and earth will pass away, but My words will by no means pass away. Matthew 24:35*

The *weapon of the Spirit* in your possession is an offensive, indestructible, weapon. Yes, technically you can use the Word for defense, such as when you are ambushed by the enemy or someone is sniping at you, but that's what you have the *ballistic shield of faith* for – defense. To win the war the *weapon of the Spirit* is best used as an offensive weapon for those Christian Soldiers who have the guts enough to "take the hill." By "hill" I mean earth. And, by "earth" I don't mean the dirt that we came out of, but "the people of earth."

Our *weapon* is loaded with a lot of good, reliable *ammunition* for various situations, for both ministry and fellowship (witnessing to the lost and supporting the body of Christ). For the lost there are verses to bring them to the Lord either by fear or by love. Some people need to hear the former, while others need the latter. There are verses to comfort believers in times of celebration, and in times of mourning. There are verses to inform unbelievers about truth, such as the universe was created and not a result of billions of years of evolution, and verses to make believers turn away from the lure of false doctrine. There are verses about raising kids, and how to use money as a tool and not let it become your master. There are verses about holding your tongue to keep out of trouble, and verses you are to proclaim. Verses about when and how to have sex. Verses about a good work ethic. Verses about everything you need to know to live a victorious life, and to take the enemy's ground. Of course, Christians have a lot of "good" excuses as to why they don't pick up their weapon and fight.

"Take a knee," because I want to tell you a little story. No, I don't mean "take a knee" like those who disrespect the flag of the United States of America. Before all of that nonsense, military personnel took a knee out in the field when a leader was speaking to his troops, so that everyone could see and hear him or her clearly without Soldiers standing in the way. It was a sign of respect.

Okay, now that that's cleared up, I have another point-making story from my life, my life in the United States Army, to share with you.

One day, while on the shooting range, the Soldier next to me was just not hitting his computerized plastic human silhouette targets that were "killable," meaning they would fall once a 5.56mm bullet hit them, despite having received excellent training from the drill sergeants.

When the sergeant, who was standing over the Soldier's fighting hole, asked him, "What is your major malfunction private? Why aren't you hitting the targets?" The private responded, "It's gotta be the rifle sergeant."

Then the sergeant asked him loudly, "What is the effective range of an excuse?"

The private was a bit confused. He knew what the effective range of the M16A1 rifle was, but not an excuse? He had never heard such a question before. I was curious as to what the answer was as well.

Seeing the private dumbfounded, the sergeant barked out, "Zero meters! Zero meters private! Stop making excuses and follow the steps we taught you!"

However, the sergeant didn't just leave it at just a tongue lashing. He patiently took the time to correct the Soldier's mistakes, and eventually the Soldier started hitting some of the targets.

Although those words were not directed toward me, that question, and the sergeant's response, influenced me greatly. For certain situations there are no excuses. And, for Christian Soldiers there are no excuses not to share the Gospel to the lost, and not to fellowship with the brethren. These are orders from our Commander in Chief. So, remember that, "Zero meters!"

That doesn't mean that everyone is going to be equal when it comes to shooting their weapon. The Soldier on my left, when it came time for rifle qualification, did pass the test. He didn't hit all of the targets, especially those the furthest away, but he did his best. When it came time for receiving the U.S. Army Weapons Qualification Badge, the private earned the Marksmanship Weapons Qualification Badge.

There are three Weapons Qualification Badges, which are worn on the dress uniform over the left pocket, and from the highest medal to the lowest they are: Expert, Sharpshooter, and Marksmanship.

What did you earn Jim? You're probably thinking.

That's a fair question.

I earned the United States Army Expert Weapons Qualification Badge. Both in the military, and in law enforcement, every time I tested, I achieved Expert. That's because I have always taken my firearms training seriously, and from day one I took the large metal sign at the entrance of the rifle range at Basic Combat Training to heart. The sign I'm talking about had a silk-screened illustration of the Expert Marksmanship Badge, and a quote from President Theodore Roosevelt, who prior to his presidency was a colonel in the United States Army having fought in the Spanish-American War. The quote was, "In battle, the only bullets that count are those that hit. A soldier who cannot shoot is a soldier who counts for little in battle."

Hitting a target in battle is not just picking up a weapon for the first time and firing at the enemy. In the U.S. Army the first step to learning about one's rifle starts with classroom instructions: the nomenclature of the weapon, ballistics, care and maintenance.

Next is learning how to safely handle the weapon. How to lock back the bolt to make sure the chamber is empty. How to insert a magazine into it and release it. How to flip the selector switch from SAFE to FIRE to FULL automatic, and back again. Many hours include field stripping the weapon, which means taking it apart for cleaning, and then reassembling it again; sometimes while being timed.

Then comes the moment that every Soldier had been anxiously waiting for, and that is going onto the live-fire range and actually firing the weapon. It's quite a thrill for the first time to be able to control all that fire power in one's own hands, while at the same time giving a healthy respect for its destructive power. However, going to the rifle range for the first time is not just flipping the selector switch to FULL and spraying the bullets at anything that's downrange for the fun of it. The first bullets to leave the weapon are to "zero" it, which means adjusting the front and rear sights in order to have the correct aim point. It's a rather lengthy process the drill sergeants take you through, but at least it's still an opportunity to shoot.

Once the weapon is zeroed, then comes getting into all of the shooting positions: standing, kneeling, sitting, and prone (lying on one's stomach while firing the weapon), and lots of "throwing lead down range."

However, marksmanship alone is not enough to be fully ready to engage the enemy. The next phase of training are combat simulations with the weapon shooting at role players. Obviously, it's not possible to shoot real bullets at the mock Opposing Force (OPFOR), but with today's technology it's possible to shoot plastic bullets at low velocity that leave a colored soap mark upon impact.

One of the questions a new Soldier is asked by a firearms instructor after he or she has learned how to use their weapon effectively is, "Soldier, are you willing to shoot and kill the enemy?"

I was asked this very question just before my last live-fire session in Basic Combat Training. This particular rifle training was purposely inserted towards the end of the war games while surrounded with the stark reality of warfare: a realistic battlefield with battle damaged buildings and overturned vehicles, role players that wore authentic enemy uniforms and used AK-47s as their primary weapon, using blanks of course, and explosions throughout the day and night. All the sights, sounds, and smells were there – minus death.

I remember that moment as if it were yesterday. It was lightly raining, and inside the muddy sandbag lined trench the sergeant was blocking my path that led to the small live-fire range that could accommodate no more than six soldiers at a time. Dressed in full combat gear underneath my rain poncho, as he looked at my wet and cold camouflage painted face, I answered him without hesitation, "Yes, I am sergeant!"

He looked at me, smiled, and then said, "Good. Keep moving forward." He then blocked the path of the next Soldier and repeated the process.

A few minutes later I was given two loaded magazines by the range staff, and was told, "Every fifth round is a tracer." This is a bullet that leaves a colorful fluorescent illuminated trail, some red, some green, that looks like a laser shot from a laser gun like in a Sci-Fi movie. In addition, this was not the typical rifle range that they had me on before, but the computerized plastic human shaped 3D targets, painted with a face and hands that held an AK-47, popped up from behind sandbags or along the tree line 70 to 300 meters out to add to the realism.

You remember how I stated that law enforcement is a paramilitary organization. Well, here's a parallel example of that Army experience. A decade later I was sitting in the Briefing Room down in the basement of the Costa Mesa Police Department. The sergeant, an "old salt," giving the briefing decided to ask every police officer around the large square table the same question. There were seven of us that evening. He started with the officer closest to him, and asked, "Williams, if you had to shoot someone on duty, would you do it?"

Williams answered, "Yes."

The sergeant asked the next officer, and then the next. I was halfway around the table, and he asked me the same question, "Wagner, if you had to shoot someone on duty, would you do it?"

"Yes sergeant," was my reply. For me it was a no brainer.

Then he came to 16-year police veteran Officer, well, let's just call him Officer Bill Jones to protect his real identity.

"Officer Jones, if you had to shoot someone on duty, would you do it?"

He answered, "No."

A few men chuckled. It had to be a joke.

The sergeant asked the question again, and Officer Jones answered, "No. No, I wouldn't."

We all looked at him in shock, and I'm sure the thoughts in everyone's heads were the same as mine. *What if I am in trouble out there, and my life depends on Bill? He's not going to shoot the suspect! Unbelievable!*

Well, needless to say, from that day forward nobody ever trusted Officer Jones again, and as I recall, I don't remember him out on the streets after that briefing. A desk job was better suited for him.

Sadly, many "Christian Soldiers" are just like Officer Bill Jones, even if they have been a Christian for many years. They don't want to "shoot" the enemy – the devil and his minions. Such a Christian Soldier, using Theodore Roosevelt's quote, "who cannot shoot is a soldier who counts for little in battle." Oh sure, they count "a little," but they are better off *in the rear with the gear,* or behind a desk somewhere. Those on the front line all need to be brave souls picking off the enemy.

This brings up a good question for you. "Are you willing to shoot someone to protect yourself or a loved one?"

I don't mean spiritually, I mean physically. It doesn't have to be a gun, because perhaps you don't own one or you are not allowed to have one for legal reasons. So, replace the firearm with a knife, baseball bat, or whatever. So, with these items in mind, let me ask the question once again, "Are you willing to kill someone to protect yourself or a loved one?"

This is the question I ask to all my self-defense students when I am teaching. I've asked this question to thousands of people over the years.

In every class there are some who say that they wouldn't kill someone in self-defense. Well, legally the intent, when it comes to the use-of-force in the United States, is to "stop" someone, even if you're armed with a firearm. Unfortunately, sometimes stopping an attacker results in killing him or her, but you get the gist. So, again, the question to you is, "Would you 'stop' a person trying to seriously harm or kill you, or protect someone you care about who is next to you?"

It's a simple YES or NO answer.

First of all, a normal person has no desire to take the life of another, not even that of an enemy. Only a sadistic or demon possessed person would take satisfaction in taking a human life.

We, who are made in the image of God, have a conscience that tells us not to murder, and "murder" being defined as *the crime of unlawfully killing a person especially with malice.*

The seventh commandment, of God's Ten Commandments, states, "You shall not murder." The Hebrew interlinear is תרצח לא *Not, you shall murder.*

Therefore, there is unlawful killing, which is murder, and lawful killing. Cain murdering his brother was murder. Moses murdering an Egyptian task master for beating a Hebrew slave was murder. God killing all the first born of the Egyptian people and animals was justifiable homicide, not murder. General Joshua and the Israelite Army wiping out all the people of Jericho, except Rehab and her family, was warfare ordained by God, thus justifiable homicide, not murder. In the New Testament Ananias and his wife Sapphira were killed by the Holy Spirit for lying to God (Acts chapter 5).

When Jesus Christ comes back to earth, riding upon His white horse, here's what happens to those who are in rebellion against Him.

WARNING: THIS SCRIPTURE CONTAINS GRAPHIC DESCRIPTIONS THAT MAY BE DISTURBING TO SOME CHRISTIAN READERS.

Note: The words in parenthesis are my own comments.

And I saw the beast (the Antichrist), the kings of the earth, and their armies, gathered together to make war against Him (our Commander in Chief) who sat on the horse and against His army (that's us, his Christian Soldiers).

*Then the beast was captured, and with him the false prophet (the one who headed up a false world religion) who worked signs in his presence, by which he deceived those who received the mark of the beast (warn your unbelieving family and friends to never take the mark or there is no possibility of ever being saved) and those who worshipped his image (American idol). These two were cast alive into the lake of fire burning with brimstone (a literal place, not figurative). And **the rest were killed with the sword which proceeded from the mouth of Him** who sat on the horse (they are justifiably killed as enemy combatants, not murdered). And all the birds were filled with their flesh (the men and women who had fought against our Lord do not receive a proper burial, which is a privilege). Revelation 19:19-21*

So, as you just read in this passage, it was justifiable homicide by God. Plus, I find it rather interesting that "the sword which proceeded from the mouth of Him" kills His enemies. From His mouth is both the *breath of life,* and also a *sword* that kills.

Wait a second! What happened to Satan? Isn't he part of the unholy trinity? Satan, the dragon, the snake, whatever you want to call him. Why wasn't he also cast alive into the lake of fire with the beast and the false prophet in our study verse? Well, that's because Satan is spared for one last battle, the last battle in angelic and human history, and you can read all about it yourself in Revelation chapter 20. I won't go into all the details here, but in a nutshell, after 1,000 years of Christ, and us, reigning and ruling on the restored earth, which will be an absolute paradise, Satan is let loose from his "prison," and some very stupid men and women, "whose number is as the sand of the sea," who never knew the horrors of the former earth, are deceived by this liar and they get duped into gathering together

PUT ON THE FULL COMBAT GEAR OF GOD

for battle against God and His saints.

The battle is over just as fast as it began, *"And fire came down from God out of heaven and devoured them. The devil, who deceived them, was cast into the lake of fire and brimstone where the beast and false prophet are. And they were tormented day and night forever and ever." Revelation 20:9-10*

So, yes, the God of the Old Testament and the God of the New Testament are the same God. He is a God of love in both covenants, and He is a Warrior King in both covenants as well. He heals, restores, and yet kills to protect His own and apply justice. The good thing for us is that He is also our Father, our daddy, *Abba.* His *sword* will never be used against us.

As we have discovered, the *sword of the Spirit* does indeed kill. It does not murder, but it justifiably, and righteously, kills both evil men and spirits.

This brings us to our next question. We know that God is holy, and He can do whatever He wants, however, "Is it a sin for a Christian to physically kill another person?"

The answer is "no," as long as it is justifiable and there is no other alternative. Did not Jesus say to His disciples, *"But now, he who has a money bag, let him take it, and likewise a knapsack; **and who has no sword, let him sell his garment and buy one.**" Luke 22:36*

One cannot buy the Holy Spirit, so the "sword" that Jesus was talking about is a physical sword for stabbing and cutting. Apparently, Peter did exactly as he was told, for in the Garden of Gethsemane ***Peter, having a sword,*** *drew it and struck the high priest's servant, and cut off his right ear. The servant's name was Malchus. John 18:10*

That was a pretty good-sized blade Peter must have had, because it severed Malchus' ear from the side of his head. I'm sure Peter was aiming to split the guy's head in two, but Malchus moved off line just enough to avoid a fatal blow.

So Jesus said to Peter, "Put your sword into the sheath." John 18:11

Jesus didn't ask Peter in horror, "What are you doing with a sword? This is a nonviolent movement I've been leading. Get rid of it!"

No, it was Jesus that told His disciples to go out and buy a μάχαιρα (pronounced mak-air-ah), the ancient Greek generic name for a sword, if they didn't own one. Peter not only purchased a μάχαιραν, sword, but the whole kit, which included a sheath. He was into tactical gear.

Although Peter gets a bad rap by a lot of preachers over the centuries for pulling his sword and using it to defend Jesus, I don't believe Peter did anything wrong. Jesus is God, and Peter was fighting for God. The problem was not Peter's action, only the timing. *So Jesus said to Peter, "Put your sword into the sheath. Shall I not drink the cup which My Father has given Me?" John 18:11*

Jesus had to be arrested and go to the cross in order to fulfill His purpose on earth. Peter was told this earlier, but he didn't understand what Jesus meant. The disciples believed that they were about to overthrow the Roman government, and usher in a righteous government ordained by God. Therefore, Peter wasn't about to let enemy soldiers take the very Leader, the Messiah, who was going to kick the Romans out of the Holy Land, even if that meant taking on the whole arresting army himself.

The book of Matthew gives us more information on this sword incident:

But Jesus said to him, "Put your sword in its place, for all who take the sword will perish by the sword. Or do you think that I cannot now pray to My Father, and He will provide Me with more than twelve legions of angels. **How then could the Scripture be fulfilled, that it must happen thus?"** *Matthew 26:52-54*

When killing is not God's will, then it's of *the flesh*. When killing is His will then it is of *the Spirit*.

You may be thinking, *Whoa! Aren't you reading a bit much into this Scripture Master Sergeant Wagner?*

Am I? Let's take a look at another example.

General Joshua was told by God to cross the Jordan River and kill every single enemy: men, women, and children. They did it to the inhabitants of Jericho, and it was time to move onto the next military target. God wanted them to take and destroy the Amorite city of Ai.

However, there was sin in the Israelite camp, and when the Israelite spies returned from their reconnaissance of Ai they reported to General Joshua, *Do not let all the people go up, but let about two or three thousand men go up and attack Ai. Do not weary all the people there, for the people of Ai are few." Joshua 7:3*

Well, the Israelites got their butts kicked, and *the hearts of the people melted and became like water. Joshua 7:5*

Once Joshua dealt with the sin that was in the camp, and got the people's heart right with God again, the next time the Israelite Army went against the Ai Army they were victorious, *And it came to pass when Israel had made an end of **slaying all the inhabitants** of Ai in the field, in the wilderness where they pursued them, and when they had fallen **by the edge of the sword until they were consumed,** that all the Israelites returned to Ai and struck it with the edge of the sword. So it was that all who fell that day, both men and women, were twelve thousand – **all the people of Ai.** For Joshua did not draw back his hand, with which he stretched out the spear, **until he had utterly destroyed all the inhabitants** of Ai. Joshua 8:24-26*

The first battle against Ai was not God's will. Yes, He wanted them to destroy the city of Ai, because that was part of God's original plan, but not until His people dealt with their sin first. The second battle, killing all the inhabitants of Ai, was God's will, and because the people's hearts were right with Him, God gave them victory.

In Peter's case, in the Garden of Gethsemane, going into physical combat mode was not God's will. If it had been time for physical combat, at the moment just before Jesus' arrest, He would have called upon the Father to provide "more than twelve legions of angels," and that's a lot of hard-core warrior angels who wouldn't hesitate to go on the offensive. Talk about "shock and awe!" One Roman legion is 5,200 infantry soldiers, 300 cavalry soldiers, and 120 auxiliary soldiers. So, that's 5,620 angels in one legion x 12 = 67,440 angels, and Jesus said that He could summon "more than twelve" legions.

To give you an idea of just how powerful a single angel is, sometime before 609 BC *the angel of the Lord went out, and killed in the camp of the Assyrians 185,000, and when people arose early in the morning, there were the corpses – all dead. Isaiah 37:36*

If one angel can slaughter the entire population equal to that of all those who currently live in Knoxville, Tennessee in one night, then imagine what more than 67,440 angels could do to the whole planet. If Jesus had wanted rescuing, He could have called for it. In fact, if Jesus wanted to just walk out of there on His own, right through their midst, like He had done in His hometown of Nazareth when the crowd wanted to "throw Him down over the cliff," He could have. Although Peter was certainly courageous for try-ing to take on a small army in the Garden of Gethsemane, Jesus didn't want his help. He was there for *"Glory to God in the highest, and on earth peace, goodwill toward men!"* That included goodwill even to the evil men that wanted to arrest and harm Him.

I'm sure Peter was a little more than confused when Jesus told Him to stop. He was told to go out and buy a sword, and then when he uses it to protect the very Man who told him to buy it, he is told to *stand down*.

Just hours before he pulled his sword from its sheath, Peter had eaten the Passover meal with Jesus, and Peter said to Him, *"Even if I have to die with you, I will not deny You!" Matthew 26:35*

Peter was indeed willing to die with Jesus, but only in battle. The very fact that Peter pulls a sword, as a small army is closing in on Jesus, indicates that he was indeed willing to die with Jesus, just as he said he would. That was one brave man. Any rational man knows that when you pull a sword on a multitude of armed men that you're not going to make it out alive, and if you do survive, then it could only be by the Hand of God. However, Peter was not willing to die with Jesus under a different set of circumstances, at least not on that night. He was not willing to be taken prisoner by the Romans, and possibly executed, for a leader he saw just give up on the cause hours earlier. It was at this time Peter denied Jesus three times before the rooster crowed.

You must be thinking, *How do you know it was a "small army" that Peter went up against?*

I know, because the Greek word used, for those who came to arrest Jesus, is ὄχλοις (pronounced oak-lo-is), which translates "crowds" or "multitudes."

It wasn't just a few Temple Guardsmen (the precursor to today's church security) that came to arrest Jesus in the dark of night, as depicted in Mel Gibson's 2004 movie *The Passion of the Christ,* but it was a whole lot of armed men who expected a fight with Jesus and his disciples. The Scriptures state, *In that hour Jesus said to **the multitudes,** "Have you come out, as against a robber, **with swords and clubs to take Me?** I sat daily with you, teaching in the temple, and you did not seize Me. But all this was done that the Scriptures of the prophets might be fulfilled." Then all the disciples forsook Him and fled. Matthew 26:55*

The Jewish Temple Guard, a paramilitary organization, most likely had gathered a posse, as indicated by the fact that some of the men were armed with inferior weapons - "clubs."

So, there's your answer. If you're going to use injuring or deadly force, it has to be God's will. Protecting yourself or a loved one from serious injury or death is justifiable homicide. A police officer that is fired upon by a suspect is justified to return fire until the threat is stopped. A hostage taker about to slit a hostage's throat has forfeited his right to life, thereby

229

giving the police sniper "the green light." There are many circumstances to justify killing another human being. This is why I believe that all able-bodied Christians had better wake up and start learning physical self-defense. That's right! You read it correctly.

I know some of the Christians reading this are freaking out right now, as if I am now going to use the sword metaphor to justify owning guns, and God forbid, even actually using them! So, before some of you close the book, in fear that you are being sucked into some right-wing Christian militia cult of some sort, hear me out. Or, "read me out."

I always tell my beginning self-defense students, "If you're not physically ready for a fight, then you're not mentally prepared for a fight."

Let me explain.

The very first self-defense lesson I teach to my civilian students is not how to punch or kick, but the Threat Zones. I allow only friends and family into my Red Zone (touching distance). For professional or social distance, I keep them in my Orange Zone (a fully extended arm's length away). For people I don't know, or don't trust, which I call "unknowns," they're in my Yellow Zone (a minimum of a full step away, and as far as I can see or hear).

In my Defensive Tactics course, to illustrate these three different zones, I set up realistic scenarios for each using two students. When I begin the Yellow Zone scenario, I have one student, playing the role of the victim, pretend that he or she is filling up their car at a gas station. Then an unknown, the second student role player, walks up to the person getting gas, and asks him or her, "Could you give me a ride? I'll go as far as you can take me, and any direction you go is fine with me. I just need to get out of town."

Most students, playing the role of the victim, continue to hold the gas pump handle while telling the unknown that he or she will not be given a ride. Yet, while talking to the unknown they do not attempt to adjust their body position at all.

Having set up this scenario thousands of times before, I know human nature and cultural habits very well, and almost everyone reacts in the same predictable manner. After the scenario is over, I ask the victim a series of questions, "Why did you keep your hand on the pump when the unknown approached you? Why did you keep your back to the car, which kept you trapped in a confined space? Why were your hands down, and not protecting your upper body?"

I educate the student, "If he would have tried to punch you, or he pulled a knife to cut your throat, his action would have been faster than your reaction. This tells me that since you were not physically ready for an attack, then you were not mentally prepared for an attack. If you had really been mentally prepared for an attack, then you would have positioned your body tactically."

To correct my students' bad habits, which they never realized they had, and this often includes many black belts, I instruct them how to get into the Alert Stance whenever they come face to face with an unknown, and then how to move from that stance into the Imminent Conflict Stance if an attack is suddenly launched against them. Once they see the easy techniques and tactics, only then do they "see" the truth of combat, and they never have a problem with managing the Threat Zone distances again.

I have learned over the years that Threat Zones also apply to Christians. Thus, I tell my beginning church security students, which also applies to all Christians, "If you're not physically ready for a fight, then you're not mentally prepared for a fight. If you're not mentally prepared for a fight, then you're not spiritually ready for a fight."

Let me explain.

Many Christians fancy themselves as "Christian Soldiers," when in fact, they are, what I call, "terracotta warriors." I'm referring to the thousands of terracotta soldiers found buried with Chinese Emperor Qin Shi Huang (259–210 BC). All of the life-size clay figures look fierce, all decked out in their ancient armor, but they don't actually fight, and any pressure will make them crack.

It is very easy for someone to say that they are "fighting" the devil and his minions, but, like James said, *Show me your faith without works, and I will show you my faith by my works. James 2:18*

In other words, *You talk the talk, but do you walk the walk?*

If someone was trying to kidnap a child, a child you don't even know, by pulling them off the sidewalk and shoving them into a car, would you physically try to stop the kidnapper? Is that not evil happening in your presence?

If a group of youth were beating up an old man or an old woman, just for the sport of it, would you try to stop them physically? Or, do you just pray?

If somewhere were to kick in your front door to do a home invasion, would you hop off of the couch, go arm yourself, and then "go Medieval on him," or just sit there and pray? Is not *faith by works* required at this time? Wouldn't refusing to physically and mentally resist a violent human being, who is obviously controlled by his evil flesh or under the influence of an evil spirit, be *faith without works*?

Some of you are thinking, *Oh, but I could get hurt or killed if I engage in physical combat!*

No kidding! Then how about something a little less physical, where you won't risk physical injury?

Answer this then. "Are you tithing to your church regularly, like the Lord requires?" (Malachi 3:10). "Are you even attending church regularly?"

"Are you helping the poor?" (Proverbs 22:9)

"Are you visiting orphans and widows in their trouble?" (James 1:27)

How about a real no brainer, like, "Are you even helping fellow Christians in their times of need?" (Romans 12:13, Luke 3:10-11, and Hebrews 13:16)

VIRTUAL REALITY vs. PHYSICAL REALITY

My nephew Gary was really into first-person video games when growing up. Those are video games where the player is actually doing the "shoot-ing." On the screen you can see your virtual arms holding the weapon on the screen or through the virtual reality headgear, and you can fire the weapon at will. Gary's favorite genre of video games was as a warrior, and it didn't matter what type of conflict either. He enjoyed being a samurai warrior slashing away with a sword just as much as being a Soldier on a modern battlefield firing bullets from a weapons and tossing hand grenades.

From these video games he had quite a virtual education, and he could tell you all about various firearms. He knew the difference between an M4 rifle and the enemy's AK-47. He also knew all of the shooting positions and combat movements. I also bought him an M4 Airsoft rifle and M9 pistol, both of which fired a 6 mm plastic projectile, and we'd go out to his backyard and I would teach him military tactics. I figured, *His father,* my brother-in-law, *was allowing him to play these "shoot 'em up games" anyway, so why not teach him the real techniques and tactics, and use the time as a teaching opportunity where I could interject the physical and moral responsibility of human conflict?* Many kids get their minds warped with these types of video games, because there is no adult supervision to give them proper guidance or put things into the proper context.

When Gary was finally old enough, and mature enough, to go out onto a real gun range with me, I told him that I would "shadow" him very closely, which means to be practically on top of him to be able to jump in at any second in case he made a mistake. He said to me, "Uncle Jim, I know how to use this pistol. I've used it many times before in my video game."

I chuckled at his naivete, and responded, "Well, firing a real gun is a lot different than a plastic video game gun or even an Airsoft gun. Let me stay close to you until I know that you can handle it."

After the first shot went off, I had to lean in suddenly and grab his arm to force him to keep the muzzle pointed down range. He did what a lot of beginners did. He got startled when the fire, noise, and recoil occurred, which

233

was scarier than he thought. This broke his concentration, and so he failed to follow through (maintaining good aim on the target to be able to take a second shot).

Gary knew at that very moment, when I grabbed his arm, that I was right. Not only that, but I could also tell that he was extremely nervous, which he hadn't been before the shot was taken, when it came time to take the second shot. He realized, for the first time in his life, through an actual physical experience, that the pistol was a deadly weapon that could hurt him. Before that, it was all fun and games. He received a good dose of reality.

Well, after a few more shots down rage at a human silhouette target, Gary relaxed, and I was able to back off a bit. Over the years he has become quite proficient in the use of pistols, shotguns, and assault rifles.

Now that I've made the comparison between virtual reality and physical reality, let's now take a look at spiritual reality.

A lot of "Sunday Warriors," think they have their spiritual life in order, and see themselves as hard-core Christian Soldiers, because they go to church on Sunday to get fed the Word, and then go about their "civilian life" until the following Sunday. That's the extent of their involvement in the "war." Yes, it's good that they show up to the "base" for the "Intelligence report" once a week, but very few church-going Christians are involved in the two "missions," the actual "combat" the Commander in Chief ordered them to do, which are **ministry** and **fellowship.**

Ministry is witnessing to the lost, thus the reason you were issued the *combat boots of the Gospel of peace.* Yet, many Christian organizations that have taken polls reveal that most Christians do not try to lead people to the Lord.

I saw a bumper sticker once that read, HOW MANY PEOPLE WILL BE IN HEAVEN BECAUSE OF YOU? That really hit me hard, because it is so true. Obviously, we don't have the ability to save a single soul, for only the Holy Spirit can do that, but we can certainly be the instrument God uses to save souls. I'd like to be in heaven and see some people that are there because I obeyed God's commandant, and I wore out my *combat boots of the Gospel of Peace* doing it.

The second mission is **fellowship,** which is strengthening or assisting fellow believers. It can be a Bible study or prayer meeting with just one other person. *For where two or three are gathered together in My name, I am there in the midst of them. Matthew 18:20* That's not just a metaphor, but God is literally in it.

Fellowship also includes serving in the church: as a greeter, in the nursery, as an usher, a parking lot attendant, picking up trash on the grounds, or my personal favorite – church security.

If you are a "wounded warrior," unable to leave your home, you can still have a ministry or be in fellowship with today's technology. Even if you are in a prison cell with no technology you can witness to the guards, and fellowship with those who have come to the Lord. Paul certainly did.

I wrote this book, because this is one of the ways I can fellowship. I want to help train you up as a Christian Soldier.

Now for the opposite. When you're not training on a "spiritual live-fire training range," or engaged in actual physical or spiritual combat where the wicked one is firing wounding or lethal *fiery darts* at you, then your Christian walk is essentially "theory," which is kind of like being immersed in virtual reality. It's easy to read about David slaying Goliath, but it's quite another thing facing today's "giants:" the giant who will publicly ridicule you for your Christian faith, the cancel culture giant who will "cancel" you for declaring Biblical truth, or the giant who tries to convince you that it is best for everyone to erase the country's Judeo-Christian history and foundation.

It's easy for the non-warrior to think or say, "Why didn't the Israelites trust God completely when the Red Sea was at their backs and Pharaoh's army was coming toward them on chariots at full speed from the opposite side? I would've been strong," but it's quite another thing when you experience financial hardship or health problems. It's easy for the non-risk takers to read about the 1st Century church, and what's happening in many foreign countries today in having to deal with religious persecution, but it's quite another thing when you see it with your own eyes with the increasing persecution against the Jews and Christians in the United States of America. To make matters worse, despite the signs of the times, it's astonishing to hear believers make the statement, "The American church will not have to go underground. At least not for a long time," as if somehow God is obligated to spare the United States of America of hardships despite its headlong plunge into paganism and all kinds of vile practices.

The only way you're going to stay strong in these trying times is to *Trust in the Lord with all your heart, and **lean not on your own understanding;** Proverbs 3:5* Therefore, once again, strap on and take up your "full combat gear." Your *patrol belt of truth* keeps you centered with a Biblical worldview, your *body armor of righteousness* keeps you right with God and man. Your *combat boots of the Gospel of Peace* are how you take the enemy's ground. Your *ballistic shield of faith* blocks the heavy frontal assaults as well as the sniping attacks the enemy throws at you, and your *helmet of salvation* protects your very thoughts – the location of your memories, your knowledge, your intellect, and your reasoning abilities. It's not just your physical brain that a helmet protects, but your "software" that is somehow embedded among all that gray matter and electrical signals.

Don't just tell people, or even yourself, what a great Christian Soldier you are. Be it! Pick up your *weapon of the Spirit* and fight. Select a target and fire! Stop the enemy from advancing. He's taking over our schools, sports, the medical community, our companies, our governments, and even our churches with false doctrines. It's a target rich battleground, if only you would get into the fight.

You know exactly what is required of you. And, if you don't know, either because you're a new believer or you've been living the Christian "civilian" life for way too long, just "Get it and go! Get it and go!"

That's what military sergeants bark out all of the time, only in a deep guttural, almost indistinguishable, way, "Get it and go!"

Get what, and go where? You may be thinking.

Well, for Christian Soldiers it can only mean one thing. **Get** your nose back into the Field Manuals – the Word of God, the *weapon of the Spirit.*

*"**Go** therefore and make disciples of all the nations, baptizing them in the name of the Father and of the Son and of the Holy Spirit, teaching them to observe all things I have commanded you; and lo, I am with you always, even to the end of the age." Amen. Matthew 28:19-20*

It doesn't get any simpler than that.

Congratulations Christian Soldier! You now have your full battle rattle, your *full combat gear of God.* You are a lean, mean, fighting machine! However, before you are deployed to war, you need to know the enemies that you will be fighting.

Just as U.S. Army Soldiers were given the "Soldier's Handbook No. 07-15" before stepping foot on Iraqi or Afghan soil, that prepared them as to what they could expect during "The First 100 Days" in country, so will you be presented with the "Christian Soldier's Handbook No. 11," as in Chapter 11, the next chapter you'll be reading, that will prepare you for what to expect during "the last days."

*But know this, that in **the last days** perilous times will come: For men will be lovers of themselves, lovers of money, boasters, proud, blasphemers, disobedient to parents, unthankful, unholy, unloving, unforgiving, slanderers, without self-control, brutal, despisers of good, traitors, headstrong, haughty, lovers of pleasures than lovers of God, having a form of godliness but denying its power. And from such people turn away!*

These all read like headlines from recent news stories. That's because they're all an accurate description of the United States of America today. The paragraph is 2 Timothy 3:1-5, but they might as well be today's news headlines.

This is what a rifle bullet can do inside a human body. It is a substance called ballistic gel, the consistancy of human flesh, for testing bullets.

American Soldiers must not only be proficent with their weapons, but they must master many tactics with them to defeat their enemies.

Soldiers must take a yearly qualification test with their weapons. Shooting is a perishable skill, and constant practice is necessary.

Many police departments in the country have a monthly firearms qualification test, which is far better than just once a year.

Of course, the enemy practices with their weapons as well. Sometimes the bad guys have more firepower than some of the the good guys do.

To stand against criminals with heavy firepower, law enforcement is armed accordingly. Christian Soldiers have the ultimate "firepower."

As more and more churches are attacked physically, they too must have more firepower where permitted by law. If they don't, then...

If a church is ready for physical attacks against their congregation, then they are also ready for spiritual attacks. Satan attacks both ways.

Your *weapon of the Spirit* has unlimited "ammunition," so use it! There is no reason to conserve prayers. So, "open fire" on the devil.

COMBAT GEAR OF THE ENEMIES

...for wide is the gate and broad is the way that leads to destruction,
and there are many who go in by it. Matthew 7:13

HELMET
OF DAMNATION

BODY ARMOR
OF UNRIGHTEOUSNESS

WEAPON
OF
ANTICHRIST

BATTLE BELT
OF LIES

SHIELD
OF UNBELIEF IN JESUS

THE 3 ENEMIES & WAR STRATEGY EQUATION

THE DEVIL

THE WORLD

THE FLESH

FIRST ATTEMPT AT
A ONE WORLD
GOVERNMENT
& RELIGION
WITHOUT GOD
(TOWER OF BABEL)

$+ t = 666$

THE COMING
ONE WORLD
GOVERNMENT,
ECONOMY,
& RELIGION
WITHOUT GOD

666

COMBAT BOOTS
OF CONFUSION

© JIM WAGNER

244

Chapter 11

COMBAT GEAR OF THE ENEMIES

Christian Soldier's Handbook No. 11

Although Paul did not take the time, nor was given the divine inspiration, to label the pieces of armor that the enemies wear, we are able to easily determine what kind of body armor they are wearing and the type of war equipment they use. "They," being **the flesh, the world,** and **the devil.** If you want to know exactly what the enemies have, or what they will do with it, the rule of thumb is to compare it to God's nature and His Word. The enemies are always the opposite.

Before we start examining their armor and equipment, I want to share with you something I learned while I was attending the police academy, the Orange County Sheriff's Training Academy in Southern California.

One of the academy instructors taught my class, the twenty-one men of Class 104, all about counterfeit money. Since the United States dollar was the world's reserve currency, American bills were the most counterfeited legal tender in the world.

The approach that the instructor took was to have us first study intensely real American currency. He taught us all about the printing process, the type of cloth that the bills were printed on, the –

That's right! American bills are not made of paper, but 75% cotton and 25% linen, and that's so they will last for a minimum of 6.6 years for the One Dollar bill, and 22.9 years for the One Hundred Dollar bill.

He had us hold the bills up to the fluorescent lights in the ceiling above us to see the watermarks to the right of the portrait and examine the embedded security thread woven into the cloth. He told us, "In order for you to detect a counterfeit bill, you must first know everything about real money."

His words resonated with me, and I realized that it was the very same method for being able to detect counterfeit religions or Christian cults. First you must know everything in the Bible, the full counsel of God, and then you will be able to recognize the lies of the enemy - *the devil.* Of course, this is why many Christians stumble in life, and that's exactly why Timothy urges us:

*Remind them of these things, charging them before the Lord **not to strive about words to no profit,** to ruin the hearers. Be diligent to present yourself approved to God, a worker who does not need to be ashamed, **rightly dividing the word** of truth. 2 Timothy 2:15*

Here's another phrase that Old English doesn't quite have the same "punch" to it as it does in the original Greek, and that is "rightly dividing." The Greek word used it ὀρθοτομοῦντα, (pronounced ortho-tom-oon-ta), which means *accurately handling.* Well, that definition makes more sense to us warriors.

Remember from the last chapter, that our weapon is the *weapon of the Spirit,* and the Holy Spirit and the Word are one in the same. Therefore, we don't "rightly divide" our weapon, but we certainly "accurately handle" it.

To accurately handle our weapon, we must know our Bible inside and out. Then, whatever God declares, we know that the enemies will be the direct opposite. Oh sure, the enemy will oftentimes cloak the lies with some truth, but how much of a meal would you be willing to eat if you knew there was just a single drop of arsenic in it?

The flesh tells us that "fornication (sex outside of marriage between one man and one woman) is not harmful," but God tells us that unrepentant fornicators *will not inherit the kingdom of God. 1 Corinthians 6:10*

The world tells us that "it's not a baby," but "just fetal tissue" until it takes its first breath, and even weeks afterwards, but God tells us, *Before I* *formed you in the womb* I *knew you, Jeremiah 1:5* which means each one of us was a person before the womb, in the womb, and after the womb.

The devil told our original parents, in the Garden of Eden, *"You will not surely die." Genesis 3:4* and there has been pain, suffering, and death ever since the moment they believed his lie.

Now, let's make a side-by-side comparison of our *full combat gear of God* with that of the enemies.

THE ENEMIES' PATROL BELT

We Christian Soldiers start by putting on the *patrol belt of truth,* which not only shapes our worldview, but it even exposes our own sinful nature to ourselves. Our three enemies' wear a *patrol belt of lies.*

What does our Commander in Chief say about lying? Well, He is crystal clear about His position. *There are six things the Lord hates, yes, seven are an abomination to Him: a proud look,* **a lying tongue,** *hands that shed inno-cent blood, a heart that devises wicked plans, feet that are swift in running to evil,* **a false witness who speaks lies,** *and one who sows discord among brethren. Proverbs 6:16-19*

Since most people are living the lie, and not "living the dream" as the popular secular saying goes, it is imperative that we speak truth to the world, that we are not deceived by our fleshly desires, and that we ignore *the devil* altogether, since there is no hope for him.

Don't forget, *the devil* was the first creature to tell a lie, and those who are not of God are like him. Jesus made this very clear when He rebuked some Pharisees, who were supposed to have been servants of God, but who in fact were self-deceived, *You are of your father the devil, and the desires of your father you want to do. He was a murderer from the beginning, and does not stand in truth, because there is no truth in him. When he speaks a lie, he speaks from his own resources,* **for he is a liar and the father of it.** *John 8:44*

THE ENEMIES' BODY ARMOR

Christian soldiers wear the *body armor of righteousness,* which means to be morally right or justifiable. Naturally, our enemies wear the opposite body armor, *unrighteousness,* which means *to be immoral and unjustified.*

So, what are some specific examples of unrighteousness? Well, here's a few verses in First Corinthians that have the word *unrighteous* in it, and also the word *justified.*

*Or do you not know that the **unrighteous** will not inherit the kingdom of God? Do not be deceived. Neither fornicators, nor idolaters, nor adulterers, homosexuals, nor sodomites, nor thieves, nor the covetous, nor drunkards, nor revilers, nor extortioners will inherit the kingdom of God. And such were some of you. But you were washed, but you were sanctified, but you were **justified** in the name of the Lord Jesus Christ and by the Spirit of our God. 1 Corinthians 6:9-11*

Are you currently practicing anything of these sins found on this list?

You probably think I'm going to bring up the most controversial sin of our day? The one that is most responsible for pushing God out of the public square and individual lives. Well, you're right, I'm going to. So, I might as well go ahead and use this specific sin as an example.

How about being an idolater? Are you an idolater?

Wait! That wasn't the one you thought I'd pick, is it?

Yes, idolatry. Are you practicing it?

Just to make sure we are clear about this particular sin, idolatry is *the worship of a physical object as a god.*

"No, no, no!" you may strongly protest. "I don't worship a god made of stone, wood or metal."

What about Greek mythology? Do you worship their false gods such as

Zeus, Apollo, Athena, Hermes, or the many others?

"Absolutely not! They were all created by the imaginations of unbelieving men a long time ago," and I'd agree with you.

Well, then. How about idolatry in the expanded context of the Biblical meaning, which means giving devotion to anything that is false, and placing it above God.

No, I don't do that either. I guess I am safe, you may be thinking in relief.

Do you believe in evolution? Do you believe the earth is billions of years old, and that all life forms today share a common ancestor? If so, that is 100% idolatry, and that would make you an idolater.

The Bible says, *Therefore, just as* **through one man sin entered the world,** *and* **death through sin,** *and thus death spread to all men, because all have sinned – Romans 5:12*

If evolution were true, then that means the Bible is not. If plants, animals, and "pre-humans" had been forming for millions of years, or even tens of thousands of years for that matter, then that means that there was **death** prior to Adam and Eve. Yet, God's Word clearly states that **death,** because of sin, **"entered the world."** Death was not a natural occurrence, but it **"entered."** Thus, death was a result.

So, you can't have it both ways. You either believe in a literal six-day creation, or you don't. Either you are putting on the *body armor of righteousness* or you're strapping on the enemies' body armor - *unrighteousness*. Remember, that the first piece of the enemies' armor starts with the *patrol belt of lies.* Now, if you're like me, you not only believe the Bible, because it is the inspired, inerrant Word of God, but you also know that true science does not support the "theory of evolution." The fossil record, DNA, the "design features" of all living and non-living things, support creation.

When God formed Adam from the dust, was he a baby or an adult? The Genesis record is clear that he was a "man." In fact, the name Adam is the Hebrew word אדם, pronounced ah-dam, which means *man.* We don't know what "age" his appearance seemed to be on his "create day," because he did not have a "birthday," yet when God breathed life into him, Adam was a fully functional man, and he started to tend (לְעָבְדָהּ, cultivate) the Garden of Eden that he had been placed in. Even secular scientists that study DNA know that humans have no common ancestor with primates. Human and chimpanzee genomes are no more than about 85% similar, which in simple English means *we're not related at all*. It's impossible for us, or any living creature, to change the genetic codes through "natural selection," whatever that means, not to mention, that no "transitional forms" have ever been discovered in the fossil record. Fish have always been fish, spiders have always remained spiders, plants are plants, and so forth. Plus, the only way fossils, coal, and crude oil could have been formed, was by rapid, cataclysmic, burial of plants and animals by mud. Hence, the Flood of Noah that "covered the whole earth" approximately 5,000 years ago.

Yes, I know, there have been a lot of fakes (lies) when it comes to supposedly "hominid" discoveries. I've actually seen the "3.18-million-year-old" "Lucy" (Australopithecus) skeleton myself in a museum, who is believed to be "the grandmother of humanity," yet she has the bone structure of an ape. So, why not just call her what she was? An ape.

When I was a child in the 1960s and 1970s my science teachers taught me that the Neanderthals, known as "cave men," were the evolutionary link just before modern man – homo sapiens. However, recent DNA testing of the remains of Neanderthals have proven that they were 100% homo sapiens, us, and that they have absolutely no link to primates. In fact, many people today who get their results back from a DNA testing company find out that they have a percentage of Neanderthal DNA. Ever since Lucy was discovered in 1974 there is still no evidence of humans evolving from any animal.

Circling back, if Adam could be created as an adult in a single day, day six, then the earth and universe, which were created in the first three days, must have also had a mature "create day" as well. If Adam was created to look, let's say 20 years old, then the light shining from the stars that are now hitting our planet could have appeared instantly at creation, even though they are billions of lightyears away.

I was brought up "at the feet of" Pastor Chuck Smith until he died in 2013, and he used to say, "If you can believe the first sentence in the Bible, then you won't have a problem believing the rest of it." Of course, the first sentence reads, *In the beginning God created the heavens and the earth. Genesis 1:1* He spoke it into existence – out of nothing!

In fact, the very first word of Genesis is the Hebrew word בראשית (pronounce beh-reh-sheet, which means *in beginning*), thus the very first letter in the Bible is ב (Bet). The very last word in the Bible, Revelation 22:21 is the Greek word Ἀμήν (pronounced Amen, which means *so be it*), thus the very last letter in the Bible is ν (Nu). Amen also happens to be the exact same word in Hebrew, אמן Therefore, the first letter of the Old Testament, and the last letter of the New Testament, and keep in mind that Hebrew is read from right to left, forms the word בן, which means *son*. The entire Bible, from beginning to end, is all about the *Son of God*. In fact, Jesus said, *I am the Alpha and the Omega, the Beginning and the End, the First and the Last. Revelation 22:13*

To protect ourselves from this idolatry, that the universe somehow "evolved," we must rely on our *ballistic shield of faith,* because nobody was around to see the beginning, neither believers nor scientists. Therefore, *by faith we understand that the worlds* (αἰῶνας pronounced ay-o-nas, *universe* or *ages*) *were framed by the word of God, so that the things which are seen were not made of things which are visible. Hebrews 11:3*

When it comes to morality, established by God, and how I ought to behave, I don't question it, nor do I need to try on the enemies' *body armor of unrighteousness* to see how it fits me. Not because I am some wise old Christian warrior poet, but because every time I have sinned, I have been

251

burned by it, and I certainly have my fair share of battle wounds because I didn't listen to Him. Therefore, I don't need to break anymore of God's laws to realize that only negative things will result from it. I now realized, after engaging in years of physical and spiritual warfare, that when God tells me "No" to a few things that I may want, it is because He wants to protect me, and that's because He loves me. He doesn't want to stop me just to prevent me from "having fun." As such, I find the *body of armor of righteousness* very comforting to wear, even if it is uncomfortable.

When I have the opportunity to engage with an "enemy soldier," specifically **the world,** I don't condemn them for wearing their *godless combat gear.* They wear it because they don't know any better. It's wrapped around them tightly. Therefore, to penetrate all that armor I, and you as well, need to strip them of their first piece of battle equipment that they put on, and that is the *patrol belt of lies.* In order to counter the lies we need only to speak truth – God's truth - the Word. If they come to understand the lies for what they are, because the Holy Spirit convicts them, then the *body armor of unrighteousness* will come off next.

On the graph titled COMBAT GEAR OF THE ENEMIES on page 244, you'll notice that there is the symbol of a lightning bolt on the *body armor of unrighteousness.* That's because Jesus said of the devil, *I saw Satan* ***fall like lightning*** *from heaven. Luke 10:18*

Satan was the first of God's creatures to rebel against Him, therefore he is our Number 1 enemy. Well, actually, we are our own worst enemy, but when it comes to outside forces, he's definitely Number 1. Before he was named "Satan," and cast down to earth, in heaven his name was Lucifer (light bearer). God gives an account in the Old Testament as to why he fell "like lighting from heaven."

*How you are **fallen from heaven,** O Lucifer, son of the morning! How you are cut down to the ground, you who weakened the nations! For you* *have said in your heart, "I will ascend into heaven, I will exalt my throne above the stars of God, I will also sit on the mount of the congregation on the farthest sides of the north, I will ascend above the heights of the clouds, I will be like the Most High." Isaiah 14:12-14*

Lucifer's sin was pride, and that pride manifested itself through rebellion, war, when a number of other angels joined him.

The name Lucifer (הילל pronounced heh-lel in Hebrew) means "star of the morning." He went from a constant bright burning star for the Lord to just a temporary flash of light that fell to the earth. This is why he, and the angels that rebelled with him, are often referred to as "fallen angels." However, after "the fall" God refers to Lucifer throughout the rest of the Bible as Satan, *adversary,* for that is certainly what he is to us. The fallen angels are called "demons."

Satan is the leader of unrighteousness, thus the *body of armor of unrighteousness* bears his symbol – the lightning bolt.

THE ENEMIES' COMBAT BOOTS OF CONFUSION

Christian Soldiers wear the *combat boots of the Gospel of Peace,* and the prophet Isaiah wrote about the feet that wear these boots, *How beautiful upon the mountains are **the feet of him who brings good news,** who proclaims peace, who brings glad tidings of good thing, who proclaims salvation, who says to Zion, "Your God reigns!" Isaiah 52:7*

Now let's contrast this with the enemies' *combat boots of confusion,* but first, I want to start off by pointing out the symbols on the enemies' boots that's shown on the COMBAT GEAR OF THE ENEMIES graph. That's right, I put a "logo" on the right boot, and a infamous number on the left boot. If a major shoe manufacturer can put the name of a false god, the Greek goddess of victory, on all their shoes, I can certainly put a worldly logo and an evil number on a worldly pair of boots. The icon I chose, and I designed it myself, is an icon representing the Tower of Babel. Many scholars believe that this tower was in the shape of a ziggurat, which is a stepped tower, but the builders never had the chance to finish the temple on top of it. I'll explain all that in a moment. Just as sport shoes prominently display the logo of the manufacturer, so too the right boot displays the maker of the old world system – Babel. Babel was not just a tower, but an entire city as well. To understand the meaning, I need to give a little history lesson.

God made man. As the population grew, most men were wicked and rejected God. God destroyed everything that breathed on the ground, save Noah, his wife, their three sons and their wives. Only eight, the number of new beginning, people were saved from the global flood by riding it out on an ark.

When Noah and his family exited the ark, God instructed him, *Be fruitful and multiply, and **fill the earth**. Genesis 9:1* He didn't say, "You may go out, but keep your population down so you don't use up all the earth's resources, which will cause 'climate change.'" Nope, God wanted the earth "filled," and nobody has the right to reduce the population by any means.

Each of Noah's sons had sons, then all the grandsons had sons, and the population grew rapidly. At first, they did as they were told, and they started to spread eastward from the mountains of Ararat, where the ark had come to rest, when "they found a plain in the land of Shinar (today's Iraq), and they dwelt there." However, they refused to go any further and "fill the earth" as commanded. Quite the opposite. *And they said, "Come, let us build ourselves a city, and a tower whose top is in the heavens; let us make a name for ourselves, **lest we be scattered abroad over the face of the whole earth." Genesis 11:4***

The tower that this early civilization was building was not so its top could physically reach God, nor even be a monument to Him, but its purpose was for astronomical observation. They were worshipping the sun, moon, planets, and stars, which is a perversion of what God created these heavenly bodies for. Even today many people put their faith into these heavenly bodies by reading their daily horoscope, instead of worshipping the True and Living God. They'll take the "advice" of inanimate objects that were created, but not the One who created them. Therefore, Babel, which later becomes Babylon, is the birthplace of false religions.

While men were constructing the Tower of Babel, God put an end to their little block party.

At that time, all people spoke the same language, and so God confused their language, "that they may not understand one another's speech." Mankind didn't want to fill the earth, *so the Lord scattered them abroad from there over the face of all the earth,* and they ceased building the city. Therefore, its name is called Babel (which has come to mean "confusion"), because there the Lord confused the language of all the earth; and from there the Lord scattered them abroad over the face of all the earth. Genesis 11:8-9

This is why there are 7,139 languages spoken today around the globe, and there are approximately another 573 extinct languages that we know of. Any linguist (a person who studies languages), who is truly honest, will tell you that they don't really know why there are so many human languages. For example, how can the tropical island of New Guinea have over 900 languages? Why is the Finnish language nothing like the surrounding neighboring countries? There are some theories, but little evidence.

One theory, that doesn't support the origins of all the languages on earth, is the "theory of evolution." If we all "evolved" from a common ancestor, we'd have many, many, dialects, but they'd all have a common root language. Yes, conquest and human migration explains some common words among various civilizations, but it does not explain all the thousands of languages on earth that have no relationship to each other. The only logical explanation for so many different human languages is exactly how it is explained in the book of Genesis. If God created man, He was certainly capable of creating thousands of languages – in an instant.

If evolution is true, as most people proclaim, then how is it that ancient cultures, that were continents apart for thousands of years, had the same technology and building ideas at the same time? They didn't have the ability to communicate with each other like they can today, let alone more than a thousand years ago. With my own eyes I've seen ancient Egyptian boomerangs in Egyptian museums, and I've seen Aboriginal boomerangs in Australian museums. You'd swear that they got the idea for this hunting weapon from each other. I've seen ancient European bows and arrows in European museums, and I've seen Native American bows and arrows in American museums. Was it a coincidence? I've climbed on the great Pyramid of Giza in Egypt overlooking the desert, and an ocean away I stood on top of the Mayan pyramid at Chichen Itza in Mexico overlooking the jungle. Come to think of it, there are also ancient pyramids in Italy, Spain, Sudan, China, Peru, Bolivia and of course Iraq (Babylon). That means pyramids are in Asia, Europe, Africa, North America, South America. Was it just because "great minds think alike?" I don't think so.

Obviously, if God "scattered them abroad over the face of the earth" all at once, then they'd all have the same knowledge they all had at Babel: musical instruments, weapons, architecture, and even religion; all sorts of false religions. However, the world does not want to believe the Biblical account of how different cultures and languages came about. So instead, they have invented the story that man originated in Africa, while still half man half ape, and spread out from there into Europe and Asia over tens of thousands of years, evolving along the way, and eventually a group of them crossed over the Bering Strait "ice bridge" during the Ice Age, and they worked their way down into South America, as if there is evidence of that.

The French have a saying that I like, and it's *plus ça change, plus c'est la même chose* (the more things change, the more they stay the same). Just as the Old World Order (Babylon) worshipped false gods, sacrificed to idols, and instituted a political system that eliminate God, the post-Christian church era will usher in the New World Order, Liberal World Order, New Babel, or whatever they're going to call it, that's not just infused with the spirit of antichrist, but is the flesh and blood Antichrist (represented on the enemy's left boot with his number "666"). The book of Revelation states that Babylon, pictured as a woman, seduces the people of earth with her "abominations and the filthiness of her fornication."

And on her forehead a name was written: MYSTERY, BABYLON THE GREAT, MOTHER OF HARLOTS AND OF THE ABOMINATIONS OF THE EARTH. Revelation 17:5

What group of people do you think this godless world system attacks today? Who do these children of spiritual prostitutes turn against? The next verse states it very clearly. *I saw the woman, drunk with* **the blood of the saints** *and with* **the blood of the martyrs** *of Jesus. Revelation 17:6*

The Bible tells us that any believer is a "saint." Therefore, this verse is talking about those believers who are on earth during the Great Tribulation. So, as you can see, the physical and spiritual warfare is only going to grow in intensity. The reason that it does is because the majority of mankind will be wearing the *combat boots of confusion* upon their feet, and this confusion goes all the way back to the Tower of Babel. *Plus ça change, plus c'est la même chose.*

THE ENEMIES' SHIELD OF UNBELIEF

Everybody has faith. Men and women commuting to work have faith that the bridges that they drive over each day are not going to collapse as they drive over them. People even have faith in nature. They have faith that when they go to bed at night that the sun will rise in the morning, even if they don't live to see it, as it always does. However, not everyone has faith that the God of the Bible *is the Creator of them and the universe. Nor do they believe Jesus' words, I am the way, the truth, and the life. No one comes to the Father except through Me. John 14:6* As such, they carry a heavy shield that deflects God's Word from penetrating their sinful hearts. This is the worldview of most of *the world,* and it's why I have placed the symbol of *the world,* a globe, upon the *shield of unbelief* in the COMBAT GEAR OF THE ENEMIES graph.

God uses the word **"world"** repeatedly in the Bible to mean the *unbelievers* – the lost. Here are just a few verses to illustrate this point:

*Do not love **the world** or the things in **the world.** If anyone loves **the world,** the love of the Father is not in him. 1 John 2:15*

*And do not be conformed to **this world,** but be transformed by the renewing of your mind, that you may prove what is good and acceptable and perfect will of God. Romans 12:2*

*For what will it profit a man if he gains **the whole world,** and loses his own soul? Mark 8:36*

Sadly, many Christian Soldiers want to keep their *full combat gear of God* on, and they certainly do not want to drop their *ballistic shield of faith* on the battlefield, but for some reason they think that they are strong enough to carry two shields at the same time. They get tempted to have *faith* and *the world* at the same time, and let me tell you, the burden and discomfort is excruciating.

Jesus prayed to the Father for us, for you, while He was on this earth, *I do not pray that You should take them out of **the world,** but that You should keep them from the evil one. John 17:15*

How do I know that this prayer was also specifically for you? Because in verse 17:20 Jesus added, *"I do not pray for these alone, but **also for those who will believe in Me** through their word.*

Our battlefield is **the world.** We have no choice but to fight and camp on it, but we are not of this world. This battlefield is not our home. It is not our

kingdom. As a Christian Soldier I have no business indulging in the evil things of this world like pornography, gossip, stabbing others in the back to get ahead in business, cheating the government on my taxes, neglecting the physical or spiritual needs of those that God puts before me, saying to someone with a jealous heart, "It must be nice," because he or she has more than I do or is blessed in a some way that I am not, or entertaining ideas of how I can get even with someone who has wronged me. These things are of **the world.**

Is it hard not to compromise? You bet it is. Some people are so weak that they not only dabble in **the world,** but they come to a point that they shed their *body armor of righteousness* and *the ballistic shield of faith* altogether and go back to the other side. They become traitors. Thank God, those individuals are few. Can we understand the pull the world has on them? Of course. At one point we were all once citizens of the other side, but we chose to fight with the resistance. VIVE LA RÉSISTANCE!

So, as tempting as it may be to go back into **the world,** and carry two shields at once, I prefer believing, in *faith,* the words of my Warrior King, my Commander in Chief, who is also my daddy, *You are of God, little children, and have overcome them, because He who is in you is greater than he who is in **the world.** 1 John 4:4*

Personally, I'm not going to do it. If I get tempted to grab the handle of an abandoned polished enemy shield, I can't, I won't. I am already firmly holding the handle of my own shield, the *ballistic shield of faith.* Yet, if for some reason I do get weak, and I reach out and pick up the war trophy laying on the field, then I pray that the weight of it will start to burn my spiritual muscles, and I'll instantly say to myself, "Why am I carrying this extra load?" and then toss it back on *the world* from which it came.

THE ENEMIES' HELMET OF DAMNATION

The helmet that our enemies wear upon their heads is a sad piece of

equipment indeed. It is the *helmet of damnation,* which bears the symbol of the eaten apple from the Garden of Eden. Okay, technically the book of Genesis refers to it as מפר (the Hebrew word for *fruit,* pronounced mi-pir), but somehow the apple came to represent the fruit that our first mother and father ate, and this is why I placed the apple symbol on the helmet found on the COMBAT GEAR OF THE ENEMIES graph.

The reason that I stated that it is "a sad piece of equipment," is because all who wear it, and all who do not surrender and join our side, will not only never experience the mercies and love of God, but they will be captured, judged, and sentenced to an eternity in hell by our Commander in Chief.

But, wait! you may be thinking, *the forbidden fruit that was eaten by mankind, by both the first man and the first woman, which represents the enemies of **the flesh** and **the world,** but why would the symbol of the apple also apply to our third enemy, **the devil** when it comes to damnation?*

Well, if you remember, it was the serpent (נחש pronounced nah-kas), called Satan after the fall, who lied to Eve to convince her to eat of the tree that God warned Adam not to eat from. Therefore, Satan is connected to this symbol just as much as our great, great, great… grandparents are. However, Satan didn't force her to eat it, but she did it for three reasons:

1. The tree was good for food.

2. It was pleasant to the eyes.

3. A tree desirable to make one wise.

Adam and Eve had plenty of fruit trees in the Garden of Eden, and they were free to eat from any of them except one. *And the Lord God* (יהוה YHVH, which is the actual name of God, yet nobody really knows how He actually pronounced it, because the Jewish scholars left out the vowels) *commanded the man, saying, "Of every tree of the garden you may freely eat, but of the tree of knowledge of good and evil you shall not eat, for in*

the day that you eat of it you shall surely die." Genesis 2:15 They were even permitted to eat of the *tree of life,* which was in the middle of the garden, but for some unknown reason they didn't. Therefore, Eve, wanting to eat from the *tree of knowledge of good and evil,* because it was "good for food," was not a valid reason. She was not starving.

As far as the forbidden fruit being pleasant to the eyes, all the trees in the garden were. *And out of the ground the Lord **God made every tree grow that is pleasant to the sight and good for food.*** *Genesis 2:8*

So, Adam and Eve had plenty of food, and all of it was pleasant to the sight. And, as far as rules and regulations, there was only one law for the entire planet – ONE! I'm paraphrasing here, but if the law had been written down with today's legal wording, it may have looked something like this:

Earth Penal Code 1 of 1: DON'T EAT OF THE TREE OF KNOWL-EDGE OF GOOD AND EVIL.

Punishment: PHYSICAL & SPIRITUAL DEATH.

Pretty simple, and rather easy to avoid, if you ask me. In hindsight, it certainly was not an unreasonable law God gave them, now that we know the full extent of the consequences for breaking it. Of course, like any penal code, there is no paragraph or two that explains all the heartache and pain a person will experience for breaking the law. It's just understood that you don't do it, and if you do it, then you'll soon discover for yourself all the negative consequences after the sentencing phase.

Let's face it, *the apple doesn't fall far from the tree.* How many people today have what they need, but they want something that they shouldn't have? They have enough money, but they want more. They have a good spouse, but they want someone else. They have a comfortable home, but they covet someone else's. They want other people or things, because it is *pleasant to the eyes.* The list goes on and on what the eyes desire, but the main reason Eve wanted to eat from the prohibited tree, which wasn't fenced off to prevent man from exercising his free will, was because it had something the other trees in the garden didn't have, and that was *the knowledge of good and evil.* This is what made this tree especially attractive.

Eve knew the law, for she had quoted it verbatim to the serpent when he was tempting her, but like billions of people after her, she was deceived. The serpent said to the woman, *"You will not surely die. For God knows that in the day you eat of it your eyes will be opened, and you will be like God, knowing good and evil." Genesis 3:4*

One of Satan's tactics is to mix in a lie with the truth.

The lie: "You will not surely die."

The truth: "You will be like God, knowing good and evil."

You know the rest of the story. *"She took of its fruit and ate."* And, since misery loves company, *"She also gave to her husband with her, and he ate."* This was the moment of the fall of mankind, and damnation.

Yes, their eyes were opened, much like Lucifer's eyes were opened when he sinned in heaven, and that's why he knew what the result would be for them if he could trip them up, for it clearly states, *Then the eyes of both of them were opened, Genesis 3:7* Yet, their eyes were opened due to rebellion, and not the righteous knowledge like God has, for He is perfect. Therefore, it was quite a stretch for the serpent to say, "You will be like God."

Ahhhh, yes, and no.

For example, I "know" that illegal drugs are harmful, but I don't "know" that by actual personal experience, because I have never experimented with an illegal drug in my life. I have not even tried marijuana. Not when it was illegal in California, nor when the state government legalized it. I have never put cocaine, methamphetamines, heroin, or all the other dangerous substances in my body. I just was never tempted by that particular sin. I "knew" then, and I "know" today, that these drugs are harmful, because I have seen people fry their brains with them and even die from overdoses. With recreational marijuana I have also witnessed people I know lose their ambition and even become paranoid because of it, not to mention that it contains all of the same toxins, irritants, and carcinogens as tobacco smoke. Likewise, Adam and Eve could have said, "Whoa! Time out, serpent! You're telling us some things that contradict what God told us. We're going to go clear all this with Him before we make our decision." But, they didn't. Neither did Lucifer when pride first entered his heart in heaven. Lucifer did not go to God and tell Him the strange thoughts he was having. Instead, he entertained the destructive thought, *I will be like the Most High.* He actually believed in his heart that he could be equal with God or remove Him altogether. Eve also wanted to "be like God."

Lucifer was once perfect, and sinless.

The angels that followed Lucifer were once perfect, and sinless.

Adam and Eve were once perfect, and sinless.

Then, all of them crossed the line. They turned against Almighty God, and basically said, "No, we're going to do what we want. We want to be like You, and You can't tell us what to do."

We see this sin nature in toddlers today, defiantly telling their parents, "No!" or refusing to obey. You don't have to teach children to be bad, because they inherently are bad. The tough job of parents is teaching their children to be good.

So, what was a perfect, sinless, Holy God supposed to have done when He expects perfection and holiness from those spirits and people He made.

Don't say, "It was bound to happen," because the majority of angels did not sin, and they remain perfect and sinless to this very day. It's all the evil ones that rebelled. They turned on their Father, the Son, and the Holy Spirit.

For Satan and the demons, their fate was sealed. God has no plan to save them, and that is because they were once face to face with God. Therefore, there is no excuse for their rebellion. They all will be thrown into the lake of fire – forever.

However, mankind is different. Although all are condemned to damnation, God made a way for boys, girls, men, and women to be saved, and it is beautifully summarized in the most quoted verse of the Bible:

*For God so loved **the world** that He gave His only begotten Son, that whoever believes in Him should not perish but have everlasting life. John 3:16*

As I stated before, it is so sad that there are those who refuse to remove the *helmet of damnation* from their head and switch it with the *helmet of salvation.* It only takes a confession and repentance of a believing heart. It's the easiest thing in the world to do, and yet it's also the hardest.

Do you remember when you went through the Gas Chamber in Chapter 3, and afterwards I gave a rather graphic description of what hell may be like? It's sad that people will not put on the *helmet of salvation,* because hell will be their "everlasting life."

Do you want to know the worst part about those who go to hell is? It's being eternally separated from God, their Creator who wanted nothing but good for them. No thanks. I'd rather spend my eternity in the very presence of Love, Light, and Liberty. As such, I'll wear my *helmet of salvation* for the rest of my short, miserable, but blessed life, and then trade it in for my crowns in heaven when that time comes, be it with the individual plan (death and resurrection) or the group plan (the rapture).

THE WEAPON OF THE ANTICHRIST

Beloved, do not believe every spirit, but test the spirits, whether they are of God; because many false prophets have gone out into the world. By this you know the Spirit of God: Every spirit that confesses that Jesus Christ *has come in the flesh is of God, and every spirit that does not confess that Jesus Christ has come in the flesh is not of God. And this is the **spirit of the Antichrist,** which you have heard was coming, and is now already in the world. 1 John 4:1-3*

The main battle weapon of the enemies (*the flesh, the world,* and *the devil*) is the **weapon of the antichrist,** and as the Scripture indicates, it is "now already in the world." We've been under attack for over 2,000 years.

ἀντι is the Greek word for anti, which means "against" or "opposite." Thus, ἀντιχρίστου (pounced anti-christ-oo meaning *antichrist*), is "against Christ" or "opposite Christ." Yes, there will be coming on the world scene very soon an actual man referred to as "the Antichrist," but we'll get to him a little bit later. The bottom line is, anyone who denies that Jesus Christ is God has "the spirit of the Antichrist." If you deny that Jesus is God, then you are against Him. *The world* is against Him. *The devil* is against Him.

My wife and I live near a small, lovely lake that we like to walk around during the evening. Halfway around the lake gives us the time to talk about the day's events, and the second half we reserve for praying. We thank God for His goodness to us. We pray for family and friends. We pray about our business. We also pray for our leaders, our community, our nation, our spiritual growth and that His will be done in our lives.

Over the years young men and women, who belong to one Christian cult or another in our city, have approached us. My wife Karen never talks to them, and I'm always polite with them, allowing them to tell me their spiel without interruption. No matter if it is a Muslim, Buddhist, or Christian cult I want to hear what they have to say. I even have the mindset, *Convince me that I am wrong about my belief in the God of the Bible.* Therefore, I truly listen.

Well, after they have spoken to me, and the Holy Spirit tells me that they are telling lies, I've learned to immediately cut to the chase, and ask them, "Is Jesus the Christ, God? Did He create the heavens and the earth?"

If they have the *spirit of the antichrist* they will never answer, "Yes." Instead, they'll have some unbiblical answer such as, "He was the brother of Lucifer," or "He was the god of earth, but we'll all be gods of our own planets one day," or "Jesus was a prophet of God."

Of course, once I ask them this question, "Is Jesus the Messiah, God? Did He create the universe?" they don't want to talk to me anymore. But, before they walk away, I tell them, without any malice, "Your god is not the God of the Bible, and only the Holy Bible is the Word of God." Then, Karen and I pray for them as they walk away from us, that their eyes may be opened. I also pray, "Lord, do not let anyone believe in the lies that they are telling people around this lake."

As a Christian, and especially as a Christian Soldier, have you noticed that you can talk to people about almost anything, as long as you are polite, and they'll engage you in the conversation. However, bring up the fact that Jesus Christ is Lord, and their *shield of unbelief* is raised instantly, unless they are a believer, or their heart has been softened. In fact, many people around the world, even in Western countries that have a Christian heritage, are now labeling any Scriptures quoted from the Bible as "hate speech," and they don't want to listen to anything pertaining to God.

The three enemies only need this one weapon, the *weapon of antichrist*. If a person denies the deity of Yeshua (His name means *He saves*), which does not allow the Holy Spirit to enter into his or her heart, the One who has the power to grant him or her a pardon from the Father, then the enemies have won. It's as simple as that. The battle is lost.

Yes, there are tactics that the enemies use to distract people from coming to the truth, like sexual immorality, drugs, power, pleasure, and so forth, but their most fearsome weapon is the *weapon of antichrist*. Yet, that weapon is rendered useless when used against a person who is "born again," *No weapon formed against you shall prosper, Isaiah 54:17*

Since *the flesh, the world,* and *the devil* are very convincing enemies, it is always a good idea to be reminded why we are fighting. We are fighting because "Jesus Christ is God," and He is coming soon! Here are few verses to prove it:

He who has seen Me has seen the Father; John 14:9

*Then the Jews said to Him, "You are not yet fifty years old, and have You seen Abraham?" Jesus said to them, "Most assuredly, I say to you, before Abraham was, **I AM.**" Then they took up stones to throw at Him; 1 John 4:57-59*

They wanted to kill Jesus, right there on the spot, because He proclaimed Himself to be God Almighty. By using the words, "I AM" the Jews He was talking to knew exactly what He meant.

1,410 years before Jesus came to earth God revealed Himself to Moses in the form of a burning bush. When Moses asked Him the question, *"Indeed, when I come to the children of Israel and say to them, 'The God of your fathers has sent me to you,' and they say to me, 'What is His name?' what shall I say to them?"*

*And God said to Moses, "I AM WHO I AM." And He said, "Thus you shall say to the children of Israel, '**I AM** has sent me to you.'" Exodus 3:13-14*

In Chapter 7 we went over the specs, *specifications,* of our *combat boots of the Gospel of Peace* that you were issued. The Gospel of John, referring to Jesus the Christ, makes His deity crystal clear for us:

*In the beginning was the Word, and the Word was with God, and **the** Word was God. He was in the beginning with God. All things were made through Him, and without Him nothing was made that was made. In Him was **life,** and the **life** was the **light** of men. And the **light** shines in the darkness, and the darkness did not comprehend it. John 1:1-5*

Did you notice that the word "life" was said twice, and the word "light" was also said twice? That means that it is legally confirmed, and based on this verse, here is a simple formula:

The Word = God = Jesus Christ

Then Jesus spoke to them again, saying, "I am the light of the world. He who follows Me shall not walk in darkness, but have the light of life." John 8:12

Jesus said to him, "I am the way, the truth, and the life." John 14:6

BOOM! You're smoked *flesh, world,* and *devil!* Those verses are tactical nukes.

So, Christian Soldier, the targets have been "softened." Disarm the enemies of their *weapon of antichrist,* which is nothing but a lie, and flip the selector switch of your *weapon of the Spirit,* the Holy Spirit, to AUTO, and FIRE!

We have already won this war! Jesus won it for us at the cross, yet, the battles continue. There are battles going on in our lives, in the lives of our families, in the lives of our friends, in our community, in our country, and throughout the entire world! So let's *put on the full combat gear of God,* and fight! Amen.

The enemies have set up many "checkpoints" to block you from doing God's work: fear, intimidation, embarassment, rejection, et cetera.

The enemy never gets tired of fighting us. They are battle hardened veterans who are intent on our destruction, but some are blind to it.

When you *put on the full combat gear of God* you can count on being a target, because you pose a *clear and present danger* to the enemies.

The enemy has planted all kinds of "spiritual land mines" that can take you out of action: lust, the love of money, cowardess, et cetera.

Don't be fooled. The enemies, like a suicide bomber, are willing to destroy themselves to destroy us. Case in point, godless socialism.

Hostages have been taken. *Jesus answered them, "Truly, truly, I say to you, everyone who commits sin is a slave to sin." John 8:34*

As Christian Soldiers, one of our missions is to rescue hostages, and the only way to do that is to go into enemy territory and get them out.

Granted, you may not get all of them out. Some will be destroyed by the enemy, and some won't want to go, but anyone freed is a victory.

Why are there so many active shooters today? *To do evil is like sport to a fool, but a man of understanding has wisdom. Proverbs 10:23*

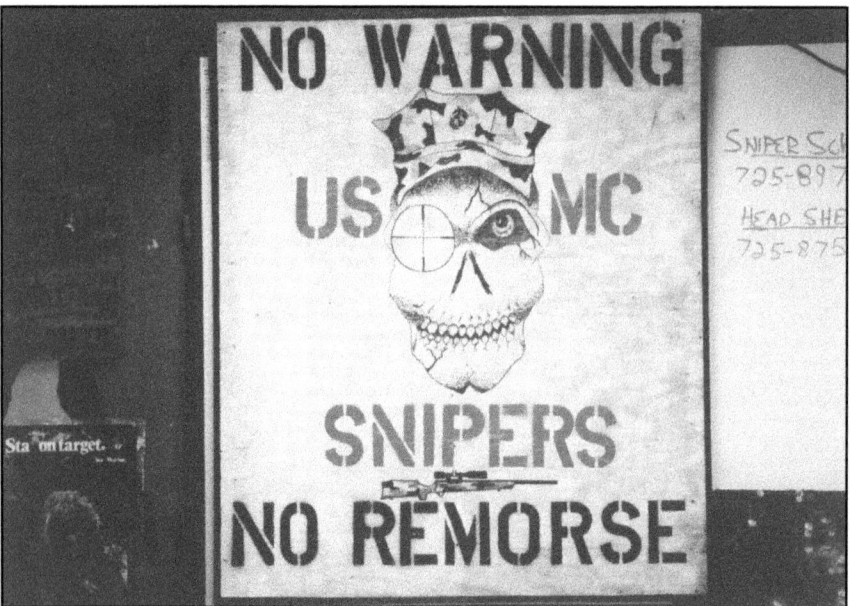

This sign also applies spiritually. We have NO REMORSE exposing lies: "There are more than two sexes," "a woman's right to choose," etc.

In the fight, don't lose your sense of humor or the ability to enjoy life. I put a traffic ticket on this Black Hawk helicopter just for the fun of it.

There's a lot of hardships being a Soldier, but it makes you stronger, like when I went through this U.S. Navy S.E.R.E. (survival) course.

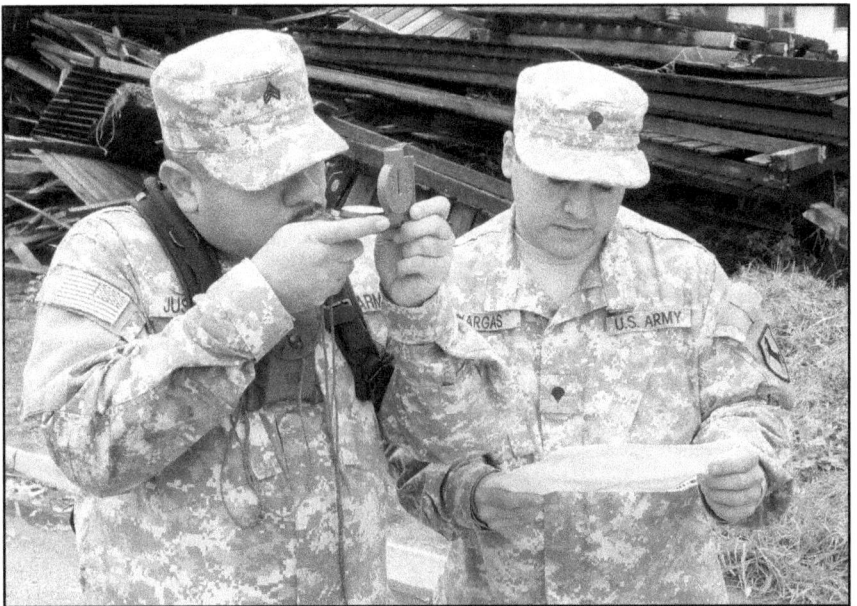

Yet, despite all the hardships, you'll never lose your way if you stay the course. You won't veer off far if you pray and read the Bible daily.

As this world gets darker and darker, a Christian Soldier's "light" can be seen better, both for exposing evil and attracting lost souls to Him.

We Christians are going to leave this earth one day, either individually (death and resurrection) or through the "group plan" (the rapture).

American Soldiers who gave their lives for their country are honored. Christian Soldiers who fight to the end will also receive their rewards.

If American Soldiers obey the legal orders of the President of the United States of America, who is also the Commander in Chief of the Armed Forces, a mere man that places them in harm's way, how much more should we Christian Soldiers obey the "Commander in Chief of Commanders in Chief" who is forever Great, Powerful, and Love.

Throughout American history most Soldiers never met their Commander in Chief, and yet they faithfully served, fought, and died based upon the decisions that were made by him.

When I was in the military I served under four presidents: Jimmy Carter, Ronald Reagan, George W. Bush, and Barack Obama. Of those four I only met one, President Bush (photo above), on January 12, 2009. It was indeed the highlight of my military career to have been invited to the White House and meet my Commander in Chief in the Oval Office, especially during wartime, for I had trained many Soldiers who were deployed to Afghanistan and Iraq. However, when I left the grounds of the White House that day, the President never thought of me again, for I was just one of thousands of Soldiers he had met during his eight years in Office, and then a week later he was no longer in power. However, not only does my heavenly Commander in Chief live inside of me (the Holy Spirit), but the thoughts He has for me *if I should count them, they would be more in number than the sand; Psalm 139:18*

That is a Commander in Chief I can serve, live for, die for, and live again for - eternal life. Amen.

INDEX

283

JIM WAGNER BOOKS

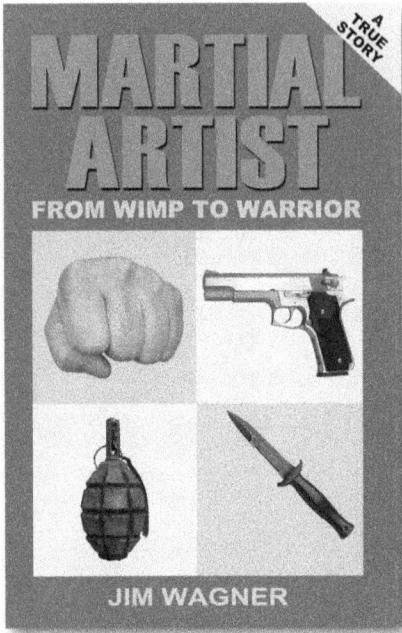

Martial Artist, and Martial Artist 2 and 3, is my autobiography. In this book you will start off by experiencing with me what is was like to be embedded in one of Europe's top counterterrorist teams - German GSG9. Then, going back in time from there, I start from the beginning on my journey from wimp to warrior.

The first step was studying the martial arts at the age of 14. The discipline, mixed with my faith in God, prepared me for the second step of the journey, joining the U.S. Army during the turbulent post Vietnam War era.

You will then "go to jail" with me as a corrections officer for two years, then into the police academy, and out onto the mean streets as a police officer. Then, my dreams come true. I become a member of my police department's S.W.A.T. team.

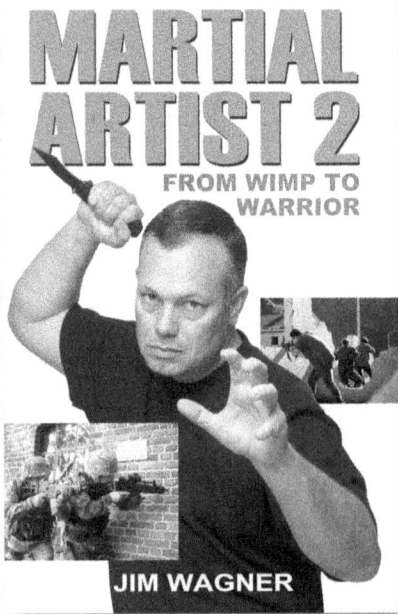

In **Martial Artist 2,** God opened a door for me, and that was writing for Black Belt magazine, which gave me fame in both the tactical and civilian martial arts communities. Along with this fame came a lot of enemies that wanted to take me down, for years to come. Some did.

I traded in my police shield for a six pointed Sheriff' badge. Soon I was promoted to the rank of sergeant and made the team leader of the Dignitary Protection Unit. Suddenly the world changed. The United States of America was attacked by Al Qaeda terrorists on September 11, 2001 and soon afterwards I found myself fighting in The Global War on Terrorism as a counterterrorist.

Next comes training the world's elite: U.S. Army Special Forces, the FBI, the Israeli police & military, and many more.

AVAILABLE NOW

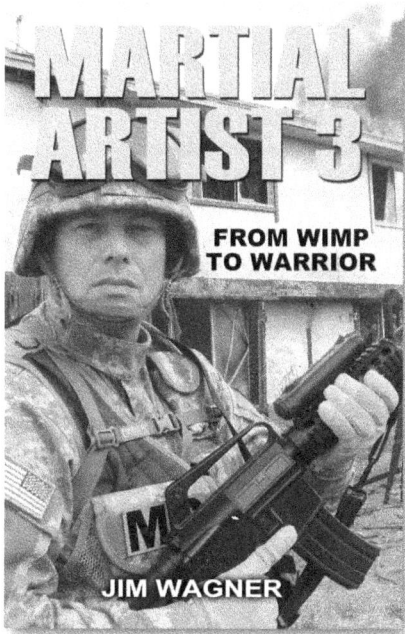

FROM WIMP TO WARRIOR

JIM WAGNER

In **Martial Artist 3** you'll travel all over the world with me as I train law enforcement agencies, military units, and civilian self-defense schools - changing the way people learn self-defense. In fact, I even open up my new headquarters for the Jim Wagner Reality-Based Personal Protection system in Solingen, Germany. I then decide to go back into the military as a Reserve Soldier for another ten years. For eight of those years the Obama Administration had gutted and weakened the United States Armed Forces, but it gave me opportunities I would have never had otherwise. Of course, it was all God's doing to prepare me for the next step of my career, and a new ministry, at a critical time in American history - the birth of church security as God's people are also attacked physically.

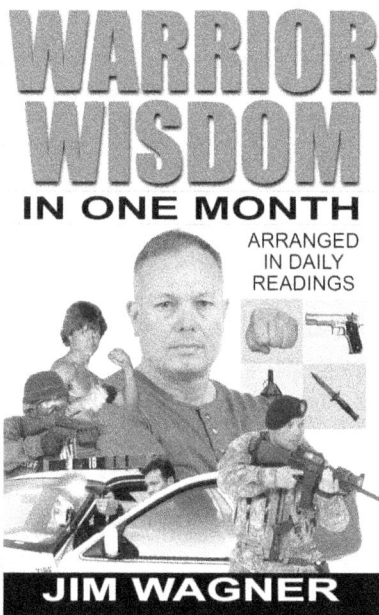

IN ONE MONTH

ARRANGED IN DAILY READINGS

JIM WAGNER

Warrior Wisdom is for any warrior or anyone who wants the heart of a warrior.

Each day of the month you'll learn a different self-defense or tactical lesson, which will take only a couple of minutes to learn. By the end of the 31 days, you'll have gained techniques, tactics, and life-saving information you'd never get from a single organization, school, academy or military unit.

Reading this book is like sitting in on a counterterrorism course, training with Special Forces, running through the police academy, picking the brains of the top self-defense instructors in the world, and being on the streets with cops arresting people, all rolled up into one book.

Everything in these pages are based on my own training and experience spanning four decades on six continents.

CHRISTIAN SOLDIER™
SELF-DEFENSE SYSTEM

PROTECT MY CHILD™
SAFETY & DEFENSE SYSTEM

SECURITY OPERATIONS™
ORGANIZATION, PROCEDURES & TRAINING

MISSIONARY SECURITY™
MATTHEW 10:16 TRAINING

CHRISTIAN UNDERGROUND™
SURVIVAL DURING PERSECUTION & POST RAPTURE

DOUBLE TIME TO
GodsArmySurvivalTraining.com

www.ingramcontent.com/pod-product-compliance
Lightning Source LLC
Chambersburg PA
CBHW071410090426
42737CB00011B/1415